When Republicans Were Progressive

★

"Dave Durenberger grew up during the challenging 1930s and '40s. It was also the beginning of Minnesota's progressive Republican Party. By learning and listening he developed an enthusiasm for and dedication to public service which he has never lost. This book is an inspiring reminder of the way politics is supposed to work."
    US Senator Nancy Landon Kassebaum Baker

"In 1990, by overwhelming margins, the Congress enacted major clean air legislation. It was the culmination of a ten-year effort led by a small bipartisan group of legislators that included Dave Durenberger. His deep knowledge of the issues and his strong powers of persuasion made possible what today seems impossible: Placing the national interest above party interest to enact legislation that benefits all Americans.

"Dave has written a book about the Minnesota Republican Party, and how it shaped him and his beliefs. At a time in our history when bipartisanship is so rare, Durenberger's book should be of interest to all Americans."
    US Senator George J. Mitchell

"While looking back, Dave Durenberger captures what is needed to lead us forward: vision, conviction, and a dedication to the greater good."
    Kathleen A. Blatz, Retired Chief Justice, Minnesota Supreme Court

When Republicans
Were Progressive

DAVE
Durenberger

with **LORI STURDEVANT**

MINNESOTA
HISTORICAL
SOCIETY PRESS

www.mnhspress.org

The Minnesota Historical Society Press is a member of the Association of University Presses.

Manufactured in the United States of America

10 9 8 7 6 5 4 3 2 1

♾ The paper used in this publication meets the minimum requirements of the American National Standard for Information Sciences—Permanence for Printed Library Materials, ANSI Z39.48–1984.

International Standard Book Number
ISBN: 978-1-68134-078-4 (paper)
ISBN: 978-1-68134-079-1 (e-book)

Library of Congress Cataloging-in-Publication Data
Names: Durenberger, David, author. | Sturdevant, Lori, 1953– author.
Title: When Republicans were progressive / Dave Durenberger with Lori Sturdevant.
Description: St. Paul, MN : Minnesota Historical Society Press, [2018] | Includes bibliographical references and index.
Identifiers: LCCN 2018022616 | ISBN 9781681340784 (paper : alk. paper) | ISBN 9781681340791 (ebook)
Subjects: LCSH: Republican Party (Minn.)—History. | Progressivism (United States politics)—History. | Minnesota—Politics and government.
Classification: LCC JK2358.M6 D87 2018 | DDC 324.277604—dc23
LC record available at https://lccn.loc.gov/2018022616

This and other Minnesota Historical Society Press books are available from popular e-book vendors.

To Charlie, Dave, Mike, and Danny Durenberger

and the memory of Elmer L. Andersen

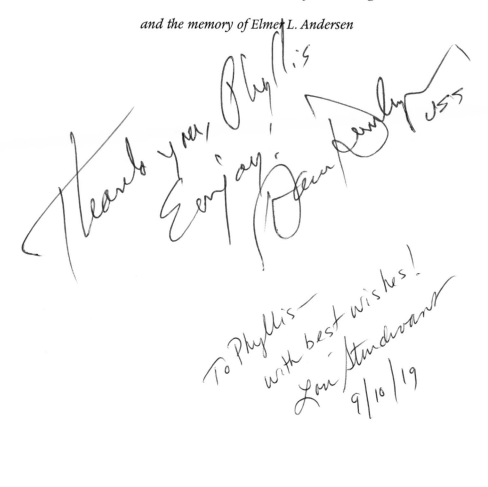

CONTENTS

★

FOREWORD

by Norman J. Ornstein

As a young person growing up in Minnesota, I was surrounded by politics. My maternal grandfather, who died of cancer the year I was born, led the Minneapolis laundry workers' union and was a key member of the "kitchen cabinet" that worked to elect Hubert Humphrey as Minneapolis mayor, launching one of the most consequential political careers of the twentieth century. My uncle served for many years in the state legislature, where he had close ties to Humphrey, Walter Mondale, Orville Freeman, Art Naftalin, Don Fraser, and other leading members of the Democratic-Farmer-Labor party.

So I started with an image of politicians with deep values, social consciences, and a reverence for democratic principles. But that image was not limited to Democrats. I was deeply inculcated with Minnesota political values of fairness, the need for and value of compromise, decency, and civility; my political role models back in the 1950s, 1960s, and beyond included Harold Stassen (before his serial presidential runs), Elmer Andersen, and Harold LeVander. As a young undergraduate at the University of Minnesota, I encountered Doug Head, the Republican attorney general of Minnesota, who spent a good deal of time with me and a handful of other political science students; I had deep admiration for him, and he became a friend. My peers and I took pride in our Minnesota culture, one that transcended any partisan divide.

That pride persisted into the 1970s and 1980s, with admirable Minnesota Republican politicians and policy makers like Arne Carlson,

Bill Frenzel, Jim Ramstad, and Dave Durenberger. Minnesota Republicans by and large were pragmatists who married their moderate conservatism with decency and a drive to solve problems by working across that divide. When I came to Washington in 1969 as a congressional fellow, I worked for Don Fraser, a Democrat, but I developed relationships with Republican representatives like Bill Steiger of Wisconsin and Barber Conable of New York, along with senators like Charles Goodell of New York, Bill Cohen of Maine, Chuck Percy of Illinois, and Mark Hatfield of Oregon. Some were more conservative in political ideology, by the standards of the time, but all were institutionalists and problem solvers. I built relationships with many of the Minnesotans, Dave Durenberger included.

Durenberger was a particularly admirable lawmaker who worked diligently in the Senate to find ways to solve important national and state problems, from health care to climate change to foreign affairs and intelligence. My Democratic friends in the Senate talked about him as one they could work with, casting aside partisan and ideological differences. But, as he and Lori Sturdevant note in this book, long before Durenberger left the Senate, the politics of the parties and the broader political culture in Minnesota and in the country were changing, and not for the better.

Nationally, the profound changes in the Republican Party and the rise of tribalism in our politics were driven, as Durenberger and Sturdevant point out, by Newt Gingrich, from his election in 1978 and rise as a disruptive force in his party in Congress through his deliberative obstructionism when Bill Clinton became president in 1993. In Minnesota, the signs were evident during the same years, with the rise of a strong evangelical and rigidly conservative set of elements. In the Clinton era, Minnesota's Independent-Republican Party changed its name back to simply the Republican Party, signaling the turn away from the center to the sharp right that paralleled the national trend.

As Durenberger notes, there were seventeen Republican senators who could fairly be labeled progressive when Ronald Reagan was inaugurated in 1981; by 1996, only four were left, and two—Arlen Specter and Jim Jeffords—would soon leave the party, while a third, Richard Lugar, would be ousted in a primary by an ultraconservative. Both parties have seen their lawmakers who hewed close to the center decline in numbers, and neither party has been angelic; politics ain't beanbag. But as Tom Mann and I have long pointed out, the polarization has been distinctly asymmetric, and the obstructionism has been as well.

There was much to lament during the Obama years about the state of our politics and the degeneration of a problem-focused center-right Republican Party into an obstructionist and more radical-right entity. But there is more to be concerned about now, in the Trump era, with a party that has transformed itself into a science- and climate-change-denying, nativist, protectionist, and nearly nihilistic engine for a president dismissive of fundamental American values. During his time in the Senate and since he left, Dave Durenberger's signature focus has been health policy. As the debacle over "repeal and replace" shows, the current GOP has no health policy and has rejected all the principles evident in the Durenberger alternatives. The country and the state of Minnesota have both suffered immeasurably as we have moved away from an era where the Durenbergers of our political system anchored the problem-solving center.

Our political environment now is not normal, and it is exceedingly dangerous. We will not emerge from it soon or unscathed. But this excellent book, part memoir and part history, reminds us that there is a different and better path that for many decades worked for Minnesota and the country. We need it back.

PREFACE AND ACKNOWLEDGMENTS

NOT LONG BEFORE HIS DEATH IN 2010, Russell Fridley, the tireless Minnesota historian and longtime leader of the Minnesota Historical Society, invited me to breakfast at the Downtowner Restaurant in St. Paul. His mission: to persuade me to write a history of Minnesota Republicans. He knew there was something unique about my party, especially the so-called "progressives," starting with Harold Stassen, the "boy wonder" governor of the late 1930s. Russ was concerned that their contributions to the state had been overlooked. He told me, "You are the last of the breed, someone who knew them all." Given the very different nature of the state Republican establishment at that time, I asked, "Why should I bother?" To which he replied with the certainty of a historian, "Because when things get bad enough, history has a way of repeating itself, and will. You 'progressive Republicans' consistently captured the unique values that are Minnesota's contribution to our democracy. You respected this state's institutions, and translated our ideas for progress into public policy." His words echoed in my mind after he was gone.

Several years later, I was pleased to learn that another veteran Minnesota political observer shared Fridley's thinking. Lori Sturdevant's willingness to be my writing partner convinced me to proceed. Lori has put in forty-plus years at the *Minneapolis Star Tribune*, making her a unique presence in our community. On the newspaper's editorial staff since 1992, Lori has also been the author, co-author, or editor of the life stories of some outstanding Minnesotans, including the one-and-only Governor Elmer L. Andersen, who was a special friend and mentor to both of us. I thought myself a gifted analyst and writer until I spent two years with Lori writing nearly sixty years of Minnesota political history and discovered her gift for conveying the same idea better than I—in half the time. That's her gift to you, our readers.

My wife, Susan Bartlett Foote, provided more inspiration as she worked daily for several years to produce her second book, *The Crusade for Forgotten Souls*, published in April 2018 by University of Minnesota Press. She tells of the unsung citizen heroes who pressed for change and the progressive Republican governor whose commitment to reform brought him and Minnesota national acclaim. To Susan I owe not only love and admiration, but also gratitude for renewed appreciation of how dependent those of us who seek to succeed at elected office are on voters' passion for change.

The true public servant owes much to lessons learned from those he or she represents. As a nearly lifelong politician, I am eager to acknowledge more than a million Minnesota voters who, on three very different occasions, put a check mark by my name to make me their United States senator. Their trust and their ideas gave me a platform from which to learn and serve them and the nation. Among this many, some stand out. Paul Overgaard, a state senator from Albert Lea, was there for me, at great personal sacrifice, when I needed him most. Gene and Susie Holderness were best friends before I made the decision to run for elective office. Gene, the most brilliant man I've known, managed my first and most challenging reelection campaign in 1982 and kept everyone's head, including mine, "screwed on right."

This book also owes much to members of both parties and their elected leaders in the Minnesota legislature and those with whom I served in the US Senate and House of Representatives. My first Senate

Finance Committee chair, Louisiana Democrat Russell Long, taught me to value the uniqueness of a Senate with two members from each state, so that "when every state is heard from, we get good national policy." I hope that idea is among the key takeaways from this book. The Senate ought not be just another House of Representatives beholden to popular whim.

Senate majority and minority leader and Republican presidential candidate Robert J. Dole schooled me on the evolution of congressional and presidential leadership and the influence of single-issue advocacy groups in today's politics. He also modeled devotion to the people he served when, at age ninety, he visited each of 108 Kansas counties to express his thanks. His fellow Kansas senator and my best friend in the Senate from the class of 1978, Nancy Landon Kassebaum, also became the wife of Howard Baker, Dole's predecessor as Republican leader. Nancy affirmed my recollection of the resistance progressive Republican senators began to feel from within our own party in the late 1980s. Most of us were out of office by the mid-1990s.

Among the many Minnesotans who helped me tell this story, none has left a legacy to this state like that of Wheelock Whitney, who died in 2016. He was a leader in commerce and finance, in nonprofit and foundation work, and in Republican politics without ever having been elected to office. Wheelock and his cousin Whitney MacMillan, the former chairman of Cargill Co., provided me an opportunity to create the National Institute of Health Policy at the Opus College of Business at the University of St. Thomas. The fond memories that so many Minnesotans have of Wheelock attest to the abiding appeal of his brand of progressive Republicanism. MacMillan is among the several dozen people to whom I am grateful for help financing this project. Their generosity truly made this book possible.

My memories of a Minnesota Republican Party that was independent of national party directives were reinforced by former party chairs Bob Brown, Chuck Slocum, and, just before he died, Leon Oistad, who also managed my 1988 campaign. The family of the late

Bob Forsythe, who chaired the party in the 1960s, contributed the story of his town hall debates with DFL chair George Farr, including the day in 1965 when he sent his son in his place because he, the Minnesota Republican chair, was in Selma, Alabama, marching with Martin Luther King Jr. into history.

The late governor Harold LeVander's children, Hap LeVander and Jean LeVander King, contributed archival material and encouragement for this project. Besides being a best friend and on Harold Stassen's "short list" of five female Minnesota Republican candidates for the US Senate in 1978, Jean served on her dad's staff and as staff chief to Governor Al Quie. Commissioners E. I. "Bud" Malone and Richard Brubacher and staff members Archie Chelseth, Larry Koll, Mike McTeague, and Fred Krohn were most helpful. Other veterans of the LeVander years in Minnesota politics cheered us on, including my former law partner, federal judge Paul Magnuson, and retired state supreme court associate justice Paul Anderson. Martha Head gathered some of the leaders of the Hennepin County "young turks" for a fascinating glimpse into the character of young progressive Republicans in Minnesota. Veteran Minnesota political reporters of my day were enormously insightful as well.

The other two victors in the Minnesota Massacre election of 1978–former governor Al Quie and my US Senate colleague Rudy Boschwitz–remain friends and sources of inspiration and insight. Scott Cottington, the Litchfield grocery store owner's "son in the back room" whom I met on my first day as a gubernatorial candidate in 1977, contributed the perspective of one of the best Republican campaign consultants in the country. Former Minnesota US representative Vin Weber added to our understanding of congressional politics in the 1980s and 1990s. Former governor Tim Pawlenty challenged us with his take on the party's story in the years since 1994.

Several key leaders of the Citizens League of the twentieth century remain active citizens in the twenty-first and were allies of this project. Ted Kolderie, Tom Swain, Paul Gilje, and John Adams put on a Saturday seminar for Lori and me about the trends that shaped the

Twin Cities a half century ago. Clarence Shallbetter and Lyle Wray helped as well.

I was ready to take on public policy formation in 1966 because I'd learned the principles of community development and leadership in the Junior Chamber of Commerce, or Jaycees. I am indebted to Don Salverda, the president of my South St. Paul Jaycee club's chief competitor, the Roseville Jaycees. He went on to serve as a Ramsey County commissioner and today oversees leadership institutes for local government administrators while breeding optimism at the Roseville Optimists Club. I was schooled in the importance of corporate social responsibility through many years of watching it in action in Minnesota. Former ADC Telecommunications CEO Chuck Denny reinforced those lessons for this project.

My memories of the way in which progressive Republicans cared for the environment were supplemented by Peter Gove, who served in both Minnesota and the federal government and turned down my staff offer to instead become a best friend and leading conservationist for life. My neighbor and veteran state capitol lobbyist Bill Strusinski helped me understand the influence of progressive Republicans on Governor Wendell Anderson and his chief of staff, Tom Kelm. So did retired Minnesota Senate secretary Pat Flahaven and Minneapolis attorney and former DFL representative Tom Berg, who wrote *Minnesota's Miracle: Lessons from a Government That Worked*, a fine book about the legislature in the 1970s.

My former US Senate staff members were willing and able resources about my efforts to bring Minnesota's progressive Republican ideas to Washington. Former chiefs of staff Tom Horner, Bert McKasy, and Rick Evans; policy staffers and committee aides Ralph Neas, Steve Ockenden, Ed Levine, Shirley Hunt, and Danny McNamara; and communications and constituent services wizards Jon and Dana Schroeder, Karen Humphrey, and Lois West Duffy all helped in ways great and small. I'm forever grateful for their love for "we the people."

Jimmie Powell and Steve Moore deserve special recognition. Jimmie began working with me as research staff to Governor Wendell

Anderson's Commission on the Arts, joined me in community affairs work at H. B. Fuller, and managed my campaign for governor. He became the person on my Washington staff and then the environment committee staff who had the greatest influence in shaping my thinking about the role of government in driving private solutions to commonly experienced public problems. He helped me write and pass some of the period's most valuable and effective environmental legislation. Steve Moore came to work as my legislative director in 1985 and remains a best friend and spiritual mentor to this day. He understood my sincerity when I confided that growing up under the influence of Benedictine fathers and brothers and Franciscan sisters at St. John's led me to believe that "the sign of God is that I will be led where I did not expect to go." In that spirit, when my Senate colleagues asked me to represent their faith commitments to the leaders of some four dozen nations, most of whose dominant religion differed from mine, I went. When asked in retirement to join a small group of Twin Cities Catholic leaders in weekly prayer, I did. They were my spiritual support team for this project.

The former state legislators who shared their stories include some of Minnesota's finest. Wayne Popham, Jack Davies, Paul Overgaard, Lyall Schwarzkopf, and Ernie Lindstrom helped Lori and me understand the legislative sessions prior to 1973; Roger Moe, Duane Benson, David Jennings, Kathleen Blatz, and Glen Taylor described the 1980s and 1990s. After his legislative service, Taylor became one of the most successful entrepreneurs in Minnesota by espousing the philosophy that success is never about winning and losing, but about shaping every contest in business, public policy, and politics so that both sides are winners. Across the aisle, DFL leadership veteran Roger Moe observed that a good legislative process is like two hundred people working on a jigsaw puzzle. The leaders on both sides see issues build over time, recognize that everyone brings something to the table, and assign a few to work out the picture on the box so everyone contributes something. The leaders' task is to encourage everyone's willingness to return to the table for the next puzzle.

Every legislative leader who contributed to this book urged capitalizing on the economics of Minnesota as one state, built on renewable natural and human resources. They join Lori and me in lamenting the rise of a version of identity politics that fosters regional resentments, dividing Minnesotans from one another and contributing to government gridlock and dysfunction.

My dismay about the change in my political party was part of the impetus for this book. But it was also propelled by my abiding faith in the wisdom of the American people and, in particular, the goodness of the people of Minnesota. As new friend Joe Cunningham reminded me, Minnesota is "think-it-over country." Minnesotans are instinctively curious, "why not try" people who have always produced informed leadership for policy change at all levels of governance. For all that they taught me through decades of public service, and for the many ways they inspire me still, I am in their debt.

Dave Durenberger

The transformation of Minnesota's Republican Party may be the biggest story I've covered during more than forty years as a journalist at the *Minneapolis Star Tribune*. A dramatic change has occurred, shifting not only the party's philosophy but also its geographic and demographic base in ways that would make it almost unrecognizable to those who led it in the middle of the twentieth century. I am persuaded that that change has had a negative effect on government in both Minnesota and the nation. It has contributed to a recurring gridlock that leaves chronic state and national problems to fester and erodes Americans' trust in the form of government they've inherited.

My newspaper duties have obliged me to describe the Minnesota Republican Party's journey from center-right progressivism to Trumpism in the increments of daily journalism, one legislative session, party convention, and election at a time. I'm exceedingly grateful to Dave Durenberger for the chance to help him tell this story with the sweep of decades it deserves. Dave and I share a deep devotion to Minnesota and an admiration for the quality of the civic life that prevailed in this state through most of our lifetimes. It's been a satisfying exercise to help him convey how Republicans in the Stassen line worked with like-minded DFLers to create Minnesota's strong civic life, how and why that political line vanished, and how concerned citizens might create conditions in which a like-minded political force might rise again.

Dave has named many of the people who shared their stories and spurred us on with both encouragement and financial support. To all of them, thank you.

Let me add particular appreciation for the Star Tribune, my employer since 1976. I began covering state politics in the year Dave first ran for the US Senate, 1978, and fell in love with the beat. Being allowed to pursue that passion for so long, first as a reporter, then as an assignment editor, editorial writer, and columnist, is rare in my profession. For this, my eleventh book project, the Star Tribune was again generous in allowing me a leave of absence and access to its electronic archives. Editorial editor Scott Gillespie and my editorial board colleagues kindly accommodated this project's demands. Their support has been a great asset.

I'm also grateful to work for the second time with editor in chief Ann Regan, managing editor Shannon Pennefeather, and the other publishing professionals at Minnesota Historical Society Press. Their coaching, editing, designing, and marketing services are first-rate. Ann bravely indulged our desire to produce an unconventional "hybrid" book—part history, part memoir, part editorial argument—and helped us achieve those aims in this volume.

All of my eleven books have benefitted from one excellent copyeditor—my husband, Martin Vos. He has also supported this project by fueling the authors with lattes, providing them with a ready sounding board, and tolerating the nights, weekends, and vacations it has consumed. Dave's wife, Susan Bartlett Foote, has been equally devoted, going so far as to share material from her own book project to aid ours. They have our abiding thanks and love.

Lori Sturdevant

When Republicans Were Progressive

INTRODUCTION

T HE STORY OF MINNESOTA'S progressive Republican Party is a poignant reminder that a very different Republican Party holds sway in Minnesota, and the country, today. Minnesota's progressive Republican Party came to power in 1938, had its heyday in the middle of the twentieth century, and faded into near obscurity by the century's end. Yet it is remembered fondly, and when the CEO of a large Minnesota company recently described it to me, his perceptive evaluation rang true. He said it "spoke for the silent majority that lives in the center, sometimes veering right on certain issues and sometimes left on others, thus making compromise both possible and admirable."

Modern Minnesota's success story sprang from the ideas and ideals of that party. It stood not for big or small government but for effective government. It prized government not for its own sake but as a practical tool for creating the conditions that allowed individuals to thrive. To a remarkable degree, it both reflected and enlarged the strengths of the people of Minnesota. It supplied their leaders and built their institutions. It nurtured a sense of responsibility for the common good in both citizens and elected officials. It encouraged citizen participation, drawing its ideas and resources from the grass roots. It provided keen competition for other political parties while respecting its rivals' contribution to the whole. It held that "working across the aisle," as well as across the state or the country, was a mark of strength, not weakness or disloyalty.

The progressive Republican Party produced governors Harold Stassen, Luther Youngdahl, Elmer L. Andersen, Harold LeVander, Al Quie, and Arne Carlson. It greatly influenced the agendas of DFL governors Wendell Anderson and Rudy Perpich. It's also the party that sent me to the US Senate in 1978. During my sixteen years there, I brought progressive Minnesota Republican values to bear on national policy.

While its antecedents arose well before the state's founding, the political organization this book describes originated with Harold Stassen. Remembered—and scorned by some—for a series of increasingly futile bids for the presidency, Stassen was far more than a perennial candidate. He was the charismatic young leader in the late 1930s who took a state by storm and made an immediate impression on national politics with a fresh, appealing Republican response to the distress of the Great Depression. He rejected both the laissez-faire ideology of a previous generation of Republicans and the left-leaning cronyism of the Farmer-Labor Party, a populist force that peaked in Minnesota in the early 1930s and outshone the Democratic Party in the state in those years. Stassen sold a generation of followers on the virtues of an efficient, professionally run government, friendly to organized labor and responsive to the needs of the downtrodden. He argued that government should be "an aid to individual initiative, not a substitute for it." He wanted Minnesota Republicans to claim as their special purview an ability to make government perform well in service of that goal. Though Stassen left state politics when he joined the navy in 1943, he cast such a long shadow that this book might have been entitled "Stassen's Line."

Stassen personally recruited the likes of Luther Youngdahl, Elmer L. Andersen, Harold LeVander, as well as future US chief justice Warren Burger to the slightly right of center party he built, and he inspired a good many more young people of ambition and ability to sign on with the Republican Party. Returning GIs from both World

War II and the Korean Conflict found it a congenial political home as they worked to build households and businesses in the 1950s and 1960s. Those "Young Turk" Republicans stood for civil rights, quality public education, adequate infrastructure, environmental protection (they called it "conservation"), and compassionate care for the physically and mentally disabled—all financed with taxes they were unafraid to raise and reform for the sake of both adequacy and fairness. They met with resistance from both an "Old Guard" within their own party and many in the Democratic-Farmer-Labor Party, created by merger in 1944. But while the DFL was also gaining strength during the 1960s, Stassen-style Republicans were in the driver's seat in state politics.

These Minnesotans believed that their state and its institutions were testing grounds for the creation of "a more perfect union." They were willing to employ government at all levels to tackle problems, forging alliances with slightly left of center DFLers and borrowing ideas from Minnesota's grassroots-based nonpartisan think tank, the Citizens League, to set public policies that were both innovative and durable. These Republicans had lives of professional and community service outside politics that helped them better understand the role of government. They approached politics and public policy with both pragmatism and a sense of purpose. They were eager to learn from people with different backgrounds, look for consensus, compromise with both the ideological right and left, and aim for what was within reach.

Minnesota Republicans took such pride in their homegrown success story that when the Watergate scandal sullied the image of the national party, they changed the state party's name to emphasize its separate identity. It became the Independent-Republican (IR) Party. That name lasted for twenty years and contributed to the 1978 election sweep that ushered me and Rudy Boschwitz into the US Senate, Al Quie into the governor's office, and a huge class of IR freshmen into the Minnesota house, resulting in a messy 67–67 balance of power in 1979.

These progressive, pragmatic Republicans were my teachers, supplying me with ideas I took to national policy making in environmental protection, health care, education, energy, trade, civil rights, intergovernmental relations, and foreign policy. That work became increasingly difficult in the last half of my Senate tenure. Republicans in the state and nation began drifting away from Stassen-style progressivism in the 1980s. As the World War II generation left the field, Democrats who were uncomfortable with their party's deepening commitment to civil rights and to a woman's right to abortion drifted into the Republican fold. They found a party whose winner-take-all rules made it susceptible to takeover by well-organized zealots. In the Minnesota IR Party, an increasingly politicized religious right found a home, particularly in rural and exurban sections of the state. The willingness of the party's new establishment to mount a primary challenge—albeit unsuccessfully—against a popular moderate IR governor in 1994, the year I left the Senate, showed how far from progressivism the party had moved.

I can measure the time that the nation has been largely without a progressive Republican influence in Washington in personal terms, by the lifespan of my granddaughter Sara Durenberger. Sara, my eldest grandchild, is now a college grad and a health professional. She was born in May 1994 on the day on which President Bill Clinton's proposed health reform legislation was to be marked up in the Health, Education, Labor, and Pensions Committee. I was striving mightily to move the committee away from Clinton's highly regulated measures to a more market-oriented approach to health-care coverage. I was facing opposition from both the left and the right. To my dismay, many in my own party had decided that ensuring the failure of the Clinton proposal was more important than improving health care for Americans.

An hour into the debate, I left the hearing room for a phone call from my son Charlie in St. Paul, who informed me that I was a new grandfather. When I returned, the committee chair, Democratic senator Edward M. Kennedy, pounded his gavel and said, "I am pleased and very happy to announce the birth this morning of Sara Marie Durenberger," and followed with her exact dimensions! Kennedy added, "Dave's concerns about being a first-time grandfather may be the cause for some of the heat he's been giving us lately on this bill." Much laughter and prolonged applause followed—along with a tear or two from me. That kind of comity was among the ingredients of the Senate I knew. It is among the casualties of the change in the Republican Party that this book chronicles.

More than two decades have passed since I left office. No one would claim today that Minnesota or the nation has two philosophically centrist major parties, one slightly left of center, one slightly right. America's political middle no longer has a party. That change has led directly to the disconcerting presidency of Donald Trump and the inability of Republican majorities in Congress to effectively respond to chronic problems that include widening income inequality, unaffordable and/or unavailable health insurance and health care, worsening epidemics of opioid addiction and gun violence, and the plight of 11 million undocumented immigrants on whose labor the economy depends. Dysfunction in Congress is a reflection of an electorate whose disdain for government at any level Republicans have been stoking for decades. Many elected officials in today's GOP have abandoned all semblance of bipartisanship. Republicans in Congress and in Minnesota have talked themselves into believing that Democrats cannot be trusted to meet their standards for reform. And Democrats are desperate to unite their fractured party around Republican failures—but not, to date, around fresh ideas.

While both parties have at varying times enjoyed electoral success in the last twenty-five years, few observers could claim that Americans are satisfied with the result. By substantial majorities, Americans have been telling pollsters for years that they consider the nation "on the wrong track." That's been true whether Republicans or Democrats are in power. As the two parties have moved away from centrist progressivism, both appear to have lost the public's trust. I don't think that is coincidental. In fact, one can claim that Trump's triumph over a field of more experienced politicians in 2016 was not an affirmation of trust in today's Republican Party but just the opposite.[1]

The good word "progressive," once associated with President Theodore Roosevelt and midwestern Republicans like Wisconsin's Robert La Follette, is now mostly identified with the left wing of the Democratic Party. Those Democrats appear to believe that every commonly experienced problem requires expanding the legal, programmatic, and financing authority of the federal government. But centrist Democrats in Minnesota have told me they see only too well the problem-solving limits of Great Society–style federal efforts that dilute the accountability of state and local elected officials. They, too, long for a progressivism that respects local and state control—the kind that once governed Minnesota. I'm confident that a revival of progressive Republicanism would be widely welcomed.

This book is not an exercise in nostalgia. Rather, it is written in a spirit of hope. The words "What Is Past Is Prologue" are carved in stone outside the National Archives for good reason. It is common in societies for ideas to come in and out of fashion and patterns to recur. That gives me hope that the progressive Republican ideas I knew in Minnesota will come back, whether in the Republican Party, the Democratic Party, or some new political organization not yet named. What humans once created can be created again, especially if history is available as a guide to those intent on producing positive change.

This book attempts to supply some of that history. More than that: it argues that the principles and practices of the party I once knew are a fitting remedy for what ails American democracy today. For this nation to flourish, it must be led by a political organization that's broadly representative of and accountable to the people, not to special-interest donors. It must engage the brightest members of each new generation, calling forth their best selves with a positive vision of public service. It must see government not as the problem, but as a tool for identifying and solving shared problems. It must seek to employ that tool deftly, with a maximum of competence and cost efficiency. It must maintain a healthy regard for the prerogatives of each level of government, recognizing that public service is often at its best at the state and local level. It must respect the distinct civic character of each state and community. It must see government as both a check on capitalism's excesses and a partner in its preservation.

Ordinary Americans have lately approached me in search of direction toward a better democracy. They ask: "What do you think? What can we do? Have you any ideas?" This book is my response. It may not be possible to go back to the future. But it is possible to look back and learn, and then use that knowledge to bend the nation's course.

1 A BURST OF CHANGE

MAIN STREETS IN RURAL MINNESOTA TOWNS are sedate places in early fall, as farmers prepare for harvest and kids return to school. A small commotion is sufficient to attract considerable notice. Imagine, then, the wide eyes and gaping jaws that would have greeted riders on several dozen horses that galloped unannounced into a sleepy town's center, tooting horns, pounding drums, shooting pistols into the air, and whooping as if they were herding cattle.

That was how the Harold Stassen campaign for governor announced its arrival in town after town in 1938. Stassen's friends and neighbors in the Hook 'Em Cow horse-riding club from the meatpacking town of South St. Paul—many of them about the same age as the thirty-one-year-old candidate—were only too happy to create a ruckus on Stassen's behalf. They were as eager as was the candidate himself to signal that this was no ordinary Republican quest for the governorship. It was a campaign brimming with youth, energy, creativity, and willingness to try something new.

The Hook 'Em cowboys' "vote roundup" added excitement and fun to Stassen's campaign stops. But by the fall of 1938, Stassen may not have needed their assistance to draw a crowd. He had become an object of fascination in his own right.

The young prosecutor from Dakota County had burst onto the state's political stage only two years earlier as chairman of the brand-new Minnesota Young Republican League. With that office as his calling card, he stumped the state to proclaim that young Republicans, born in the twentieth century and shaped by a cruel depression, possessed ideas more expansive than their elders' about the rightful role of government in American life. Stassen initially attracted skeptical notice when he announced a bid for governor in November 1937. But he then shocked his party's establishment by gaining enough delegates to block an endorsement at the Republican state convention. That sent the GOP's four-way gubernatorial nomination contest into a wide-open primary on June 20. Stassen won with amazing ease, besting the party's 1934 and 1936 gubernatorial nominee, Martin Nelson, by nearly fifty thousand votes. Minnesotans had never before seen a young politician rise so rapidly. Harold Stassen was a phenomenon people wanted to see for themselves.[1]

That included George and Isabelle Durenberger. My parents were small-town Minnesotans at the time of Stassen's rise. My father was the first in his family to attend college, arriving at St. John's University by Greyhound bus from Le Sueur, Minnesota (home of the Jolly Green Giant), in early September 1924. Like all the students, he walked a mile from Minnesota Highway 52 to the campus, midway between two small towns in central Minnesota's predominantly German-Catholic Stearns County. "Big George," as he was known, graduated in 1928. His athletic prowess landed him a job at his alma mater as a coach that same year. By 1930, he was college athletic director.

My dad was fortunate to have a reliable job during the Depression and to marry my mother, Isabelle Cebulla, in 1933. Her father, Ferdinand "Fred" Cebulla, came to a farm outside Delano, Minnesota, in 1899 from Pilchowicz, Poland, with all but one of his siblings. He went to work for the Great Northern Railroad at age fifteen, working his way across the country laying track and up the corporate ladder to become an officer of the company by the time he retired fifty years later. I was given his first name as my middle name when I was born in 1934—at a time, I used to say, when "I was all my parents could afford to have." That's not quite true; four other children soon followed.

George's best friend from St. John's was Fred J. Hughes, a St. Cloud attorney and one of Stassen's earliest supporters. Through Fred, the Durenbergers were introduced to Republican politics and became admirers of Stassen's brand of Republicanism. All during my child-hood, I associated the names Harold Stassen and Fred J. Hughes with Republicanism, and I believed they represented the values of my family as much as did the ideas I acquired at daily Mass and my public grade school, which was taught by three Franciscan nuns. On a recent tour of St. John's with my grandchildren, we met a priest who had been my St. John's Prep boarding school classmate. He told our kids, "We all envied Dave because he got to go home for dinner every night," and added, "and we always knew he was a Republican." More precisely, a Stassen Republican.

Harold Edward Stassen was an imposing figure, easily spotted as he emerged from his campaign car. He stood well over six feet tall and possessed broad shoulders, a rich baritone voice, a leonine head, an expansive smile, and large farm-boy hands capable of memorable handshakes. He also possessed keen intelligence and amazing drive. Born April 13, 1907, the third son of truck farmers William and Elsbeth Mueller Stassen of West St. Paul, young Harold was raised in a house-hold that prized hard work, education, and Baptist piety.

Both his mother and his paternal grandfather were among the one out of four Minnesotans in 1910 who were foreign-born—his mother in Germany, his grandfather in Austria. Those northern European roots were common in Minnesota. In 1900, two-thirds of the state's foreign-born residents came from just three countries: Germany, Sweden, and Norway. The Scandinavians and Protestant Germans who chose Minnesota brought with them communitarian impuls-es nurtured by both their Lutheran faith and their experience with parliamentary democracies. The German Catholics who settled in Stearns County also possessed a zeal for community life. These tra-ditions meshed well with the ideas of Minnesota's founding settlers from New England, who brought with them a tradition of highly participatory democracy via town meeting governance. Many—though not all—of the new German Americans in Minnesota believed that their new homeland should not be divorced from the old, an idea that would come to be called internationalism.[2]

By the time Stassen was fifteen, his father was ill and he was managing the family farm. He was also already studying at the University of Minnesota, where he enrolled after graduating second in his class

Harold Stassen and his father, William Stassen, about 1939. *Courtesy of MNHS Collections*

at St. Paul's Humboldt High School. His father, who survived his illness and went on to play leading roles in local Republican politics, would later boast that his son had the kind of academic prowess that allowed him to earn top grades without regular class attendance. At the university, Stassen was a champion debater, orator, and marksman; his rifle squad won three national championships in a row with him as its sure-shot captain. Fellow students would marvel years later at his gargantuan capacity for work. He held a variety of physically demanding jobs, including a stint as a night Pullman conductor on a train from St. Paul to Chicago, in order to support himself and pay for law school, in which he enrolled immediately after completing his bachelor's degree.[3]

Stassen graduated from law school in 1929, at the tender age of twenty-two. Just a year later, he was the successful candidate for Dakota County attorney, making him the county's top criminal prosecutor. It was the same year in which another county attorney, Hennepin County's Floyd B. Olson, would win the governorship for the upstart Minnesota Farmer-Labor Party. Stassen was well aware of his new office's potential as a political springboard.

He also saw how the Great Depression was ravaging the lives of his friends and neighbors on the small farms that then dominated Dakota County, just south of St. Paul. At one point he dissuaded dairy farmers angry about low prices from their plan to block a highway, promising that he would help them negotiate higher prices for their milk—a promise he kept, free of charge. Dakota County's proximity to St. Paul exposed it to organized crime, an ill effect of Prohibition and the Depression. Stassen's name appeared frequently in headlines as he investigated and prosecuted a spate of gang-related bank robberies and murders that rattled nerves in the countryside.[4]

The Depression undoubtedly solidified in Stassen a political philosophy that had been taking shape since his youth. One might say he was born Republican—raised in a Republican household in a state where the Republican Party had been the dominant political force for more than a half century.

Minnesota became a state in 1858, its politics marked from the start by the searing national debate over slavery that gave way to the Civil War in 1861. Antislavery and pro-union sentiment ran strong in Minnesota. Republican governor Alexander Ramsey made Minnesota the first state in the union to offer troops to President Abraham Lincoln, on April 12, the day after Confederates shelled Fort Sumter. The 82 percent casualty rate the First Minnesota Volunteer Infantry Regiment sustained at Gettysburg sealed in blood the state's loyalty to the party of Lincoln for the remainder of the nineteenth century. Republicans were the state's establishment party, the party of choice for both the founding New Englanders and many of the newcomers. It accommodated both captains of the state's burgeoning timber, flour, and iron industries and the small farmers and eager entrepreneurs who flocked to the state after the Civil War and the scarring US–Dakota War in the Minnesota River valley in 1862.

The party was sufficiently dominant to offer a "big tent" to a variety of ideas and personalities—not all of them harmonious. While Republican patronage strengthened the party's control, "rifts within the Republican Party were more serious politically than Democratic rivalry," historian Theodore Blegen noted. In general, Minnesota Republicans stood for nationalism rather than state's rights; for suffrage for African Americans (but not yet for women); and for business expansion, unfettered and sometimes actively encouraged by government. Friendly regard of railroads in particular was an early Republican staple and a sore spot within the party as the decades unfolded.[5]

Minnesota's nineteenth-century Republicans were, however, united in fidelity to strict notions about limits on government's role in solving the shared problems of a population. Not even a plague of locusts could bend those notions. The state's most popular nineteenth-century governor, John S. Pillsbury, took office in 1875 at the midpoint of a four-year siege by Rocky Mountain locusts in the southwestern quadrant of the state. The grasshoppers were destroying crops and inflicting stunning damage, consuming clothes hung out to dry and the wooden handles of garden tools. The prairie was depopulating; pioneers who tried to hang on were in dire straits. Whole communities were destitute. Pillsbury, a big-hearted patriarch in the Minneapolis milling family, was so much inclined to help that he issued a widely circulated Christmas appeal for donations and spent his own funds to collect and distribute them. He also visited the region at his own expense, dispensing cash and at one point giving a struggling farmer his own overcoat on a bitterly cold day. He met with other governors of afflicted midwestern states and helped finance the distribution of a pamphlet containing the best scientific advice of the day for combating locusts—advice that in hindsight appears largely worthless. He went so far as to declare a day of prayer in April 1877 to call on God to "stay the pestilence."

But Pillsbury was unwilling to do what would come naturally in Minnesota in the twenty-first century if a large segment of the state were similarly stricken. He did not ask the legislature to appropriate money for relief. He and other Republicans rejected direct government aid to the citizenry as too prone to the "moral hazard" of dependency. They also considered unacceptable providing any aid to the schools, cities, and counties that were unable to collect property taxes from impoverished farmers. The plague would end in mid-1877, with many of Pillsbury's contemporaries claiming that his day of prayer had been his most effective response to the infestation.[6]

A new century brought new ideas. Rifts within the GOP coalition widened. Farmers and laborers increasingly chafed at an economic system that seemed stacked against them. They came together in new associations, giving rise to politically potent labor unions, cooperatives, and third parties. Minnesotans began electing an occasional Democrat, first Governor John A. Lind in 1898, then popular Governor John A. Johnson, elected to three terms beginning in 1905.

Meanwhile, about the time baby Harold joined the Stassen family, a new strain of Republicanism emerged. In the White House, President Theodore Roosevelt was rattling the Republican business establishment with a willingness to employ the federal government in efforts to rein in the oligarchs' power, particularly over government itself. He drew heavily from ideas that sprang from the Midwest. Wisconsin's Robert La Follette (first as governor, then US senator) and Indiana's US senator Albert Beveridge argued that government should be controlled by the people rather than large business interests and should be a tool to better the lot of working people in an increasingly industrialized nation. When Roosevelt broke with the Republican Party to run against his former protégé President William Howard Taft for a third term as president in 1912, he gave his new party a name and a platform that would long outlast that year's campaign. He called it the Progressive Party.

Its platform was an agenda that like-minded American politicians in both major parties would trot out for the remainder of the twentieth century. Among its ideas: Women's suffrage. Direct election of US senators. An income tax and inheritance tax. National health service. Social insurance for the elderly, disabled, and unemployed. Veteran's pensions. A minimum wage for women. An eight-hour workday. Limits on judges' ability to end labor strikes. The creation of a cabinet-level Department of Labor. Workers' compensation for workers injured on the job. Limits and disclosure requirements on campaign contributions. An open meeting requirement for government bodies. Candidates chosen by the voters via primary elections. Lobbyist registration and disclosure of expenditures. Initiative, referendum, and recall.[7]

Roosevelt lost the 1912 presidential election, and his third-party foray had the unintended short-term consequence of tightening the conservative grip on the Republican Party, both in Minnesota and in the nation as a whole. But Minnesota was among six states Roosevelt won. Progressive ideas had been planted deeply in the state.

Progressive ideas would not dominate Minnesota's Republican Party in the quarter century after Theodore Roosevelt's last hurrah, however. Rather, those ideas were embraced in larger measure by Minnesota's next and most successful third party, the Farmer-Labor Party. It emerged in 1918, and by the time Stassen was a student at the University of Minnesota, it was led by an amalgam of socialists, labor activists, economically aggrieved farmers, and a smattering of communists. It was also gaining strength as the postwar prosperity enjoyed elsewhere in the country failed to extend to the midwestern farm belt.[8]

Stassen often told in later years of witnessing a skirmish on a cold December day in 1921 during a labor strike at the meatpacking plants near the South St. Paul stockyards, not far from his boyhood home. He watched in horror on the second day of the strike as a picket line of strikers—men and women he knew—were roughed up and forcibly pushed aside by armed National Guard troops. They had been ordered to the scene by Republican governor J. A. O. Preus, the scion of a prominent family of Lutheran clergy, at the request of the plant owners. The packinghouse owners, intent on breaking the Amalgamated Meat Cutters and Butcher Workmen union, had announced that any worker who joined the strike had forfeited his job. Stassen's father, a local Republican Party leader, was offended by the use of troops against average Minnesotans who were simply trying to preserve their incomes through a nonviolent work stoppage. The strike would end sixty-four days later with union members reluctantly giving in to wage concessions and union leaders facing criminal charges for violating a court order to end the strike. The episode left young Stassen with an enduring belief that government owed workers a fairer response to their plight.[9]

The privations of the Great Depression renewed that sentiment in the still-young Dakota County prosecutor. But Stassen had a sufficient brush with communist agitators during a 1934 strike at the same meatpacking plants to stiffen his opposition to the communist cause. Stassen was alarmed by Farmer-Labor governor Floyd B. Olson's tolerance of communists within his party and his 1934 avowal at his party's convention, "I am frank to say what I want to be. I am a radical." Olson was increasingly talking about government takeover of key industries and a revolutionary break with capitalism. Such talk worried even some elements of Olson's political base, and some of the state's employers called for his resignation. The situation was ripe for revival of the progressive Republicanism that Theodore Roosevelt had embodied in 1912.[10]

Enter the Young Republican League. Established in Minnesota in the fall of 1935, the league's founding documents made no secret of its desire to be "a source of new personnel and fresh ideas for the Republican Party." Its first state chairman, Harold Stassen, was chosen in March 1936. Almost immediately, he began stumping the state to recruit members and announce to anyone who would listen that a new generation had arrived to reshape the state GOP.

Then the trajectory of the Farmer-Labor Party changed. Olson died of stomach cancer in August 1936. He was succeeded after the 1936 election by Farmer-Laborite Elmer Benson, a rural banker who had been Olson's banking commissioner and who had served a brief stint in the US Senate, courtesy of a gubernatorial appointment when the seat became vacant in December 1935 due to incumbent Thomas Schall's death in a Washington, DC, traffic accident. Benson possessed all of Olson's radicalism but little of Olson's personal charm or political finesse. Furthermore, Benson presided over a surge in state debt, state employment featherbedding, and preferential contracting to the benefit of Farmer-Labor cronies. Benson quickly became so unpopular that he barely survived a Farmer-Labor primary challenge by Hjalmar Petersen, who had been lieutenant governor in 1936 and completed Olson's term that year. Benson's positions on the left and the old-line conservatism of the Republican establishment on the right opened a wide philosophical gap in the middle for Stassen to occupy. He could present himself to the voters in 1938 as both a Republican and a reformer.

Stassen's stump speeches portrayed Benson as a divisive, radical figure who had failed to respond effectively to the renewed economic downturn that Minnesota and the nation experienced in 1937–38. Although he usually did not name Benson, Stassen clearly accused him of "preaching class hatred, bitterness and intolerance" and "a bigoted labeling of all who disagree as ignorant or dishonest." The Republican candidate scolded him for excessive partisanship and invited Hjalmar Petersen's Farmer-Labor supporters to his side. He vowed reforms that would end the cronyism and excessive patronage that the Benson administration had exhibited.

But the Stassen message was more than a critique of the Farmer-Labor incumbent. At his party's September 2 state convention, Stassen said he intended to "present a progressive, common-sense program" and offer "a new course to better conditions and more jobs in Minnesota." As if to underscore how different his course would be from the one set by the last Republican to serve as governor—Theodore "Tightwad Ted" Christianson—Stassen said his first concern would be increasing government help for the indigent. "We shall not be niggardly in extending the helping hand of government to care for our fellow men who are forced to be dependent on us," Stassen told Republican delegates. He spoke favorably and presciently about state assistance to the elderly, including support for their health-care costs.[11]

He sounded a more familiar Republican theme when he said his next task would be "securing more jobs in private employment" lest people receiving government help "spend their lives on this government sidetrack." But his notions were activist ones. Government could finance industry-spawning research at the University of Minnesota, he suggested. Tax credits could encourage industries to beef up research and development. State government could play a role in promoting Minnesota-made products around the world. It could step up tourism promotion—he suggested a "Governor's Day" at the start of the tourist season. He vowed as governor to exhibit "an active interest" in businesses that might locate or expand in Minnesota. Economic development should be a responsibility of state government and its chief executive, Stassen said—a view that would influence Minnesota governors for the rest of the twentieth century and beyond.[12]

Stassen also charted a new, middle-ground course on labor relations, announcing to GOP convention delegates that he disapproved of both "short-sighted, reactionary employers" and "radical labor agitators." For perhaps the first time, the pro-business Minnesota Republican Party had a candidate for governor who supported "full recognition of the rights of labor to organize and to bargain collectively through representatives of its own choice." Running just four years after a Teamsters' strike had left four men dead on the streets of Minneapolis, Stassen wanted labor peace and fairness for workers like the neighbors he had seen on picket lines in South St. Paul. "We shall never permit the National Guardsmen's bayonets to be used as an employer's weapon to crush those who labor," he said. He expressed interest in inviting labor and business leaders to work together to craft a "labor relations code," mentioning the example of three other nations many Minnesotans were inclined to favor–Norway, Sweden, and Denmark.

It was a fresh message, and a winning one. Stassen knocked Benson out of office with a stunning 60 percent of the vote in a three-way race. Benson came in second with 34 percent, and Democratic Party candidate Thomas Gallagher ran a distant third with slightly less than 6 percent of the vote. Republicans running as conservatives on the state's nonpartisan legislative ballot reclaimed a majority in the Minnesota house and added to their majority in the senate. The Farmer-Labor Party's heyday had ended. Six years later, it would merge with the Democratic Party to become Minnesota's Democratic-Farmer-Labor Party, or DFL.

The sense that a generational torch had been passed was keen at the state capitol in 1939. At age thirty-one, Stassen was hailed as the "boy wonder," the youngest governor elected in US history. Meanwhile, in the Minnesota house, a new thirty-year-old speaker took the gavel.

It's likely a testament to Stassen's appeal that house speaker Lawrence "Duck" Hall, an attorney from St. Cloud and another of my father's friends and classmates at St. John's, switched from the liberal to conservative caucus that year in order to join the new conservative majority. It's also a testament to Hall's leadership ability that he won the house's top job immediately after switching caucuses. The new governor and speaker were like-minded allies, eager to make their marks. At St. John's University in Collegeville, the Durenberger family rejoiced.

More than youth was being served in 1939. Stassen had promised reform, and he was under pressure to deliver. His inaugural message on January 3 reaffirmed many of the positions he had taken during his campaign. But he brought fresh emphasis to a proposal that would become a premier accomplishment—the professionalizing of state government via establishment of a merit-based civil service employment system.

Stassen understood that a major reason Minnesotans rejected his predecessor after only two years was their objection to state hiring and contracting practices they considered corrupt. He recognized that, by and large, voters were not seeking an end to the Farmer-Labor Party's activist policies. It was cronyism, not liberalism, that had offended Minnesotans. Self-dealing is a high political crime in Minnesotans' eyes. They see it as almost a personal betrayal. Stassen shared that judgment. He placed a high value on government and considered its redemption a noble mission—not to mention a politically advantageous one.

After a nod to his desire for bipartisanship, Stassen's inaugural speech turned immediately to a call for a new state hiring process: "One of our first and most important problems is to raise the standards of public service and to improve the morale of state government. A place on the state payroll must be based upon doing a good day's work for the people of the state for a day's pay received," he said. He vowed to base hiring decisions in his administration on applicants' "fundamental integrity," ability, and interest. But that vow would only be as good as the governor who made it. For lasting change, he said, the legislature must enact nonpartisan, merit-based civil service employment policies.[13]

The idea was far from new in Minnesota. The first bill to create a civil service employment system in state government had been introduced in the senate in 1889. A 1913–14 commission and a 1925 interim legislative committee recommended such a system, spelling out details such as how a three-member oversight board would be chosen and how various state jobs would be classified for compensation.

Governor Harold Stassen, 1939. *Courtesy of MNHS Collections*

But moves to actually implement such a system had been repeatedly blocked in the legislature, most recently in 1937, when the idea was promoted by a new civic interest group, the Minnesota Civil Service Council.[14]

But Farmer-Labor allies controlled the state house in 1937. In 1939, a big conservative majority was in charge in both chambers—100 of 134 members of the house, 56 of 67 members of the senate. The political impediment to the creation of a civil service system had evaporated. Just nine weeks after its introduction (a fast pace by legislative standards), the civil service bill was on its way to Governor Stassen's desk. It created a Department of Civil Service administered by a gubernatorially appointed three-member oversight board, which was empowered to hire a director based on scores on an exam, not political connections. The bill described the essentials of a merit-based hiring and compensation system for more than ten thousand classified employees. It specified that "the political or religious opinions or affiliations of an applicant shall not be considered."[15]

Minnesota was not the first state to enact civil service reform; in 1940, sixteen other states had systems that bore at least some similarities. But the reach of the Minnesota system was wider than in many places. More than three decades later, Minnesota's 1939 civil service reform law was still receiving national acclaim. "This fundamental reform has transformed the nature of Minnesota politics," wrote syndicated columnist Neal R. Peirce in 1973. He credited the law with making politics "a highly honorable profession in which citizens participate as willingly as in a united fund drive or PTA. There simply are no 'bosses,' and virtually no one goes into Minnesota politics out of a patronage motive. By taking politics out of the back room and engaging thousands in political activity, from women to college students, Stassen made the governmental process in Minnesota a superior instrument of the people's will."[16]

Stassen's desire to improve government operations was evident in another major achievement of 1939, the reorganization of state government into a structure resembling its current form. Small, patronage-driven fiefdoms such as the commissioner of purchases, the board of audit, the state printing commission, and the comptroller budget commissioner were eliminated, replaced by a Department of Administration charged with budgeting and controlling state purchasing. (That unit today is Minnesota Management and Budget, or MMB.) That change did much to advance state government accountability, efficiency, and respectability in the public's eyes. It also strengthened executive-branch control over state coffers. The new, powerful commissioner of administration, a gubernatorial appointee, was granted the power to unilaterally cut spending—or "unallot"—during a budget period when revenues were falling short.[17]

True to his campaign word, Stassen also pushed through the legislature a Labor Relations Act unlike any that would have been contemplated by the anti-union Republicans who dominated the state prior to the Depression. He took issue with those in his own party who wanted to end labor strife with a tough anti-union bill. At one point, he met all through the night with Republican hard-liners to convince them to drop a punitive measure that would have essentially abolished union shops and outlawed picketing. He, too, wanted fewer strikes, he argued. But he sought a way to deter strikes before they happened, by increasing the chances that collective bargaining would lead to agreement. That kind of strike prevention would give Minnesota an economic advantage, he said. It would also signal to working people that the Minnesota Republican Party no longer considered strikes illegitimate. Rather, Stassen Republicans saw strikes as undesirable and, with smart state intervention, preventable. That was a position many of the state's working people could get behind.

Stassen dubbed the result of his efforts the Minnesota Labor Peace Act, though in popular parlance it was known as the "count-ten law." It required that before a strike or lockout could occur, the party intending to initiate the work stoppage had to file written notice with a new office—the state labor conciliator—then wait ten days. During that time, negotiations would continue under the conciliator's direction. Further, if the dispute involved "a major public interest," the governor could get involved, appointing a fact-finding commission and extending the waiting period an additional thirty days. While the conciliator had no power to stop strikes or lockouts, the slowdown the law required seemed to work. The number of man-hours lost to strikes in Minnesota was down by more than two-thirds by 1942, *Life* magazine reported. It worked politically, too. Stassen won reelection handily in 1940 with 52 percent of the vote in a three-way race.[18]

Already, Stassen was a national figure. Soon after winning a second term, he was elected chair of the National Governors' Conference (today's National Governors Association). He was a hit at the 1939 Gridiron Club annual dinner, at which he introduced the Washington press corps to his brand of progressive Republicanism. "Government, in our view, must supply a cushion against the harsher features of a free economic system, but it cannot successfully furnish a bed on which society can go to sleep," he said. (His speech was so well received that a player in the following skit suggested that President Franklin Roosevelt should change Stassen's birthdate by executive order so that the thirty-two-year-old would be thirty-five and hence eligible to run for president in 1940.)

He made another big splash in 1940 as the keynote speaker at the Republican National Convention. That spot had been secured for him at least in part by Minnesotans who ranked among the national Republican Party's kingmakers, John and Eleanor ("Juty") Pillsbury, of the milling family, and John and Elizabeth Cowles, owners of the *Minneapolis Star Journal*. They touted him in part because his anti-isolationist views matched those of their preferred 1940 Republican presidential nominee, Wendell Willkie. In short order, Stassen was not only a keynote speaker but also a Willkie floor leader at the convention and chair of Willkie's campaign advisory committee.[19]

Isolationism—the idea that the United States should assiduously avoid involvement in European conflicts—was the dominant view among midwestern Republicans in the years after World War I. It is no coincidence that the nation's leading voice for isolationism in 1940 and 1941 was a son of Minnesota, aviator Charles Lindbergh, whose father and namesake, Charles A. Lindbergh, represented central Minnesota in the US House for ten years. The senior Lindbergh had opposed the nation's entry into World War I and retained enough favor with Minnesota voters that, had he not died in 1924, he might well have been elected governor that year.

But among the Durenbergers and many other progressive Minnesota Republican families in the year after war erupted in Europe, a contrary view was emerging. Many of us had familial roots in other lands. Gratitude for the freedom we found in this country helped us value government and public service. We were grieved by the rise of fascism and decline of democracy in Europe. If the United States could do something to stop those trends, we thought it should.

Stassen's 1940 convention speech gave voice to that idea. "Our forefathers erected here a great lighthouse for liberty," he said. "Once again, the black shadow of despotic force falls over the world. . . . Even as we meet, lights are going out in Europe. Black houses of dictators take the place of lighthouses of freemen. It is our grave responsibility to keep burning brightly the light of liberty." He stopped short of calling for US military intervention in Europe. But he had provided a philosophical frame for the shift in Republican thinking that would follow the attack on Pearl Harbor on December 7, 1941.[20]

After Willkie lost to FDR in 1940, Stassen's name began swirling as a potential presidential contender in 1944. That's why his announcement in the fall of 1942 made national news. Still just thirty-five years old, Stassen was a shoo-in for a third two-year term as governor. But he did not intend to serve a full term, he announced. His plan was to resign from the governorship after the 1943 legislative session and enlist in the US Navy. "This war will be fought by young men of my age, and I want to be with them," he said. He had already attained the rank of lieutenant commander in the Naval Reserve and had been taking correspondence courses to learn such naval rudiments as navigation and gunnery.[21]

Life magazine dispatched reporter Jack Alexander to Minnesota to inquire about Stassen's unconventional move. As Alexander noted, naval officers seemed to be in ample supply that fall; good governors were not: "His departure from Minnesota will deprive the state of a progressive governor who rescued it from a revolutionary Farmer-Labor junta gone crazy with power and pickings; who restored its financial standing and its state pride and, through an enlightened labor policy, has enabled it to function efficiently as one of the country's leading guns-and-butter states." Alexander proceeded to extol the butter produced by Minnesota dairy farmers and guns and ships built with ore mined on Minnesota's Iron Range. Then he revealed the real reason for his interest in Minnesota's governor. Stassen, he wrote, was "one of the few Republicans extant who could conceivably win a presidential election."[22]

Stassen was true to his word. He resigned the governorship in April 1943, leaving the state's executive branch in the hands of his personally chosen lieutenant governor and a future US senator, Ed Thye of Northfield. He was off to the South Pacific to serve as administrative assistant to Admiral William "Bull" Halsey. After nearly two years on the USS *Missouri* handling the admiral's correspondence, he was chosen by President Roosevelt to serve on the US delegation to the San Francisco conference that drafted the charter of the United Nations. From March to May of 1945, he played a leading role in conference, and he would live long enough to be the last surviving signatory of the charter. It was work that he would remember as a high point in his life. Soon after the UN conference ended, he was back on the deck of the *Missouri* for the signing of the US–Japan peace treaty by Halsey and Emperor Hirohito. Days later he led an expedition to free American prisoners of war in Tokyo, including Minnesota survivors of the Bataan Death March.[23]

Though Stassen briefly returned to Minnesota after the war, his direct service to his state was over. While he remained the de facto leader of the state GOP's dominant faction in 1946, his own focus was on national politics. He embarked on a presidential campaign in 1948 that nearly succeeded in winning him the Republican nomination. In 1952 he was again a serious contender, though even in Minnesota he could not overcome the popularity of General Dwight Eisenhower.

Stassen made seven more increasingly marginal bids for president. His feeble last hurrah was in 1992. Those repeated campaigns made him the butt of comedians' jokes and cost him respect in some quarters. But he was not deterred by detractors. Stassen maintained that a national campaign afforded him the opportunity to propose policy solutions to critical problems, even when he had little chance

Young Stassen supporters, 1947. *Courtesy of MNHS Collections*

of winning. He once told me—with specific examples—that each time he ran for office, his policy proposals influenced the thinking of both Democratic and Republican candidates. The same was true when he ran for governor one last time, in 1982. The winner of that election, DFL governor Rudy Perpich, was intrigued by Stassen's proposal to attract a major indoor theme park to Minnesota. Perpich later credited Stassen for sparking the idea that became the Mall of America in Bloomington.

Stassen's greatest Minnesota legacy may lie in his influence over a generation of Republicans who came of age watching a charismatic young governor transform both his own party and its rivals. It can be fairly argued that the 1944 merger of the Democratic and Farmer-Labor parties into the modern Minnesota DFL would not have happened had Stassen not moved the state Republican Party to the philosophical center and proved that he could hold it there. The "boy wonder" governor was a giant in the eyes of young loyalists, whose ranks included a future US Supreme Court chief justice and several future Minnesota governors. One of the latter, Elmer L. Andersen, would recall late in life the "natural leader with a big voice and bold ideas that captivated people. He captivated me. . . . In sheer intellectual capacity, he is the ablest person I have known."[24]

I count myself among the young Republicans who were part of the Stassen line, though my election to the US Senate came thirty years after his closest presidential bid. Stassen moved back to Minnesota in 1978 and briefly ran for the US Senate seat held by DFLer Wendell Anderson that year—but only after naming four well-known Republican women as his preferred candidates, including Jean LeVander King, daughter of former governor Harold LeVander. I came to know and regard Governor Stassen as a friend. His commitment to sound public policy rooted in Minnesota values was important to me, and his advice mattered as I established my own positions on national security policy. Stassen lived long enough to see his progressive lineage flower, then fade. He died in 2001 at age ninety-three.[25]

2 POSTWAR PROGRESSIVES

HAROLD STASSEN WAS OFF TO the presidential sweepstakes after World War II. But the hold Stassen had on the Minnesota Republican Party remained firm—remarkably so, given that the old guard he had humiliated in 1938 and marginalized in the ensuing years had not disappeared. It lived on in the legislature, nursing its resentments and biding its time.

Its time was not 1946. That year's key Minnesota political decisions were made not in November, but in February—and not at the state capitol, but about ten miles away, in Harold Stassen's South St. Paul living room. My friend Bernhard "Pete" LeVander, the brother of the future governor who would be my boss, was among the fifteen or twenty Stassen loyalists—all young, all men, mostly military veterans—who participated in several intense conversations about whose names would top the state GOP ticket. It was an assemblage with considerable political and intellectual horsepower. Included in the circle, for example, was future US Supreme Court chief justice Warren Burger, who, like Stassen, was born in 1907, grew up as a farm kid in rural St. Paul, and put himself through college and law school. Pete LeVander's 2006 memoir describes lively discussions that ended with much deference to the group's undisputed leader. When Stassen decided, all that was left for his team to do was to determine who

Governor Stassen awaiting Minneapolis election returns with Senator Edward Thye and Luther Youngdahl, 1950s. *Courtesy of MNHS Collections*

would be dispatched to inform the as-yet-unwitting gubernatorial designee of the role he would play in that year.[1]

Harold's decisions: US senator Henrik Shipstead had to be defeated. Governor Edward Thye was the man to take him out. Running for governor in Thye's stead would be associate justice Luther Young-dahl of the Minnesota Supreme Court—who at that moment was not present, not a candidate, and not much aware that his name was under consideration. The group's unanimity says much about the confidence Stassen's machine had in both its boss's judgment and its own capacity to execute his will. So does this: the US senator they resolved to unseat was an entrenched four-term incumbent—and a Republican.

Henrik Shipstead had not always been a Republican, though that was the party affiliation he claimed as a young man. A tall, affable dentist of Norwegian heritage from Glenwood, Shipstead shifted to the liberal caucus in the Minnesota house when he represented Pope County for one term, 1917–18. He ran unsuccessfully for governor in 1920 as an independent. When he won a US Senate seat in 1922, it was as a member of the growing Farmer-Labor Party. Shipstead knew how to ride a political wave. That year, the Farmer-Labor Party elected two members of the US House and also sent Magnus Johnson to the US Senate to complete the term of Senator Knute Nelson, a legendary figure in Minnesota politics who had died in office.

Shipstead also knew when to jump off the wave. Saying he was dismayed by the socialist elements in the Farmer-Labor Party—and likely also persuaded by the Stassen Republican surge in the 1938 election—Shipstead switched parties again. He ran for a third term in 1940 as a Republican and won reelection handily over the still-unpopular former Farmer-Labor governor, Elmer Benson.

Like many Minnesota Scandinavian Americans, Shipstead was an isolationist during the run-up to World War II. That alone put him at odds with the young governor of the party he rejoined. But Shipstead's 1945 vote against the United Nations Charter in the US Senate—one of only two no votes in the body—escalated their disagreement to enmity. "He took this hard," Pete LeVander said of Stassen's reaction to Shipstead's vote. Stassen, after all, had been among the charter's drafters. "He felt it was wrong. He felt that Shipstead wasn't representative of the feeling of the people of Minnesota. So we decided that one of the chores that the guys that came out of the service had to get done was to get Shipstead out of there," LeVander said.[2]

Thye—whom Stassen had left behind as governor in 1943 and who was elected in his own right in 1944—evidently was happy to do his part in this scheme. So were the state's Republican primary voters.

Thye ousted Shipstead in the July 8 primary by a 3–2 margin, ending his political career.

Youngdahl required only a little more persuasion. A week's consideration and a Saturday night home visit by Stassen himself were all it took to land Youngdahl as a candidate for governor. Even though it meant giving up work he loved on the state's high court, Youngdahl answered a call that he may have understood to have emanated from a rank higher than even Stassen occupied. A son of a devout Lutheran family, Youngdahl had promised his late father that he would set his own political ambition aside to yield to his elder brother Oscar. Oscar Youngdahl represented Minneapolis in the US House for two terms, from 1938 to 1942, but lost the 1942 Republican primary to Walter Judd, who would go on to a twenty-year congressional career. That was the last time Oscar's name had been on a ballot. But Luther, who took a seat on the Minnesota Supreme Court in 1942, honored his promise until Oscar died on February 3, 1946. The very next day, Pete LeVander paid him a visit as an emissary from the Stassen machine. Luther told Pete he would not have considered a gubernatorial candidacy if his brother had not just died, relieving him of his vow.

Stassen considered Youngdahl a prize catch, one he'd been trying to land on the state GOP ticket for some time. Youngdahl, not Thye, had been Stassen's first choice as a running mate and heir apparent in 1942. His appeal was grounded in a good name, good looks, and good character. The tall, blond, athletic son of a Swedish immigrant Minneapolis grocer, Youngdahl was raised a middle child in a blended family of ten siblings and half-siblings, each of whom had excelled academically, athletically, and/or professionally. Oscar Youngdahl was not the only familiar name in the family. By the mid-1940s, Reuben Youngdahl, Luther's younger brother, was becoming well known as the charismatic senior pastor of Mount Olivet Lutheran Church in South Minneapolis, which was on its way to becoming the largest Lutheran congregation in North America. Another brother, Carl, was the popular head of the music program at Augustana College in Sioux Falls, South Dakota.[3]

Youngdahl's Scandinavian heritage and Lutheran piety were deemed political plusses. By the 1940s and with Stassen as the only exception, Minnesota had been electing Scandinavian Americans to the governor's office for fifty years. (They would continue to do so until 1982, when they installed second-generation Croatian American Rudy Perpich in the office.) Taken together, people of Norwegian, Swedish, and Danish ancestry comprised Minnesota's largest ethnic group. The vast majority of them considered themselves Lutherans, though that denominational label applied to a plethora of synods and sects of varying philosophies and practices. A 1952 census of religious denominational affiliation in the state found more than 760,000 Minnesotans identifying as Lutheran. That was a quarter of the state's 2.9 million people and more than any other denomination—including my own Roman Catholic Church—could claim.[4]

The communitarian values of all those Scandinavian Lutherans contributed a heavy dose of what Temple University political scientist and Minnesota native Daniel Elazar called moralism—and I would call progressivism—to Minnesota's political culture. In Elazar's telling, moralism in politics emphasizes the commonwealth and the public interest. It says government is legitimate as long as it is a positive force in the lives of its citizens. It values rather than scorns politicians as agents of the public good—but also demands exemplary conduct from elected officials. The Youngdahl name's association with Lutheran leadership functioned as a seal of approval for voters keen on keeping corruption and self-dealing out of state government.[5]

As his 1955 biographer described him, Youngdahl was "an excellent example of the Nordic type of personality that has been idealized in Minnesota cultural traditions." He was deeply religious but not holier-than-thou; highly intelligent without being arrogant or eggheaded; unfailingly polite but a forceful speaker on the stump. And, like many in his tribe, his political leanings were liberal and moralistic—more so, perhaps, than the Stassen machine bargained for.[6]

The hold that machine had on Minnesota politics in 1946 is evident in Youngdahl's easy victories that year. Youngdahl—whose name previously had been on only judicial ballots—clobbered former Farmer-Labor governor Hjalmar Petersen in the Republican primary, then sailed past Harold Barker of the new Democratic-Farmer-Labor Party (created by a Farmer-Labor and Democratic merger in 1944). Youngdahl received nearly 59 percent of the November vote. Thye held the senate seat for the GOP by a similar margin.

Petersen's emergence as a Republican in 1946 illustrates how easily Minnesota politicians shifted their party loyalties in the first half of the twentieth century. The many moves from one party to another attest to the parties' philosophical similarity. They may also say something about the consequences of Minnesota's decision in 1913 to drop party designations at the legislature—a circumstance that continued until 1973. One might claim that as a result, Minnesotans at mid-

A billboard sponsored by the Governor's Interracial Commission at the 1948 Minnesota State Fair. Governor Luther Youngdahl is third from left. *Courtesy of MNHS Collections*

century didn't take party labels and loyalty as seriously as did politicians and voters in other states.[7]

The Stassen team assumed that Youngdahl would govern much as their leader had from 1939 to 1943–namely, that he would emphasize improving the economy, increasing government efficiency and professionalism, and extending a GOP hand of friendship (if not a full embrace) to organized labor. Those themes were indeed present in Youngdahl's 1947 inaugural message. But the new governor also announced an intention to build up the state's human resources, "the greatest assets of our state." His goal was to make state government the tool of "an enlightened citizenry, showing concern for its handicapped and needy members, courageously attacking the problems of education, housing, public health, youth conservation and racial discrimination–here is a goal that is worthy of all the thought and energy at our command."[8]

Minnesotans soon saw that Youngdahl's notions about building human capital had a decidedly moralistic bent. He wanted to save Minnesotans from their sins, starting with the sin of gambling with slot machines. The "one-armed bandits" were legal and pervasive in the state in those years–surprisingly so, given that they are technically considered lotteries, which were then prohibited in the state constitution. Minnesotans in the mid-1940s had an estimated eight thousand slot machines at their disposal throughout the state, scattered in bars, restaurants, resorts, and clubs in all but four of the state's eighty-seven counties. The annual "take" from slot machines was pegged at $4 million, or about $54 million in today's dollars.

Youngdahl's aversion to slot machines was said to originate with a 1938 vacation on Gull Lake near Brainerd, where he was shocked by the rowdy behavior he observed in a gambling hall at Bar Harbor, reputed to be Cass County's bawdiest resort. His work as a municipal judge during the Depression also shaped his views. In 1950, he told a US Senate committee investigating organized crime, "In my years on the bench, I had frequent opportunity to see the evil consequences that result from the racket. The lure of a possible jackpot induces many to play who can ill afford to do so, and families have gone hungry or poorly clad as a result." As he campaigned in 1946, he fretted about the "disillusioning aftermath of war," particularly among young people, and sought a "bolstering of our moral and spiritual resources." Removing the temptation to gamble would fill that bill, he argued. He asked the 1947 legislature to ban slot machines.[9]

Many in both the Republican old guard and the party's Stassen wing did not share Youngdahl's anti-gambling fervor. The party's rank and file included owners of the resorts and other establishments that happily offered their patrons mechanical games of chance and derived profits from the machines. But neither was the conservative-controlled legislature inclined to reject a top priority of the new governor on whose coattails some had ridden in the 1946 election. It passed Youngdahl's anti–slot machine bill on April 24, 1947. Notably, its chief sponsor in the house was not a member of the conservative caucus, but liberal representative Alfred Otto of St. Paul. One of the measure's most visible advocates was the young DFL mayor of Minneapolis, Hubert Humphrey, who was waging an anti-gambling crusade of his own in the state's largest city.[10]

Youngdahl followed that legislative success with a tough-talking meeting on June 25, 1947. He summoned the state's eighty-seven county sheriffs and some county attorneys to the state capitol to hear the recommendations of a citizens' committee Youngdahl had recruited to help implement the new slot machine ban. It was a blue-ribbon group headed by the prominent general counsel of the Pillsbury Company, Bradshaw Mintener. The lineup pitted Twin Cities blue bloods against rural sheriffs who were well aware of the popularity of gambling in their communities. They were being asked to confront their friends and neighbors and remove a source of their livelihoods.

A magazine account three decades later reported that "a wild affair" ensued. Sheriffs challenged Mintener, who chaired the meeting, about what was and was not gambling. Mintener sent a hasty plea to the governor to join the meeting and help him keep order. Youngdahl–a physically imposing figure–arrived with his jaw set. He bravely told the lawmen that not only would slot machines have to go, but all other forms of "hard gambling"–which he deemed un-constitutional–would no longer be tolerated. The new law specified that any establishment found in violation of that ban would lose its liquor license, a crippling penalty. Youngdahl said he would insist that the law be fully enforced. He implied that he had the power to remove from office any sheriff who did not comply–a questionable notion given that sheriffs are elected, not appointed by the gover-nor, but one that got the sheriffs' attention. Despite bitter opposition, Youngdahl got his way. Soon my dad was witness to a slot machine being hauled out of a café he frequented in little Avon, Minnesota– and Youngdahl was receiving national notice for his willingness to use state government to eradicate vice.[11]

The slot machine ban may be the best remembered of Youngdahl's gubernatorial achievements. But he did a good deal more to en-trench in Minnesota minds the idea that state government has both a rightful role and a duty to play in the betterment of people's lives. "Our values must stem from the fatherhood of God and the brother-hood of man," he argued in his second inaugural address on Janu-ary 6, 1949. "We must stop gauging our success by the production of machines or dollars of income. We have got to understand that important as it is to produce efficiency in the factory, it is even more important to build character in its workers and to turn out a prod-uct that will strengthen our nation." The policies he promoted that year and again in 1951 ran the liberal gamut–corrections reform for juveniles, public housing for the indigent, aid for the disabled, racial integration. He brought racial integration to the Minnesota National Guard and sought a Fair Employment Practices Act barring job dis-crimination on the basis of race eight years before the legislature was ready to adopt it.[12]

The initiative that may have been closest to Youngdahl's heart—and ultimately the cause of some heartbreak—was his drive to modernize mental-illness treatment. That rich topic deserves a book of its own—and it has one, courtesy of my wife, Susan Bartlett Foote, and the University of Minnesota Press. Susan's book, *Crusade for Forgotten Souls: Reform of Minnesota's Mental Institutions, 1946–1952*, published in 2018, tells how Youngdahl joined forces with a cadre of citizen activists and medical professionals in an effort to transform the treatment of both the mentally ill and the developmentally disabled populations at state institutions.

That work was the centerpiece of the governor's 1949 and 1951 legislative agendas. The goal, he said in his 1949 inaugural message, was to make each state mental hospital "a house of hope, rather than a habitation for the living dead." He outlined an ambitious improvement plan—research-driven therapies, appropriately trained personnel, sufficient staffing to allow for forty-hour workweeks, enlarged facilities to eliminate overcrowding, food of equal quality for both patients and employees, out-patient services, post-hospitalization care, and consultation and coordination with the courts, schools, and welfare agencies. It was a plan to yank mental-illness care out of the Dark Ages and into the twentieth or maybe even the twenty-first century.

Youngdahl did not hesitate to support spending increases for the improvements he sought. His proposed 1950–51 biennial budget included a whopping 42 percent increase in general-fund spending, with the big cost driver a more than doubling of the state's "mental institution" budget, from $15 to $31 million.[13]

Fortunately for Youngdahl and his progressive successors, the state's revenue deck had been stacked in favor of an activist state government in 1933. That year, Governor Floyd B. Olson pushed the state's first personal income tax through a Depression-panicked legislature. Under any other economic circumstances, a gubernatorial call for an income tax would have run into fierce opposition in the conservative-controlled senate. But at the bottom of the Depression, an income tax based on ability to pay was preferable to the unforgiving property tax, which was levied on real estate and personal property without regard to the income of the owners. In 1933, property taxes were often going unpaid, and delinquent taxpayers were being pushed out of their homes and off their farms. Conservatives sought to make the new tax revenue neutral to the state, pairing it with a reduction in the state property tax. Olson accepted that plan provided that the new tax was dedicated to school funding. At a time when many school districts were unable to pay their teachers, that dedication made the new tax politically palatable. The school funding dedication was in statute, not the constitution, and eventually was removed by the legislature. But the income tax proved a boon to progressives who wanted government services to grow apace with the economy. Unlike the property tax, which can produce more revenue only if elected officials raise the levy, income tax receipts swell automatically as incomes and population grow. With the economy humming in 1949, Youngdahl could call for more state spending without asking legislators to raise the income tax rate. He asked only for comparatively small tax increases on tobacco, beer, and liquor—taxes that conveniently conveyed a moral judgment.[14]

Nevertheless, Youngdahl's eagerness to spend more state money on sick and needy Minnesotans ran into resistance within his own party. He had faced a primary challenge by the GOP old guard in 1948 in the person of state auditor Stafford King. King was an affable, long-serving functionary allied with the conservative legislators who considered Youngdahl a big spender. King was at midterm in 1948 and so could take a shot at Youngdahl without giving up a post he would hold for thirty-eight years, longer than any other Minnesota state auditor. Youngdahl easily bested King in the Republican gubernatorial primary. But the governor was on notice that his party was not united behind his agenda.

Youngdahl responded by building up another source of lobbying muscle—a well-chosen committee of citizen advocates. While likely not the first Minnesota governor to enlist willing, well-placed citizens in a legislative cause, Youngdahl took what was then an unusual step

when he deployed his Citizens Mental Health Committee to bring reluctant legislators around. Formed in 1948, the committee was ready
in 1949 to follow the governor's bidding in establishing local chapters, the better to pressure individual legislators for mental health
reform. He also found key allies among the state's growing cohort
of mental health professionals, including those at the University of
Minnesota. The mental health issue brought academic research into
the legislative process to an extent seldom before seen, also setting a
precedent.

Youngdahl also brought his own considerable persuasive skill to
bear. Time and again, he went on the radio and accepted speaking
engagements to appeal directly to Minnesotans. In language worthy
of his brother's pulpit, the governor stirred Minnesotans' compassion
for the vulnerable and reminded them of their moral duty to provide
succor to "the least of these."

That lobbying combination yielded remarkably positive results in
1949. The legislature appropriated all but $2 million of the governor's
request, bringing to state mental hospitals a forty-hour workweek,
more staffers, a new staff training regimen, improved nutrition, and
more. Opponents in the conservative caucus—Youngdahl's fellow
Republicans—went along in the end for fear of being called out as
anti-humanitarian by a popular governor in the 1950 election. And
popular he was. Youngdahl won 60.7 percent of the vote over DFLer
Harry Peterson, his largest share in three elections.

But that year, the nation was back at war, this time on the faraway
Korean Peninsula. The mood in Minnesota and the nation shifted.
The confidence and economic progress that characterized the immediate aftermath of World War II slipped. Youngdahl's 1951 request
for more staff and an enlarged research budget at the state's mental hospitals foundered as conservative legislators insisted on little
or no new spending. His top request, funding for a new residential
facility for Minnesota's developmentally disabled population, was
also spurned, albeit with a ploy today's legislative observers will
recognize. A small amount of planning money for the building was

approved—$100,000 of the $6.5 million requested—so legislators could say that they had not entirely rejected the project.

Youngdahl would be out of office only a few months later. Angered and disappointed by the 1951 session, the fifty-five-year-old governor experienced high blood pressure and was under doctor's orders to "take it easy." In mid-June, thanks to the intervention of DFL US senator Hubert Humphrey, Democratic president Harry Truman offered Youngdahl a judgeship on the Federal District Court of Washington, DC. Youngdahl abruptly accepted the offer and left the governorship in the non-progressive hands of lieutenant governor C. Elmer Anderson of Brainerd. His elevation added to the irritation the Stassen group already felt toward Youngdahl for refusing to publicly back one of their own, state senator Ancher Nelsen of Hutchinson, over Anderson for lieutenant governor in the 1950 Republican primary. Anderson edged out Nelson by just 7,095 votes in what turned out to be a costly loss. It would be nearly ten years before Minnesota again had a governor in the progressive Stassen Republican line.

Progressive Republicans did not disappear in the legislature, however. By the time Youngdahl left Minnesota, other Republicans of the Stassen lineage had arrived and were challenging the old guard's grip on state lawmaking. The new chair of the Senate Welfare Committee in 1951 was state senator Elmer L. Andersen of St. Paul, an early campaign aide and friend of Stassen. Andersen, owner of H. B. Fuller Company, a St. Paul–based adhesives manufacturer, earned victory in a February 1949 special election, just in time to bolster Youngdahl's base of support for the mental health initiatives. Through the 1950s, Andersen would work to maintain Youngdahl's gains in mental health treatment. He also picked up where Youngdahl left off in seeking a state statutory ban on racial discrimination in employment. Andersen saw the Fair Employment Practices Act through to enactment in 1955. Two years later, he spearheaded the legislature's first attempt to bring some order to the messy, fragmented governance of the rapidly growing Twin Cities metro area, which was well on its way to including more than two hundred municipalities sprawled over first seven, then eleven counties. Andersen carried the bill creating the Metropolitan Planning Commission. It was mostly advisory to local governments, but it was the start of something big.[15]

Another case in point: Art Gillen of South St. Paul. First elected to the state house in 1942 while still a law student at the University of Minnesota, Gillen was locked into the Stassen orbit as a neighbor and, after 1949, a partner in the law firm Stassen founded. By the 1950s, that firm was known as Kelly, LeVander, and Gillen, and Gillen was an active member of the state senate. He worked with Andersen on fair employment practices legislation and tried to push a stodgy institution into the modern era by compelling the redrawing of district lines after each decennial US census. The failure to regularly "redistrict" the legislature allowed rural legislators to exert clout disproportionate to their share of the state's population, shortchanging the fast-growing suburbs. Gillen was a popular and persuasive fellow. But it would take a US Supreme Court decision in the 1960s to finally move Minnesota's legislative district lines.[16]

One of the postwar era's most important moves in a progressive direction was a change in state education funding policy in 1947—and that came with the arrival of Representative Stanley Holmquist from Grove City in the state house. Holmquist—whose wife, Edith, was the sister of Elmer Andersen's wife, Eleanor—was a former school superintendent as well as the owner of a successful chain of lumberyards in west-central Minnesota. He ran for office in 1946 in part because of disgust with the legislature's practice of authorizing state aid to schools at one level and actually paying a lower sum, a practice that had become a bad habit during World War II. As one commentator described it, legislators prior to 1947 believed they had fulfilled their constitutionally assigned responsibility to provide a "general and uniform system of public schools" if they sent sporadic state assistance to school districts that fell into financial distress.[17]

As a rookie legislator, Holmquist helped sell the idea that the state's obligation extended to all of the state's students. He promoted the notion that a school's state aid allotment should be based on its enrollment, and that the per-pupil funding should be greater for secondary school students than for those in the elementary grades. That idea was adopted, along with a formula for allotting state aid in proportion to a school district's capacity to generate funds via the property tax. Property-poor districts were to receive more state help than rich ones. The premise was that the quality of a Minnesota child's education should not depend on the property wealth of his or her community. That would prove to be a powerful principle.

Holmquist's formula offered no guarantee that state funding would keep up with the actual per-pupil costs of instruction. But it set an important pattern of enrollment-based aid distribution that would serve Minnesota well as school populations exploded during the baby boom years. And it solidified an expectation that the state would be a financial partner to schools as they entered a period of widespread consolidation. The era of the one-room rural schoolhouse was coming to an end. Progressive Republicans like Holmquist wanted state government to ensure that consolidation produced not only savings for taxpayers but also better education for students.

Ideas like these had a new, homegrown source in the postwar era—the Citizens League. Springing from a network of mostly Republican young Minneapolis businessmen that jelled in the 1940s as the Good Government Group, the Citizens League was founded in 1952. It was an era in which civic and cultural organizations of all kinds flourished and often interacted. For example, the spark for taking the Good Government Group to something bigger and better organized was said to have come from a 1951 sermon preached by the Reverend Richard Raines at Hennepin Avenue Methodist Church in Minneapolis, then the state's largest Methodist congregation. In a pew that day was the construction company owner who would become the league's first president, Stuart Leck. The Citizens League started strong, with 250 people in attendance at its formal organizational meeting on February 14, 1952. The meeting was hosted by

North American Life and Casualty Company across the street from Hennepin Church, which attested to the substantial corporate support that existed for the project. Within the first four months, membership swelled to nine hundred, and it would keep growing until it surpassed 3,400 in 1990.[18]

From the start, the Citizens League was unique in both Minnesota and the nation. Strictly nonpartisan and intentionally broad-based in membership, the league set out to engage interested citizens in studying public problems and crafting recommended remedies. It dabbled initially with endorsing candidates for office, but members quickly determined that they would avoid controversy and be more

A Citizens League event in the fall of 1957 at Centennial Plaza, Minneapolis. *Courtesy of Citizens League*

effective if the group steered clear of electoral politics and established a reputation for independent issue analysis.

Though it received financial backing from a number of leading Minnesota businesses, the league's agenda was not set by corporate interests—at least not overtly. The strongest businesses in the Twin Cities were homegrown, led largely by Minnesota natives. Many of them were heirs of Minnesota pioneers who still embodied their forebears' zeal for creating a city and state with enviable prosperity and quality of life. What's more, nasty labor strife, which became violent in 1934, had damaged the reputations of an earlier generation of Minneapolis business leaders. Though business hostility to labor unions lingered in many quarters, the new leaders that emerged after World War II were more inclined toward Harold Stassen's accommodating view of organized labor. By the 1950s, bonds of familiarity and trust connected the local captains of industry to many of the people who signed up for Citizens League work. Quite a few were their employees. Business leaders continued to be the financial patrons of the old guard Republicans in the legislature, quietly—for no law yet compelled campaign donation disclosure—sending copious amounts of campaign cash to the likes of powerful house majority leader Roy Dunn and house appropriations chair Claude Allen of St. Paul. But the CEOs evidently felt no need to exert a heavy hand in the new public policy organization being assembled in Minneapolis.[19]

Likewise, the special interests that lobbied at city hall and the legislature also did not hold much sway on the new league. League members were individuals, not corporations, and the study topics were chosen by the members via surveys and representation on standing committees. That independence "stands against the prevailing conception of politics and policy-making in America," observed the late John Brandl while he was dean of the Humphrey School of Public Affairs at the University of Minnesota in 2000. Rather than fostering competition among rival interest groups, the Citizens League tapped the "public spiritedness" of individuals in search of consensus about the common good.[20]

While it relied heavily on volunteers, the young organization was wise enough to know it needed competent professional staff to keep citizen-led projects advancing. Its founding executive director, attorney Ray Black, oversaw its rapid growth and established patterns of operation that would serve it well. His lawyerly style of fact-finding and arriving at recommendations became the norm for league study committees, of which there would be a jaw-dropping four hundred in the organization's first forty years.

But the league came into its own in 1958 with the hiring of executive director Verne Johnson. He was masterful at bringing people together and inspiring them to expansive new notions about what public policy could be. A former aide to Republican US representative Walter Judd, Johnson had served one term, 1953–54, as a member of the conservative caucus in the Minnesota house, representing a district in Minneapolis.

Johnson was among the Minnesota Republicans in the postwar era who were conspicuously trying to make government work for a rapidly changing state. Urban voters who saw their growing region's need for effective government took note and rewarded Republicans for their efforts.

3 INTO THE SIXTIES

I N 1960, JUST 1.2 PERCENT of Minnesota's population of 3.4 million were people of color. But the movement for racial justice that was sweeping the rest of the nation in 1961 did not bypass the state or the office of its new Republican governor, Elmer L. Andersen. In the 1960 election, Andersen ended the six-year gubernatorial run of Orville Freeman, besting Freeman by a 22,000-vote margin—nearly the same margin that put the state in the Democratic column for president. Freeman was a cofounder of the Democratic-Farmer-Labor (DFL) Party, tightly allied with Minnesota's US senator Hubert Humphrey, one of the nation's leading voices for civil rights. Andersen vowed that in Minnesota, the Republican Party would not take a back seat to the DFL on equality under the law regardless of race. It would live up to its heritage as the party of Abraham Lincoln, the president who ended slavery.[1]

The fifty-one-year-old owner of a midsized St. Paul adhesives manufacturing company, Andersen may have struck some as an unlikely civil rights champion. But "Elmer L." (so called to distinguish him from C. Elmer Anderson) was a wise man with a big heart borne of childhood struggles with polio and economic adversity. Born in Chicago, he was the third of four children of a Norwegian immigrant father and a mother with Swedish and Norwegian ancestry. Their marriage ended in separation; Elmer moved to Muskegon, Michigan, with his mother and siblings at age five. There, Andersen's mother had unstinting support from two sisters and the Lutheran Church, to which she was devoted, plus the enterprise of her sons as they grew older. She died of pneumonia in 1925 as fifteen-year-old Elmer kept vigil at her bedside.

Elmer came to Minnesota as a traveling salesman for a school furniture company in 1928. He quickly fell in love with his adopted state, so much so that in later years he would liken his attachment to Minnesota to a religious conversion. Despite the gathering economic gloom of the early 1930s, he put himself through the University of Minnesota while continuing sales trips to cities along the Great Northern Railway line. He also met and married Eleanor Johnson of Minneapolis, whose quiet strength would enlarge his own through seventy-two years of marriage. Nine years after they were wed, they had saved enough to buy controlling interest in the small adhesives company for which he worked, H. B. Fuller. Under Elmer's leadership, it would not stay small for long.

But business success was never sufficient to satisfy either Elmer's desire to be of service or his interest in politics. He was tempted, but declined, when newly elected Governor Stassen invited him to take a place in his administration in 1939. Ten years later, when senate majority leader Charles Orr died of a heart attack in the first days of the legislative session, Elmer didn't hesitate. He was the top vote-getter among twenty candidates who competed in the hastily called non-partisan primary election; he won the runoff election on February 8, 1949. For the next five legislative sessions, he was among the most liberal members of the conservative caucus. He was an ally of Governor Luther Youngdahl in modernizing treatment of the mentally ill, a reformer in the state's response to chemical dependency, and the senate sponsor of a nation-leading program for special education for disabled and exceptional children. He also staked out a role in the awakening civil rights movement as the sponsor of the Fair Employment Practices Act of 1955, which made Minnesota only the fifth state in the nation to outlaw racial discrimination in employment. Elmer left the state senate in 1958 to tend to his business—or so he claimed. A year later, he confirmed the rumor that he would run for governor in 1960.

Elmer's campaign themes reminded Minnesotans of what they had liked twenty years earlier about Stassen-style Republicanism. His recipe for addressing the state budget deficits that were becoming chronic did not involve slashing government spending to the detriment of education or social services. Rather, Andersen vowed to

Future governor Elmer L. Andersen on the campaign trail, about 1960. *Courtesy of MNHS Collections*

bring business-style efficiency to government operations. He decried Governor Freeman's decision to call out the National Guard on the side of organized labor during a meatpacking strike in Austin, Minnesota, in 1959—a move that was overturned by a federal court order but that Freeman continued to defend, handing Elmer a campaign talking point. But Elmer was friendly enough with organized labor to mount a serious bid for support on the union-dominated Iron Range. Though he did not carry northeastern Minnesota, the eighteen thousand votes he gained in the region over the 1958 GOP candidate for governor helped him buck the DFL tide in 1960.[2]

In 1961, a major civil rights bill came before the legislature. The Fair Housing Act, an antidiscrimination companion to the Fair Employment Practices Act Elmer championed in 1955, aimed to end the practice of denying home mortgages and apartment rentals to people of color on the basis of their race. It had strong backing from Minnesota's Protestant, Catholic, and Jewish communities and the state DFL Party. Yet it had gone nowhere in each of the previous two sessions, despite DFL Governor Freeman's support and liberal control of the state house. The liberals remained in charge of the house after Elmer's election, giving fair housing advocates reason for optimism. What's more, the new governor's support for tougher antidiscrimination laws was well known. Andersen included a reminder of his position in his January 4, 1961, inaugural message: "I urge the adoption of legislative prohibitions as extensive as may be required to ensure fair housing opportunity to all citizens regardless of race, color, creed or national origin. . . . Safeguarding the civil rights of all of our citizens, granting to each equal dignity and freedom of opportunity, is of the greatest importance, and not only at home. It tells all the world where we truly stand."[3]

Elmer soon showed again where he stood. As the 1961 session moved into its crucial final weeks, the Fair Housing Act, sponsored in the senate by future Minneapolis mayor Don Fraser, was bottled up in the Senate Judiciary Committee. Old guard Republicanism was well represented on the committee. It was chaired by Thomas Welch, an attorney and World War I veteran from Buffalo, Minnesota, who had served in the legislature since 1939, and included Claude Allen of St. Paul and Donald O. Wright of Minneapolis—budget hawks who had been nemeses of both governors Stassen and Youngdahl.[4]

But also on the committee was one of the most influential lawmakers in state history, Gordon Rosenmeier of Little Falls. The son of a Danish immigrant who had served as senate majority leader in the 1920s, Rosenmeier was a very able Stanford University–educated lawyer who cast himself as chief custodian of the institution and defender of rural power at the capitol. He caucused with the conservatives but went out of his way to avoid being called a Republican, boasting that he never attended the party's precinct caucuses. He and Andersen had frequently clashed while Andersen represented a Ramsey County district in the senate. But the two genuinely liked and respected each other. Notably, they had been allies on the Fair Employment Practices Act, a measure Rosenmeier had publicly backed since Youngdahl first proposed it in 1949. Andersen knew that with Rosenmeier on the committee, the housing bill had a chance. Another committee seat was occupied by Alf Bergerud of Edina, who was a few years away from becoming CEO of the Red Owl chain of grocery stories. Like many employers in the Twin Cities, he was sympathetic to the civil rights cause.[5]

When Minneapolis Urban League lobbyist Josie Johnson—who would go on to become a beloved matriarch in Minnesota's civil rights movement—appealed to the governor for help in dislodging the bill, Elmer was happy to comply. But he knew better than to do what some rookie governors might have done. He didn't summon reporters to castigate the recalcitrant senators or threaten retaliation if they did not advance the housing bill. Rather, he opted for a less visible course of action. While Josie watched, Elmer reached for stationery and a pen and wrote a personal note to each member of the Judiciary Committee. He drew on his personal relationships, Josie's advice, and his knowledge of senate procedures and traditions in tailoring each individual appeal. His message to the bill's opponents: Even if you can't support the bill, please don't let it die in committee. This bill means a lot to people. Please allow it to get to the senate floor.

The notes were hastily delivered. The crucial committee vote was scheduled for the next morning. In those days before video broadcast of committee hearings, it fell to Josie to bring news of the result to the governor's office. She flew into his office late the next morning, cried, "It got out! It passed!" and gave Elmer a hug he had earned. The Fair Housing Act became law in Minnesota that year, with considerable support from members of the conservative caucus.

More than fifty-five year later, Josie can be found most Sunday mornings on the left side of St. Peter Claver Church in the heart of St. Paul's historic Rondo neighborhood, while I occupy a seat "just right of the center" across the aisle from her. At the appropriate part of the service we hug, and I assure her that Donald Trump and the Republican Congress cannot reverse her life's accomplishments for civil rights.

As the fair housing issue demonstrated, Stassen-style progressivism was back in vogue among Minnesota Republicans in the early 1960s. Andersen's gubernatorial influence was part of the reason. But several larger forces were also easing the old guard's grip.

Demographic change played a major role. The generation of GIs that went to war in the 1940s and early 1950s came home, married, and raised families, spurring a big 14.5 percent jump in the state's population in the 1950s. The bulk of that growth occurred in the Twin Cities, where Minneapolis was experiencing a housing shortage and suburbanization was in full swing. Greater Minnesota gained about 90,000 people in the 1950s, compared with 340,000 in the seven counties that included and surrounded Minneapolis and St. Paul.[6]

By the early 1960s, the World War II and Korean War generations had matured into civic leadership positions that included elective office. The experiences that shaped their view of government differed markedly from those of their parents and grandparents. They had witnessed as children and teens in the 1930s the harsh downside of unrestrained capitalism. They were aware that New Deal interventions in the economy, while not perfect, ended the economic freefall and made a positive difference in struggling lives. Then, as teens and young adults, they had been part of the biggest government mobilization in American history, much larger than their fathers had experienced as doughboys in World War I. While they saw government's flaws up close during World War II, they also saw it unite a nation around a noble purpose and succeed in achieving a lofty goal. They came back from that war persuaded that government could be a useful tool for solving all manner of problems. The Cold War of the 1950s sealed in them a belief that a robust federal government—at least in its military capacity—is essential to security. Parenthood and the mobility that suburban living requires made them willing to support a larger state government, provided its resources were fruitfully spent on education and transportation.

Minnesota Republicans also faced a newly competitive political environment in the 1950s. The Democratic-Farmer-Labor Party, born in 1944 out of the ashes of the Farmer-Labor Party that Stassen vanquished and the never robust Minnesota Democratic Party, was able to win a US Senate seat in 1948. But that seat was claimed by the uncommonly gifted Hubert Humphrey. Republicans consoled themselves with assurances that Humphrey was an exception to the political norm and that the long Republican dominance in Minnesota was too deeply ingrained to be dislodged. In 1954, that faith was shattered. DFLers took four statewide offices—governor, lieutenant governor, attorney general, and secretary of state—and control of the Minnesota house. The DFL had rid itself of its far-left faction and emerged as an effective center-left party, able to compete throughout the state. Some Republicans, particularly in Minneapolis and its suburbs, argued that their party should position itself nearer to the political middle, too, to compete for the same votes.

That growing urban chorus struggled to be heard at the state capitol during the 1950s. Like many states in the first half of the twentieth century, Minnesota had grown lax about redrawing legislative district boundaries to reflect population changes. No change in district lines was made between 1913 and 1959, in spite of Art Gillen's efforts through the 1950s. This was no mere case of forgetfulness or laziness. Rather, it was an early manifestation of political rivalry between the state's rural and urban regions. The 1913 boundaries gave rural representatives power that they knew they would lose to the cities if more recent population counts were used to equalize district populations. With no court ordering them to do otherwise, they kept redistricting off the legislature's agenda.

It took a US District Court order in 1958 to get them to act. But the changes made in 1959 were based on nine-year-old counts and made no serious attempt to equalize district populations. Rather, a few extra seats were allotted to a few large counties. The inadequacy of their work was evident when the 1960 census results were released. The most populous state senate district in Minnesota included more than four times as many residents as the least populous one. A majority of the state's population—the urban dwellers—were represented by only about a third of the members of the 1961 Minnesota house.[7]

With a series of landmark rulings between 1962 and 1966, the US Supreme Court would insist that legislatures around the country equalize their districts' populations after each national census. Those cases led to a flurry of new lawsuits against foot-dragging legislatures. In Minnesota, a new court order came in 1964. It took two years and a special session, but in time for the 1966 election, Minnesota's legislative map fell into compliance with the high court's "one man, one vote" principle.

But already in the 1960 and 1962 elections, GI-generation Republicans were winning enough seats in the legislature to be deemed an informal subcaucus in their own right. Newspapers gave them a name that stuck—the Young Turks. All smart, some sassy, most from the Twin Cities, they were open to new ways of using government to solve problems. All were men. The American women's movement's second wave was still a decade away. But since Stassen's era, local

GOP party units had been led by equal-status cochairs, one male and one female. That structure afforded women more opportunity for genuine leadership inside the party than DFL women had at that time.[8]

The Young Turks were a remarkable group that quickly made a big impact. Attorney Doug Head of Minneapolis was the cohort's first success story and paved the way for more. A native of the tony Lake of the Isles neighborhood in Minneapolis, Head was among the many victims of childhood polio in his generation and walked with difficulty for the rest of his life. But his limp did not slow him down. He possessed a brilliant mind and a drive to succeed that his struggle with polio may have reinforced. After earning his undergraduate degree at Yale University, Head returned to Minnesota for law school, where his study group included future vice president Walter Mondale and future federal district judge Harry McLaughlin.[9]

He also joined the Young Republican League. The organization that Harold Stassen launched and rode to the governor's office in the 1930s stalled a bit during World War II while young Minnesotans were otherwise engaged. But after the GIs came home and many enrolled in college with the aid of the GI Bill, the YRL took off. By the late 1950s it had swelled to five hundred politically ambitious members in Hennepin County and was rapidly organizing county-based chapters around the state. This was no mere social club or debating society. It was intent on becoming a modern, professional political machine. Young Republican League members in Minneapolis like Lyall Schwarzkopf, Wayne Popham, George Thiss, Bill Erickson, and Leonard Nadasdy were intent on running league members for office—particularly the legislature—and on training league members in the ways of winning convention endorsements and elections. In 1958, they muscled aside older league members in state organizational elections and set to work identifying and recruiting like-minded candidates for elective office.[10]

None of those activists were full-time politicians—yet. Popham was an attorney. Thiss played a role in his family's business, Thiss Luggage. Schwarzkopf was a field secretary for the Minnesota State

Medical Association. Nadasdy was a public relations representative for North Central Wool Marketing Corporation, which his father served as general manager for twenty-five years. Those day jobs afforded ample time for politics on nights and weekends; Schwarzkopf and Nadasdy's work assignments in Greater Minnesota allowed them opportunities to spur the formation of county-level Young Republican Leagues. By 1960, the Minnesota YRL had five thousand active members. Nadasdy, the state YRL chairman, was preparing a bid for the national YRL presidency in 1961. He and his fellow state league officers were eager to demonstrate their mettle with a winning legislative campaign in 1960. Doug Head was only thirty years old. But he was ready and willing to be the YRL test case.

"All of us who had experience running elections pooled our knowledge and ran a textbook campaign," Schwarzkopf recalled years later. "There was never any leader calling the shots. We were all equal. When Doug wanted to run, we were all there to help him." Though a first-time candidate, Head emerged as the top vote-getter in a four-way race for two seats, topping the vote total of longtime DFL incumbent Sally Luther. One YRL volunteer on the Head campaign, Caroline Burdick, kept careful notes and wrote a campaign manual based on the experience. "It outlined the necessary organization, campaign tools, the timing and the use of those tools, the follow up, and how to get out the vote," Schwarzkopf said. "This was the first written campaign manual the YRL or the Minnesota Republican Party ever had."[11]

That manual was put to good use in 1962. By then, Nadasdy had won the national YRL presidency and Schwarzkopf had succeeded him at the state YRL helm. The organization, funded by membership dues and the state party, employed a full-time executive director and worked closely with the new chair of the "senior party," YRL veteran Robert Forsythe of Edina, a former aide to US senator Ed Thye and an assistant cabinet secretary in the Eisenhower administration. Together, they aggressively recruited candidates and conducted campaign schools, training candidates and their campaign managers in the finer points of running for the legislature.[12]

Meanwhile the state GOP's "senior party" had been building a sophisticated grassroots network and was employing it to good effect. In 1959 the Neighbor to Neighbor program, the pet project of state GOP chairman Ed Viehman, outstripped any previous state party attempt to employ volunteers to identify potential voters and donors and turn potential into reality. Party volunteers were supplied with donation cards bearing the names and addresses of known Republican voters in each precinct and were asked to make an in-person solicitation and request a cash donation, thereby assessing each voter's loyalty to the Republican cause and seeking information to enlarge the donor base. Tragically, Viehman, a former radio broadcaster, died of complications of colon cancer in 1961. But Neighbor to Neighbor would endure, establishing a grassroots base that would endure for several decades and become the envy of political organizations around the country.[13]

Schwarzkopf himself was among the 1962 candidates, running for a house seat in South Minneapolis. He had ample YRL company all over the state. The YRL effort was key as the 1962 election brought conservatives back into control of the Minnesota house with a solid 80–55 majority. Forty-five of the eighty conservatives were freshmen, a stunning turnover. Among them were a number who would go on to larger responsibilities: Bill Frenzel of Golden Valley, who would serve ten distinguished terms in the US House; Arlen Erdahl of Blue Earth, a future secretary of state, congressman, and Peace Corps administrator; Gary Flakne, who would serve as Hennepin County's top prosecutor; Robert Ashbach, a future state senate minority leader; and Schwarzkopf himself, a future Minneapolis city coordinator and gubernatorial chief of staff. Other YRLers elected to the state house that year included John Tracy Anderson of St. Paul, Paul Overgaard of Albert Lea, John Yngve of Plymouth, Salisbury Adams of Wayzata, Bill Kirchner of Richfield, Thor Anderson of Minneapolis, and Otto Bang of Edina; Wayne Popham and Harmon Ogdahl of Minneapolis and Harold Krieger of Rochester were elected to state senate.

The Young Turks likely would not have described themselves in

State representative Bill Frenzel, about 1965. *Courtesy of MNHS Collections*

1963 as progressive or liberal, Schwarzkopf said. Rather, they saw themselves as a force for modernizing state and local government to adjust to the many changes in Minnesota that the postwar decades were bringing. They wanted to make government work better for people like themselves—families raising and educating young children in fast-growing urban and suburban communities. "We basically were interested in governing well, because we thought government was important," Schwarzkopf said. "We didn't want people dependent on government, but we wanted a decent safety net for those who needed it. We wanted good schools, good roads, a clean environment, and we were willing to make changes to make government work better."[14]

The Republican legislative class of 1962 ran for office expecting to help Governor Andersen advance his agenda. But Minnesota voters upended those plans. Andersen lost his reelection bid in what is still the closest gubernatorial election in US history. DFLer Karl Rolvaag, who had been lieutenant governor for eight years, wrested the governorship from Andersen with a mere ninety-one-vote margin. An election that close inevitably triggers a recount. This one lasted until mid-March 1963. Andersen stayed in office until a special three-judge panel ruled on the disputed ballots the recount discovered. He sent the legislature a budget calling for more spending on education and mental health, the same issues he had championed in the state senate. He was on hand to see the conservative-controlled legislature approve one of his top recommendations, sending to the 1964 ballot a state constitutional amendment assuring the nascent taconite industry on the Iron Range a minimum of twenty-five years of stable taxation at a rate comparable to other manufacturers. Voters approved that guarantee, giving the Iron Range economy a new lease on life.

When Rolvaag replaced Andersen, the progressive Republican movement in Minnesota hit a speed bump. Meanwhile, the national Republican Party's direction was changing. That was evident as early as June 1963 at the Young Republican League's national meeting in San Francisco (the city which thirteen months later would host the Republican National Convention). Nadasdy's term as president was ending, and as his successor, the Minnesotan backed Idaho state representative Chuck McDevitt. McDevitt was also the choice of New York governor Nelson Rockefeller, who was pursuing a presidential nomination in 1964. Mounting an unexpectedly strong challenge was District of Columbia YRL chairman Donald "Buz" Lukens, a US Air

Force Reserve officer and congressional staffer. Lukens was the favorite of the presidential candidate who was emerging as Rockefeller's most potent rival, Arizona senator Barry Goldwater. Top Goldwater aides, including F. Clifton White, head of the Draft Goldwater movement, poured money and resources into Lukens's bid, turning the contest into a bellwether for the 1964 main event. The national press treated it as such, adding intensity to a contest that included walkouts, credentials fights, and ultimately a brief fistfight on the convention floor. When it was over, Lukens had defeated McDevitt by two votes.

It was a foretaste of intraparty battles to come. Many Minnesota Republicans watched with growing concern the next spring and summer as Goldwater racked up delegates in state primaries and conventions. An heir to an Arizona department store fortune, Goldwater held political views that contrasted sharply with Stassen-style Republicanism. Goldwater rejected the idea that the federal government had any responsibility for social welfare—including racial equality—or the workings of the economy. He was no isolationist. But his hawkish anti-communist and anti–United Nations views were at odds not only with those of Democratic president Lyndon Johnson, but also with those of his Republican predecessor, President Dwight Eisenhower. Minnesota had no presidential primary in 1964, but state GOP leaders were convinced that if it did, Goldwater would have badly trailed Rockefeller and/or the other moderate Republican in the race, Pennsylvania governor William Scranton.

After Goldwater nearly clinched the nomination with a victory in the June 2 winner-take-all California primary, worried GOP leaders from Hennepin and Ramsey Counties huddled at the Ambassador Motel coffee shop in St. Louis Park. They feared that a Goldwater candidacy would not only fail to capture Minnesota's ten Electoral College votes but would drag down Republican candidates up and down the ballot. They worried that the 1962 gains in the Minnesota house were at risk, as well as Minnesota's four Republican members of Congress. Those fears would intensify a few weeks later when President Johnson tapped US senator Hubert Humphrey as his running mate.

Humphrey had surged into the national spotlight that spring as the Senate architect of the Civil Rights Act of 1964, one of the century's most significant legislative achievements. Humphrey succeeded with a bipartisan coalition. Notably, all of the Minnesotans in Congress—Republicans and Democrats—voted for his bill. Republicans like US representative Al Quie, whose Norwegian immigrant grandfather joined the Union Army during the Civil War because of his staunch opposition to slavery, were keen to convey that they were on the side of racial justice.

At the Ambassador Motel a strategy was hatched to show the voters that Minnesota Republicans were not all in league with Goldwater. The Minnesota national convention delegates who could not countenance the prospect of a Goldwater presidency would cast their nomination ballots instead for a favorite son candidate, former US representative Walter Judd. It was a fitting choice. Judd was an internationalist much in the Stassen tradition who had served as a medical missionary in China before a twenty-year career in the US House. Redistricting in 1961 ended his career by putting him in a Minneapolis district no Republican could win. But Judd remained a genuine favorite in Minnesota, admired for advocating that US foreign policy should serve the goals of peace and human rights for all.[15]

When the roll was called at the Cow Palace in San Francisco, the Minnesota tally was eighteen Judd, eight Goldwater. Schwarzkopf, the convention's floor manager for the pro-Judd forces, also managed to get one vote from Alaska for the former Minnesota congressman. The Minnesota delegation came home with a talking point it could use all fall as the Johnson-Humphrey landslide they feared materialized. Whether that made a difference to voters is hard to say, but the results were affirming: All four of Minnesota's Republican members of the US House kept their seats, and conservatives lost only two seats in the Minnesota house. By contrast, five of Iowa's six Republican congressional seats flipped to the Democrats. The seeds of the notion that Minnesota Republicans could break from the national party and chart their own course had been planted.[16]

Governor Harold LeVander with schoolchildren in the governor's reception room, Minnesota State Capitol, 1967. *Courtesy of MNHS Collections*

4 THE HEYDAY

B Y 1966, thirty years had passed since Harold Stassen began stumping Minnesota for the Young Republican League. Twenty-three years had elapsed since he left the governor's office. Yet Stassen's imprint on Minnesota's Republican Party endured. Witness the choice the party made for governor that year. It bypassed John S. Pillsbury Jr., a charismatic insurance company CEO with one of the most familiar surnames in the nation, in favor of a lesser-known lawyer who got his start with Stassen, Harold LeVander.[1]

It's a reach too far to claim that LeVander's link to Stassen swayed state convention delegates in his favor. But LeVander's tie to Stassen was crucial to his rise to the prominence a gubernatorial bid requires. And Stassen's mentoring through several decades of personal and professional friendship shaped LeVander's thinking about government's role and responsibilities.

The middle son of a Swedish immigrant clergyman, Karl Harold Phillip LeVander was born in 1910 in Swede Home, Nebraska. The family moved to Minnesota when its three gifted boys were young. Each was dispatched after high school to Gustavus Adolphus College in St. Peter, Minnesota, for undergraduate education with a Swedish Lutheran undertone. Eldest brother Theodor became a speech professor at another Lutheran college, Augustana of Rock Island, Illinois. Harold, too, was an able verbal communicator, so much so that he won a national oratorical contest while also finding time to play football, compete in track as a hurdler and pole vaulter, and serve as student body president. After graduating from Gustavus in 1932 he went to the University of Minnesota Law School, then to work at the Stassen and Ryan law firm and the Dakota County attorney's office in 1935. He had come to adulthood with a deep-seated sense of responsibility and purpose that could only have been enhanced as he watched the Great Depression scar Minnesota lives. He vowed to apply his considerable intellect and determination to making a stable life for himself and those he loved.[2]

Youngest brother Bernhard—known to his friends as Pete—followed Harold's footsteps into law. He also seized on his brother's connection to Stassen. While Harold kept the South St. Paul law firm growing and prospering after Stassen's departure, Pete went to work as the governor's research assistant and, later, his Department of Social Welfare director. While Stassen pursued the presidency, Pete chaired the state Republican Party. In 1954, he ran unsuccessfully for attorney general. If bets had been laid in the 1950s on which LeVander brother would wind up as governor, the smart money would have been on Pete.[3]

Harold made a name for himself in less conventional ways. He taught speech at Macalester College to make extra income—and got a huge bonus there when he met Iantha Powrie, the sister of one of his debate students and a high school speech teacher. The earnest lawyer and vivacious teacher were married in 1938. For many years thereafter, LeVander supplemented his income as a regular on Minnesota's small-town speaking circuit, providing for a family that would include three children, son Harold Jr. (Hap) and daughters Jean and Dyan.[4]

After Stassen left the law firm in 1939, it was renamed Kelly and LeVander and became Dakota County's premier firm, one that owners of small businesses and farms trusted for legal help with land transactions as the county became increasingly suburban. LeVander was in the thick of that transformation as president of the South St. Paul Chamber of Commerce and the South St. Paul United Federal

Savings and Loan Association in the 1950s. His legal clients also included many of the state's rural electric cooperatives and the Minnesota Association of Electric Cooperatives. They brought him in contact with scores of community leaders around the state at a time of rapid growth not only in the Twin Cities but also in the state's mid-sized regional centers. His legal work contributed to establishing the first nuclear power plant in rural America, in Elk River, Minnesota.[5]

I can attest that he was a good judge of talent. He hired me in 1959. I was graduating from the University of Minnesota Law School that year and had met LeVander just once, when he spoke at Jax Café in northeast Minneapolis to the law fraternity of which I was chancellor. But I was close to someone who knew him well. Fred Hughes, a family friend and alumnus of the school that was also my home base, St. John's University, had been a contemporary of LeVander at the University of Minnesota Law School. In the late 1950s, he headed a prominent law firm in St. Cloud. Hughes's devotion to the Republican Party kept him in frequent contact with the LeVander brothers. He gave me the entrée I needed to land a job at the firm, which was by then called LeVander, Gillen and Miller. It was a busy midsized firm with a family feeling that made me quickly at home.

By the 1960s, an amazing number of Minnesotans had at some point heard LeVander's stock commencement/civic-holiday speech, "What's Right with America." It was an unabashed paean to American democracy, ending with a recitation of the lyrics of Irving Berlin's "God Bless America." The message was patriotic, not partisan. But the traditional values it promoted were ones that resonated well with Republicans in the small towns of Greater Minnesota as anxiety grew over the Cold War and race relations in America's cities. LeVander's old-time patriotism was a comfort to his listeners. He left them with no doubt that he was a staunch Christian and capitalist, a firm believer in the value of education, and an idealist who saw little that needed correction in the way Americans elected and organized their government. He left his listeners feeling good about the country—and about him.[6]

LeVander's endorsement by the state GOP convention in June 1966 didn't come easily. It took two days, sixteen ballots, and, ultimately, a backroom deal for him to best Pillsbury. Unlike later internecine Republican contests, this one was not a tussle between philosophical moderates and conservatives. Rather, the split ran along geographic lines, with Pillsbury preferred by Hennepin County's Young Turks and LeVander by legislators and party leaders in Greater Minnesota. The rival convention campaign managers were emblematic of that division. Pillsbury's top convention aide was future US representative Bill Frenzel of suburban Golden Valley; LeVander's was state representative Paul Overgaard of Albert Lea. At the national level, a reprise of the 1964 Goldwater-Rockefeller contest was already in the offing, with former vice president Richard Nixon replacing Goldwater as the conservative champion and Michigan governor George Romney joining New York governor Nelson Rockefeller in wooing moderate Republicans. It says much about Minnesota's distance from that contest that Pillsbury had the endorsement of both Nixon and Romney, yet the convention went for LeVander.

National political handicappers likely didn't give LeVander much chance of victory. After all, Minnesota was home to the sitting Democratic vice president, Hubert Humphrey. But DFLers were sorely divided in 1966. Governor Karl Rolvaag, an old-shoe party operative who had served eight undistinguished years as lieutenant governor before becoming governor, maintained the same lethargic style through four years as governor. Criticism swelled that he was indecisive, ineffective, and given to the same flaw that had done in Governor Elmer Benson and the old Farmer-Labor Party—excessive cronyism. Later, Rolvaag would reveal that he had suffered from alcoholism during his governorship. That disorder was whispered among party insiders as they schemed to supplant him with lieutenant governor A. M. "Sandy" Keith, a telegenic young attorney from Rochester, Minnesota. Keith won DFL endorsement in a bruising twenty-ballot convention battle. A week after the GOP convention, Rolvaag announced he would "let the people decide" and enter the September DFL primary election. That decision assured that the DFL would be a house divided at least through the summer and potentially until November. Rolvaag won the September 13 primary with deceptive ease, besting Keith more than 2–1. Minnesotans have an aversion to politicians who display excessive ambition. That was the rap on Keith. But the DFL governor remained politically wounded.[7]

LeVander had one other major asset: the Minnesota Republican Party. It was well on its way to becoming what national political observer Neal Peirce would describe in 1973 as "one of the best financed, most professional political organizations in the entire United States." In truth, it was not one organization but several, all striving to attach average Minnesota citizens to the Republican Party in ways that went well beyond casting a vote. The Young Republican League that Stassen founded was a major force. But also on the scene were the Teen-Age Republican League, the College Republicans, the Minnesota Federation of Republican Women, a Minnesota affiliate of the National Council of Republican Workshops, and a smattering of loosely allied business and professional Republican men's clubs.[8]

In addition, the party itself was an organized presence with local units in every part of the state, even the DFL stronghold of northeastern Minnesota. It organized its major donors into a group called the Elephant Club that met frequently and engaged notable speakers, bringing a loyalty-building social and educational component to fundraising. The labor-intensive Neighbor to Neighbor program was paying off, and not just financially. By the early 1970s it would boast of raising $400,000 a year from more than sixty thousand Minnesotans whose identification with the GOP intensified with every $5 or $10 contribution. Peirce called it "the nation's most outstanding effort to broaden the base of political financing."

Those funds supplemented the state party's $1 million annual budget and paid for the deployment of a staff of thirty-five professionals—a huge force by today's standards. To be sure, large staffs were needed to manage communication in many pre-internet enterprises. But staffing at that level also reflected the state party's decision to emphasize grassroots organizing and person-to-person contact over mass-market messaging. Television advertising by and for campaigns was in use in 1966, but it came more slowly to geographically expansive Minnesota than to more population-dense states. Print and radio ads were prevalent, often tailored to local circumstances. Direct mail was coming on strong as a political tool, one that both major parties in Minnesota would eagerly employ. It provided person-to-person messaging that suited a state that prized political participation. By 1966, as a Dakota County Young Republican I'd door-knocked nearly every home in South St. Paul in the even-numbered years since 1960!

The Minnesota GOP's people power was regarded with envy by the political opposition. As DFLer David Lebedoff wrote in his 1969 book about the 1966 campaign, *The Twenty-First Ballot: A Political Party Struggle in Minnesota,* the Democratic Party's strength nationally was its grassroots reach, while Republicans in much of the country relied on a small cohort of big-money donors. That pattern did not apply to Minnesota, Lebedoff wrote: "It is the Republicans who now ring the doorbells, who see that all their people are registered, who provide the volunteer labor for a big campaign. The DFL had seen this type of effort atrophy among its membership."[9]

The Minnesota Republican Party took its own governance seriously. It was a grassroots party, built from the bottom up. The precinct caucus was the biennial "town hall meeting" to which all were welcomed, and many were put to work. Party leaders encouraged community-level task forces around the issues of the day. Their members were prepared to participate in party platform discussions and encouraged to be delegates at the next-level Republican conventions—counties or legislative districts ("basic political organizing units" or BPOUs), followed by congressional district and the state convention.

That process created the party's remarkable 1966 platform, Programs for People. Assembled by a committee headed by a prominent Minneapolis attorney and state senator, Wayne Popham, the thirty-six-page platform is a strikingly progressive document by twenty-first-century standards. Springing from the agenda championed by the legislature's Young Turks—of which Popham was one—it reads like a blueprint for legislation and, in some passages, like the legislature's own bill summaries, which likely were those passages' origin. It called for increases in state funding for public schools, higher education, college student financial aid, medical education and research, services for the mentally ill and developmentally disabled, and environmental protection. It eloquently endorsed racial equality under the law as "at the root of the entire existence of the Republican Party" and backed government sanctions against discrimination in employment and housing. It included detailed recommendations for "removing all barriers which keep the American Indian in Minnesota from enjoying the same rights as all other citizens"—highlighting a regional civil justice issue more than a decade before it would rise into wider public consciousness.

While the platform also called for a reduction in the state income tax burden, "particularly in the middle-income brackets," it did not seek a smaller state budget. Neither did it endorse the establishment of a revenue source that had become a fiscal workhorse in most other states, a retail sales tax—even though a growing number of Republican legislators believed the state needed the fiscal boost that ever-growing sales tax receipts would bring. Rather, the platform proposed to petition the federal government to send a fixed portion of federal income tax revenues back to the states to be used as each state saw fit. That idea was then being promoted by Walter Heller, the University of Minnesota economist who had served Presidents John Kennedy and Lyndon Johnson as chair of the Council of Economic Advisers. That likely explains why the same idea appeared in the 1966 DFL platform. But "revenue sharing" resonated with the Republican view of federalism and the financing of state and local government services. It had strong appeal for LeVander—and for me.

That wasn't the only parallel between the two major-party platforms that year. In fact, they were so similar that a side-by-side catalog of their nearly identical passages held in the Minnesota Legislative Reference Library, undated but clearly contemporary, runs to eighteen single-spaced typewritten pages. The two platforms were in accord on a number of matters that fifty years later would be points of deep disagreement between the two parties. For example, both platforms supported public employees' unions and the elimination of a ban on strikes by government employees. Both supported the creation of a new state government agency, a Department of Human Rights, to enforce antidiscrimination laws and the transformation of the Railroad and Warehouse Commission, an industry-dominated relic of the nineteenth century, into a modern Public Utilities Commission to regulate monopoly providers of electricity and telecommunications services. Both favored expanding the voting franchise to those between eighteen and twenty-one years of age; the GOP platform went on to support a reduction in residency requirements for voting, arguing for laws that "permit the widest possible exercise of the right to vote." In the name of public safety, both parties favored compulsory periodic motor vehicle inspections as part of the annual registration process—a requirement that would prove so unpopular that both parties would be eager to repeal it not long after its implementation. Popham attested a half century later that all those similarities arose without a bit of collusion. It was simply the case that Minnesota's two major parties thought that much alike in the mid-1960s.[10]

The Republican Programs for People platform was at its most innovative as it described the changes it favored in the governance of the sprawling Twin Cities metropolitan area. The metro area was then experiencing its most rapid growth since pioneer days. The population of the seven-county region swelled by nearly 30 percent in the 1950s and 22 percent in the 1960s—a rate far outstripping that of the rest of the state and the nation as a whole. The need for sewers, roads, schools, solid waste removal, and other services exploded along with the population. As the GOP platform said, "the history of political, economic, and social development of Minnesota has depended on strong local control." But it went on to acknowledge that the need for efficient and orderly provision of basic services was increasingly outstripping local governments' capacity to provide them. "The 1967 Legislature must find some immediate solutions in such critical areas as sewage disposal, mass transportation, and open land acquisition," the platform said. While it did not describe its preferred remedy in detail, it made clear that Republicans were ready to create "a new urban authority" that would be responsible to the people and "have sufficient delegated powers to act effectively in its assigned area of responsibility." These Republicans weren't interested in merely tweaking existing government structures. They were willing to make bold moves for the sake of getting ahead of problems that if neglected would only cost more to solve later.[11]

This remarkable platform lacked one thing: the stamp of the party's candidate for governor. It appeared to have been written with a different gubernatorial candidate in mind, either Pillsbury or Elmer L. Andersen, whose late-starting bid for a comeback landed him in third place in the GOP convention's balloting. LeVander had campaigned vigorously among GOP activists in the run-up to the convention, speaking to Republican groups large and small all over the state. But his speech was what one campaign aide called an "old-fashioned stem-winder" that emphasized such verities as respect for the law and the need for strong families that exercise parental authority. Those were popular themes among Minnesotans in unsettled 1966, especially among those who had appreciated presidential candidate Barry Goldwater's law-and-order emphasis in 1964. But they did not add up to a gubernatorial plan for action.[12]

The speech LeVander delivered around the state in the fall was similarly vague. He was not a creature of the legislature or state government and did not pretend to be one. Instead, he invoked timeless virtues—integrity, efficiency, compassion—with a speech entitled "Let's Be Proud of Minnesota Again." LeVander was every bit the high-minded preacher's son on the stump, vowing that "the most essential task of my daily routine will be to see to it that every act, every decision be governed by principle, not political expediency." He typically added a dismissive allusion to the programmatic theme of President Lyndon Johnson and his Minnesota vice president Hubert Humphrey: "We are more concerned with a good society than a Great Society."[13]

The speech put LeVander in the moralistic lineage of Youngdahl and the progressive lineage of Stassen and Andersen. Like Stassen, LeVander spoke of his respect for labor and of a desire to modernize the "housekeeping functions" of state government agencies. Like Youngdahl, he decried the underfunding of services for the mentally handicapped. Like Andersen, he extolled the duty of government to "maximize the dignity of each and every citizen of our state" regardless of race or religious difference. One of his chief criticisms of the Rolvaag administration was that the DFLer had ordered a 5 percent cut in state spending on education, a "political cutback" that "crippled our schools." A note from a campaign aide appended to a surviving copy of the speech advises the candidate, "You must constantly work for an image and impact of having a constructive, progressive, and exciting program to replace the feeble, fumbling, foggy, and farcical Rolvaag."

I was a part-time, unpaid field worker in that campaign, concentrating on the Sixth and Seventh congressional districts in north-central and northwestern Minnesota. I visited places where I had personal contacts, then hurried back to South St. Paul to help keep the law firm functioning in the boss's absence. College, law school, the Young Republican League, the Knights of Columbus, and a year as president of the South St. Paul Jaycees (during which we were named the outstanding chapter in the country in our population division) had given me a good-sized network of acquaintances throughout the state. Turning those friends into campaign allies was an enjoyable pursuit, I discovered, even though it meant time away from my family and the work that was piling up in the office. But I wasn't pitching Harold's ideas for state government as I met with local newspaper editors and clusters of friends. I was selling Harold himself.

We made the sale. LeVander soared past Rolvaag in the November 8 election, topping him by a decisive 72,650 votes. It was a thrilling triumph that made young campaigners like me feel that politics was an endeavor we had mastered. That sense was bolstered in South St. Paul, where several of us Jaycees had worked to unseat state senator Paul Thuet Jr.—the liberal caucus minority leader—and replace him with our friend and former Jaycees president Rollin Glewwe, Harold Stassen's nephew. We allowed ourselves to think that politics was a fun and effective means of community development and that our team was firmly in charge.

I was well aware that the governor-elect had only sketchy plans for governing. Yet I was shocked after the election when he called me into his office and announced, "I need someone to go with me to the capitol to be my executive secretary, somebody I know and trust. I believe you'll enjoy it." As a husband and father of three small children and a fourth due the following April, one of my immediate qualms was about the position's relatively low salary, $11,500 a year. Harold offered to supplement my compensation from his own funds. With that assurance and at the urging of my wife, Judy, I took the job.

I tried to project more confidence than I felt as I got busy hiring other staffers and participated in the selection of a number of the state agency heads (called commissioners) that serve at the pleasure of the governor. Archie Chelseth, who had worked with Elmer L. Andersen, was chosen to be research director, and Bob Hinkley would be press secretary, with Jean LeVander, the governor's elder daughter and a new Gustavus grad, as his speechwriter.

It says much about the political spirit of those days that we did not seek to replace every agency head who had served under Rolvaag. I was party to moving Rolland Hatfield, who had served the Rolvaag administration as commissioner of taxation, to commissioner of administration, then the top finance job in state government. To head taxation, we tapped Rufus Logan, a longtime professor of economics at LeVander's alma mater, Gustavus Adolphus College. I was pleased to find Ray Olsen, a visionary former Bloomington city administrator, at the helm of the State Planning Agency, a new office that had been created a few years earlier at the instigation of the state senate's lord of government organization, Gordon Rosenmeier. We kept him in that post.

We wanted more emphasis on business development and recruited a successful investment counselor, William J. O'Brien of St. Paul, to head a renamed Department of Economic Development. We wanted to signal that progressive Republicans valued organized labor, so we appointed E. I. "Bud" Malone as commissioner of labor and industry. Malone had been an officer of the International Brotherhood of Electrical Workers Local 160 for ten years, and in that role, he negotiated union contracts with several of the suburban electrical cooperatives that the LeVander law firm represented. Harold came to know and respect Malone as they went toe-to-toe in those contract talks.

Jerry Olson, who had been our post-convention campaign manager, took our assignment as liaison to the legislature, aided informally by state representative Paul Overgaard, our convention manager. I didn't work directly with legislators, but I was on hand at a pre-inauguration meeting with key Republican legislators at LeVander's sprawling South St. Paul ranch-style house. That made me a witness to an exchange that I suspect was without precedent between legislators and a new Minnesota governor. They asked: What do you want us to do? What do you feel strongly about?

"We'll pass the party platform," LeVander said simply.

Few governors before or since put so much trust in the handiwork of their party's convention delegates. LeVander was expressing genuine respect for the party that had carried him to victory. Still, the 1966 GOP platform bore a strong Young Turk stamp. LeVander was signaling that he had more affinity for the progressive, urban-oriented members of the conservative caucuses than some of the GOP delegates who endorsed him might have known.

That gubernatorial affirmation coincided with the seating of the most urban-oriented legislature the state had yet seen. Redistricting in 1966–done under court order to finally be consistent with the US Supreme Court's "one person, one vote" requirement–finally allowed the post–World War II population gains in the Twin Cities to be fairly represented in the state house and senate. The Young Turks, most now seasoned by several terms of service, were intent on addressing the needs of a growing population. On several key issues, they had forged working alliances with a number of long-serving great elks of the conservative caucuses. They also had support from Republicans in Greater Minnesota who understood that the whole state benefits when the metro area thrives and that outstate forces could help resolve a few persistent disputes among metro legislators. The Young Turks wanted to raise the level of discourse and policy analysis at the legislature, pushing for the creation of a nonpartisan House Research office–a talent powerhouse to this day. Pent-up progressive energy was ready for release in the legislature's new majorities. The governor could either follow their lead or get out of the way.[14]

On no issue was that spirit more evident than the push for Minnesota to become the forty-fourth state in the nation to collect a retail sales tax. The idea to make a 3 percent sales tax the centerpiece of the Tax Reform and Relief Act did not come from the governor. Nor was it included in the 1966 GOP platform. But even before the 1967 session convened, legislative leaders signaled to Minnesotans–and to us in the governor's office–that they were keen to put a sales tax on the books that year. New senate majority leader Stan Holmquist told the *St. Paul Pioneer Press* that a failure to consider a sales tax would amount to "shirking one's responsibility." During the first week of the session, house speaker Lloyd Duxbury told a reporter he was "ready to consider" a sales tax "that would have property tax relief for homeowners as its primary goal."[15]

Property tax relief—that was the goal propelling the sales tax. Since the 1950s, the property taxes that paid for schools, police, fire, and other local services had been high and rising, particularly in suburban areas. The state was also at the property tax trough, collecting a levy to pay off state bonds and cover a portion of teachers' pension costs. Other taxes could have been targets in 1967 if the goal of the legislature's GOP majorities had been simply to lessen the burden on taxpayers. For example, the legislature's conservatives might have pushed to reduce the state income tax, then highest in the nation for married couples with two children and incomes of $10,000 a year. Or they might have sought to reduce spending. A 1966 comparison of Minnesota's per-capita state and local spending with the other forty-nine states found Minnesota well above average on K–12 schools and higher education, highways, and public welfare. It stood near the average in every other category save one, police and fire services.[16]

But if Republicans in the 1967 legislature were worried about too much government spending or income taxes that soaked the rich, they did not bring those concerns into the legislative fray. Rather, in early March, the chairs of the tax committees in both chambers scheduled hearings on tax reform bills built around establishing a 3 percent sales tax. Senate tax chair Donald O. Wright—a crusty Minneapolis attorney then serving his fortieth year in office—was fully on board. "This bill is not introduced as a gesture," he told a reporter. "This is real serious business. This is what we have to do to keep this state alive."[17]

They faced one major obstacle: my boss. Harold LeVander had vowed on the final full day of the 1966 campaign that he would not sign a sales tax bill unless it referred the matter first to a popular vote. In a state with no initiative and referendum provision in its constitution, that represented a major departure from usual lawmaking practice.

Just as the GOP platform had been silent on a sales tax, so had LeVander ducked the issue through most of the campaign. Many of his allies, including Overgaard, suspected that Harold privately agreed with the argument that Minnesota needed to rely less on the property tax, which is unrelated to income and hence can force people who suffer a loss of income out of their homes. Raising a state income tax that already was the most burdensome in the nation was also not a good option, particularly for the party whose political base included the state's most affluent taxpayers. The virtues of the sales tax: it is paid in small, politically tolerable increments; its revenue stream grows automatically with the economy; and while more burdensome to the poor than the rich, this can be tempered by exempting necessities such as groceries, clothing, and prescription drugs or by providing a refundable tax credit to low-income people. Sales tax advocates argued that it could reduce the state's total property tax burden by at least 10 percent—potentially more for middle-income homeowners—plus help businesses expand if at the same time the legislature would eliminate property taxes on business inventories and equipment.

None of those arguments for a sales tax were made by the 1966 Republican candidate for governor. But that didn't keep Rolvaag from raising the issue. Opposition to the sales tax as a regressive way to pay for government had been DFL dogma in Minnesota since the 1930s, when Governor Floyd B. Olson insisted on an income tax rather than a sales tax to fill depleted government coffers at the bottom of the Great Depression. As the governor's race tightened in the polls, Rolvaag and other DFLers insisted that electing Republicans would guarantee a sales tax "forever." Two days before the election, when the *Minneapolis Tribune's* Minnesota Poll showed LeVander trailing Rolvaag, LeVander was urged by his top campaign aides to respond to Rolvaag's sales tax charge. The next day, LeVander issued a statement saying a sales tax was not needed now and would be "irresponsible"—and promising to veto it if he was elected unless a referendum was required for it to become law.[18]

True to his word, Governor LeVander proposed a record $1 billion biennial budget for 1968–69. It included $104 million in property tax relief. That sum was derived from existing revenue and was made possible by a $130 million forecasted surplus, the fruits of a strong economy and the inflation that was beginning what would be a pro-longed climb. But tapping the state surplus for property tax relief would come at the expense of education and other programs most Republican legislators favored. It wasn't going to fly with a head-strong legislature. Some of the early sales tax bills included a referendum, as a sop to LeVander. But the referendum disappeared as the bills advanced. "The Legislature is responsible for making laws," Senate Tax Committee chair Wright huffed when a reporter asked about that change. "The governor is not a member of the legislature. There is no occasion to consult with the governor at any time about the making of a law. It is not fitting to go and ask the advice of the executive department."[19]

From that point forward, positions hardened. By early April, Wright was attacking LeVander as "just as wooden-headed as Karl Rolvaag" and openly threatening to orchestrate an override of a gubernatorial veto, which requires a two-thirds majority in both chambers. "This thing has got to be solved. You can't go on taxing people out of their homes," Wright said.[20]

That position was bolstered in early May from two sources. First, a Citizens League task force cochaired by two prominent Minneapolis attorneys, DFLer David Graven and Republican John Mooty, weighed in with strong endorsement of a 3 percent sales tax to be used for property tax relief according to a formula it described in considerable detail. It returned two-thirds of the sales tax's receipts to schools and local governments. The league's task force called for an income tax credit to ease the burden on lower-income households, but added that it also liked the alternative of simply exempting from the tax food purchased for home consumption, clothing, and prescription drugs. The league's recommendations were quickly drafted into bill form and carried as an amendment to the senate tax bill by Senator Wayne Popham, the 1966 GOP platform chair.[21]

Days later, Minnesotans themselves weighed in via the *Tribune's* Minnesota Poll. A poll several months earlier had asked respondents a straightforward yes-or-no question about a sales tax, and predict-ably, "no" won a majority, 57 percent. But in May, the poll asked Min-nesotans whether they would support a sales tax if food, shelter, and other necessities were exempted, and if the proceeds were directed to schools and local governments in order to ease the property tax load. When asked that way, a strong 65 percent majority gave the idea an affirmative nod.[22]

That was enough political comfort for a majority of legislators. Speaker Dirlam told reporters he intended to move the sales tax bill into conference committee with the senate and "we'll see" what the governor opts to do. The house's bill for a 3 percent sales tax, exempt-ing groceries, clothing, and prescription drugs, passed on May 11 with a 78–53 vote—ten votes more than needed to pass, but twelve votes shy of the number needed for a veto override. The senate followed suit on May 17 with a version of Popham's Citizens League bill. It won by a 39–27 vote—six short of the threshold for a veto override.

As the conference committee began its work, three working days remained in the regular session. Representative Paul Overgaard, LeVander's loyal ally in the house, paid the governor a visit to ask what he wanted done on the sales tax bill. Overgaard recalled that day in a 2007 interview: "When [LeVander] was conflicted, he had a habit of mashing his cigar between his thumb and forefinger, and kind of rolling it. I told him, 'I'll do what you'd like, but you've got to tell me what you want.' As I recall, the silence that followed lasted an awful long time. I repeated my statement. 'If you want this bill to be overridden, it will be. If you want your veto sustained, I think I can put that together.' He didn't even look at me. He just twirled that cigar." Decades later, in 1992, Overgaard visited LeVander as the former governor struggled with his final illness and asked him again what he had wanted that weekend in May 1967. Even then, Overgaard said, LeVander refused to answer.[23]

The bill that came to LeVander's desk in the middle of the af-ternoon on Saturday, May 20, lacked the referendum he required. Within forty-five minutes, the governor stood before TV cameras to announce his veto. "I'm not sure he was against what we enacted," Overgaard said. "But he was a man of his word. When he announced that he wasn't going to support the sales tax without a referendum, that was it. He wasn't going to sign it."

A 96–37 override vote passed in the house with six votes to spare only three hours after LeVander's veto. But things weren't moving as quickly in the senate—thanks in part to a delaying maneuver orchestrated by an ambitious liberal senator from St. Paul, Wendell Anderson. "Stay off the board! Don't vote!" Anderson urged his fellow DFLers, going desk to desk to prolong the electronic vote. The board stayed open for eighty minutes with the forty-five-vote override threshold unmet. Midnight came and time ran out for action on bills during the regular session. The tax bill appeared to have died.

LeVander could have left it at that and spared himself further grief over the issue. But too many provisions of importance were embedded in that tax bill. He called a special session on May 23, the day after the constitutionally required ceremonial adjournment. Its purpose, he said, was action on a tax bill, even as he renewed his vow to veto a sales tax that lacked the referendum he desired.

Minnesota watched as the same exercise was repeated. A tax bill practically identical to the one vetoed on May 20 arrived again on LeVander's desk on May 31. The governor vetoed it on the morning of June 1. But this time, the override train could not be stalled. Just six hours later, both chambers had acted. The vote was 93–41 in the house, 47–20 in the senate. Republican majorities had bucked their own governor to establish the state sales tax as part of the most sweeping tax reform measure the state had seen in a third of a century.

The new tax was far from universally popular—and LeVander's opposition to the move was lost on some of those who disapproved. "Pennies for LeVander!" retailers and customers sometimes muttered as they dug a little deeper when making purchases after the tax went into effect on July 1. In August—in time for state fair distribution—DFLers were circulating a pamphlet prepared by the party's state chairman, George Farr, suggesting that LeVander had been party to

LeVander opposed the sales tax, but his opponents distributed "Pennies for Lavender" stickers in protest in 1967. *Courtesy of MNHS Collections*

"a conspiracy with GOP lawmakers" to enact the new tax. "Or was [the governor] so ineffective that neither he, his staff, his whole official family and his political party were not able to persuade anyone from their own group to support him?" Farr asked. It was an uncomfortable question for those of us on LeVander's team.

It strikes me as unfair that the 1967 session is remembered primarily for the sales tax dispute, when the same year produced so many examples of constructive cooperation between the executive and legislative branches of state government. Headlines about sales taxes dwarfed those about bold steps Republicans took that year to solve long-festering problems—steps that seem even more remarkable a half century later than they did from my vantage in the governor's office at the time.

The myriad problems associated with urban sprawl in the seven-county Twin Cities area were addressed with the creation of the Metropolitan Council, a regional entity that was then and is still unlike any other in the nation in structure and scope of responsibility. It was not to be an all-purpose government; municipalities and counties would retain their existing responsibilities. It was not a council of elected officials representing subordinate jurisdictions. That approach, the designers thought, would leave council members loyal to their political bases rather than the region as a whole. Rather, it was a council consisting of fourteen (later, sixteen) citizen members appointed by the governor with the consent of the senate, plus one salaried, (initially) part-time chair. The idea—which was controversial then and remains so today—was to make the Met Council accountable to state government, fulfilling the state's goals for Minnesota's largest population zone. Senator Rosenmeier held strongly to this view; in 1970, the Minnesota Supreme Court upheld this interpretation.

It fell to me in the governor's office to screen and recommend the governor's original fifteen council appointees. My orders were to find people who could represent not only the unique populations and needs of the metro area but also the politics of each of the legislatively described districts. I wasn't just looking for Republicans or LeVander loyalists. Our slate was well received. For the chair, LeVander tapped nationally renowned University of Minnesota law professor Jim Hetland. With that appointment, LeVander set the bar very high, underscoring the position's importance despite its part-time status and salary.

The Met Council's primary mission was to bring order and efficiency to the region's development. Its directive was to craft a region-wide development guide and to review the long-range comprehensive plans of municipalities, townships, and special districts. If the jurisdictional plans were in conflict with the region's plan, the council had authority to suspend the plans from special districts and to negotiate changes that eliminated conflicts among the municipal and township plans. The special districts were single-purpose regional government entities overseeing airports, mosquito control, sewers, and water treatment. These were already in existence and would continue their work. Shortly, a transit agency would join them. The council would appoint from its membership one person to serve on these and any similar commission established by the legislature. The idea was to better coordinate their work, not supplant them.[24]

Not every recommendation from the new council was welcomed. One of the first was that the region's growth would require a second major airport in the northern suburbs, to be financed with fees paid by the airlines. The idea raised the hackles of Minnesota's own Northwest Orient Airlines. Its president and chair Donald Nyrop told the governor that he would move the airline's headquarters to Seattle if the state acted on that recommendation. To prove he meant it, Nyrop repeatedly parked himself on a seat just outside my office door until LeVander persuaded the council and the Metropolitan Airports Commission not to proceed.

The same legislative session also created the Minnesota Pollution Control Agency and the state Department of Human Rights. Both put Minnesota well ahead of other states in responding to two growing public concerns, environmental protection and civil rights. Both were expansions of government—by Republicans—to more effectively solve problems that had grown beyond the reach of existing government tools.

It must be acknowledged that while my boss supported both new agencies and went so far as to mention the need for a pollution agency in his inaugural address, the impetus for their creation came from the legislature. And the legislator who did the most to put them into final form was conservative senate titan Gordon Rosenmeier—without whose support bills of this nature could not have won senate approval. Liberals faulted Rosenmeier as too slow to respond to the state's needs. But a contemporary said, "His approach to new legislative ideas [was] that of a potter who receives a block of clay and thinks about it a long, long while, gathering ideas that will guide him in forming the final product."[25]

The state's inability to respond adequately to a pair of massive oil spills in the bitterly cold winter of 1962–63 made the case for the Pollution Control Agency by showing the need for a stronger regulatory response to pollution. But it took several events on LeVander's watch for us to grasp the breadth and depth of Minnesota's concern for clean air and water. First came the decision by Northern States Power Company to build a coal-fired power plant on the St. Croix River on the dubious theory that one of the highest smokestacks in the country would reduce the health threats of air pollution. It was followed by St. Paul's approval of a metal refabricating plant called North Star Steel on Pig's Eye Lake on the Mississippi, across from South St. Paul.

Both of those moves triggered an outpouring of objection from people we were beginning to call "environmentalists."[26]

Then came growing realization that Reserve Mining Company's daily dumping of 67,000 tons of mineral waste into Lake Superior likely was not benign, as the company claimed. Reserve, the state's largest taconite pellet producer, had obtained permission to use the big lake as its waste dump in 1947 and ramped up to full operations in 1956. By the 1960s, the lake from which Duluth and other North Shore communities drew their drinking water was turning a cloudy green near Silver Bay, Reserve's home. The *Minneapolis Tribune* and reporter Ron Way were all over the governor for his cautious response to findings that the tailings were causing pollution. LeVander was fearful of straining the steel industry's always-fragile corporate commitments to Iron Range mining. After both quiet persuasion and public pressure, the governor did call on the Pollution Control Board to hold fact-finding hearings on Reserve's compliance with its permit. Eventually, the PCA sued Reserve to stop polluting the lake.[27]

Ever wonder about the origin of those interstate highway sound barriers? The portion of Interstate 35W from downtown Minneapolis south through Richfield and Bloomington into Dakota County was completed during the LeVander years. Soon after that stretch opened, I received a call from a *Tribune* political reporter angry about highway noise in his neighborhood. I went to his home along with a state Highway Department district engineer and heard the din for myself. The department surveyed every home adjacent to 35W from downtown to the Crosstown Highway in Richfield and recommended that where earthen berms could not be raised, they should build walls. They did and still do.

The Department of Human Rights evolved from state measures outlawing discrimination, first in employment, then in housing, that dated from 1955. The 1967 bill was sponsored in the senate by Keith Hughes of St. Cloud, the son and law partner of LeVander's best political friend, my mentor Fred Hughes, and in the house by Gary Flakne, who went on to become Hennepin County attorney, the county's chief prosecutor. Both were able lawyers in the progressive Republican tradition.

Both of the new agencies were set up to include gubernatorially appointed citizen boards to share in governance. That was in keeping with our party's ideas about sharing power widely rather than concentrating it in a few hands. Those boards were considered a check on excessive involvement by elected officials and special interests. It says much about the distance the GOP has come since then that in 2015, Republicans took the lead in abolishing the Pollution Control Agency's citizen board. It had run afoul of powerful agricultural interests in August 2014 when it ordered an environmental impact statement for a proposed 8,850-head dairy operation in Stevens County. The fact that the governor who appointed board members was a DFLer did not help the board survive. "What role does the legislature have in appointing them?" one Republican legislator said as he explained his eagerness to abolish the board. Regrettably, a chance to take power away from a DFL governor evidently mattered more to these latter-day Republicans than preserving a citizen-based check on special interests.[28]

5 BIPARTISAN MIRACLE

THE LATE 1960S are remembered as a creative and constructive period in Minnesota state government—a testament to the quality of governance provided by a Republican governor and a Republican-controlled legislature. Those aren't the words that leap to mind as one recalls the condition of the rest of the nation—or of Minnesota's other major political party—from 1966 through the early 1970s.

The civil rights movement that had emphasized nonviolence in the early part of the decade gave way by 1967 to a "long hot summer" of urban unrest that included a night of arson on Plymouth Avenue in Minneapolis that July. At the same time, opposition to US involvement in the Vietnam War caught fire and quickly became a full-blown protest movement, especially on the nation's campuses. Minnesota's Democratic-Farmer-Labor Party, still nursing self-inflicted wounds from the 1966 Rolvaag-Keith gubernatorial primary fight, was torn asunder again by conflict over the war. DFLers were compelled to choose between the rival presidential candidacies of two of their own. US senator Eugene McCarthy, an outspoken Vietnam War critic, challenged President Lyndon Johnson in the New Hampshire primary in 1968 and came close enough to beating the sitting president that he is credited for nudging Johnson out of the race. When Johnson stepped aside in late March, Vice President Hubert Humphrey dove in. Shocking events in rapid succession—the assassinations of

Martin Luther King Jr. in April and Robert Kennedy in June; a bloody street war between police and protesters at the Democratic National Convention in August; and a hard-fought election campaign that led to a very narrow victory for the Republican candidate, former vice president Richard Nixon—made 1968 an agonizing year.[1]

Nixon's victory produced no special joy for us in LeVander's office. Humphrey was a respected figure even among the state's Republicans; were it not so, he would not have carried Minnesota by nearly 200,000 votes. Many Minnesota Republicans were of like mind on national issues with several Republican governors—George Romney of Michigan, William Scranton of Pennsylvania, James Rhodes of Ohio, Nelson Rockefeller of New York—who had been possible presidential contenders that year. As the national GOP convention approached, LeVander was among many leading Minnesotans who believed that Rockefeller had a better chance of both winning and governing than Nixon. LeVander spoke on Rockefeller's behalf at the convention, and I was tasked with trying to persuade some of our state's party regulars who preferred Nixon to change their minds. I was successful in one memorable case. Our national committeewoman, Rhoda Lund, who with her husband, Russell, founded Lund's grocery stores, told me shortly before her death that Russell had never forgiven her for changing from Nixon to Rockefeller "just for LeVander." A few Minnesotans were also attracted to a late entrant in the Republican contest, California's new governor, Ronald Reagan.

LeVander can be called progressive by today's standards, but a more apt label might be "federalist." He was at heart a believer that the nation is best served when state governments are allowed to be as effective as possible. He appreciated the role the federal government can play in the nation's economic development, including the rural electrification program and its citizens' income security. But he was wary of federal overreach. For example, he was a reluctant backer of Elmer L. Andersen's efforts to create a new national park, Voyageurs, near International Falls. I played a role in persuading my boss to get on board. A highly successful St. Cloud businessman and conservative Republican, Bill Holes, supported the park. He and I met over lunch and designed a strategy for convincing the governor. We had invited other business leaders who shared our view to a meeting at which they told LeVander that his support would be a legacy in the making. A key argument was that Eighth District US representative John Blatnik would support the park if LeVander did, even though many of Blatnik's constituents opposed taking a million acres out of private use and off of local tax rolls. That finally sold Harold.

But the governor was concerned about the dominant liberal Democratic thinking in Washington, shared by Humphrey, McCarthy, and the senator who succeeded Humphrey in 1965, Walter Mondale. LeVander worried about the impact of inflation on the federal income tax bite and the incentives for increased federal government spending. He believed state governments—most of which were required to balance their budgets every two years—were more fiscally accountable and more responsive to matching government's response with public need.

Minnesota Republicans were too busy addressing the problems of a fast-growing state in those years to be much diverted by national drama. In the early years of statehood, Minnesota's remote location relative to the rest of the nation allowed it to develop habits of independence and self-determination. Despite the arrival of modern transportation and communication, those habits persisted well into the twentieth century. A national observer as astute as syndicated columnist Neal Peirce took note of Minnesota's independent attitude in the early 1970s and attributed it to a vigorous and varied industrial base, much of it locally owned and controlled.[2]

By the 1960s, many of the state's best-known industrial firms had moved from family to shareholder ownership. But the Daytons of Dayton Hudson (now Target Corporation), the Pillsburys of the Pillsbury Company (now part of General Mills), the Bells and Crosbys of General Mills, the McMillans of Cargill, the McKnights of 3M, the Heffelfingers of Peavey, and others still resided in Minnesota and were much engaged in civic affairs. When a business achieved a certain size, its leader could expect a call from a veteran Minnesota business leader like Kenneth Dayton, the most visible of the five Dayton grandsons of the retailing giant's founder, who would explain Minnesota's expectations for personally engaged corporate leadership and encourage the following of suit.

At about the same time—and not at all coincidentally—a number of these firms added vice presidents of corporate affairs (or a similar title) to their executive teams and assigned them to help guide the region's development. As Ted Kolderie, then head of the Citizens League, describes it, their role was less to influence the community on businesses' behalf than to bring the community's needs to the attention of the corporation. For example, the Daytons hired Oakland city manager Wayne Thompson to come to Minnesota in 1965 to help advance several large community development projects. Within a few years, Thompson headed LeVander's commission on government reorganization and spearheaded the founding of a corporate philanthropy network initially called the Five Percent Club because its members pledged to give 5 percent of each year's pretax profits to charity.[3]

Meanwhile, burgeoning new businesses were taking their places alongside the region's legacy firms. Upstart technology and medical device businesses like Control Data and Medtronic were in their infancies but growing rapidly. Big-league baseball and football arrived in 1961; NHL hockey came to town in 1967. Regional boosterism was part of their DNA. One of the state's leading Republican activists, Dain and Co. CEO Wheelock Whitney, helped rally corporate sponsorship and provided board-level guidance for all three teams—and still found time to run for the US Senate in 1964.

The result, Peirce observed, was "among Twin Cities leaders . . . a deep orientation to change—and a determination not to be engulfed by that change, but rather to make it work constructively." He might have been describing the attitude of the Minnesota Republican Party in those years—and since a majority of business leaders considered themselves Republican, in effect, he was.

Minnesota's 1969 legislative session was routine by comparison with the more consequential sessions that preceded it in 1967 and followed it in 1971. But compared with the exercises in gridlock and futility that have characterized the first decades of the twenty-first century, it bore significant fruit. The '69 session is notable in part because it would be the last time in the twentieth century when Republicans—still labeled conservatives—would simultaneously control the governor's office and both chambers of the legislature.

It's also noteworthy for the agenda LeVander and the legislature pursued—one strikingly different from latter-day GOP aims. For example, the 1969 legislature sought to allow more people to vote, requiring employers to give employees paid time off to vote and sending to the 1970 general election ballot a constitutional amendment lowering the voting age from twenty-one to nineteen. The idea of restricting access to the polls by requiring voters to show a government-issued ID card would have been anathema then. Another example: as inflation borne of war drove interest rates higher, the legislature capped home mortgage interest rates at 8 percent over the objections of the banking industry. A package of consumer protection laws passed despite business opposition.[4]

Higher education was a booming enterprise as the baby boomer generation reached college age, and Republicans went on a building spree in response. There was never a question about whether the public sector should strive to meet the growing demand. Democrats and Republicans quarreled over how much to build and how quickly to build it, but not over government's responsibility to provide reasonably affordable higher education. The governor saw post-secondary education's availability throughout the state as critical both to business development and to the retention of the state's homegrown talent.

Under the able house leadership of Representative Rod Searle of Waseca, the 1969 session added a new junior college in Faribault and a technical college in Dakota County. In an unusual show of legislative deference to a citizen governing board, legislators that year also authorized the Junior College Board to choose the site of one additional junior college from among five possibilities. Those new schools were to be the nineteenth and twentieth members of a two-year college network that had grown rapidly in the 1960s under both Republican and DFL governors. New two-year colleges and technical schools emerged from each legislative session in the 1960s; a new state college, Southwest State in Marshall, was added in 1963; and major building projects enlarged the University of Minnesota's Twin Cities flagship campus.

In a harbinger of things to come in state higher education, LeVander and the legislature created a central coordinating office for the state's colleges. We called it a "system," though the term was not yet deserved, and installed as its first chancellor G. Theodore Mitau, a highly regarded Macalester College history professor who had escaped Nazi Germany as a teenager by enrolling at Macalester. Mitau was associated with two prominent Minnesota Democrats, Hubert Humphrey and Walter Mondale. That was no impediment to his appointment by a Republican governor.[5]

LeVander's legal work with rural electric cooperatives left him with an abiding interest in economic development in Greater Minnesota. He imagined Minnesota as including eleven geographic regions, each made distinct by its renewable resources, geographic features, and mineral deposits. Accordingly, he asked the legislature to create eleven economic development regions to encourage counties to jointly plan their economic futures. It was an idea that eventually became a national network of such regional entities, enabling state, local, and county governments to coordinate social and economic development programs.[6]

In 1968 Nixon employed a law-and-order theme to winning effect. It didn't sell as well with the Minnesota legislature, despite a growing revulsion for increasingly violent antiwar demonstrations. LeVander let it be known that he had no sympathy for street protests as a means to change national policy. He was spared from deciding the fate of one measure that the law-and-order crowd favored. A bill that would have allowed police officers to stop and frisk someone suspected of a crime or of carrying a concealed weapon was stopped in the senate by the firm hand of Judiciary Committee Chair Rosenmeier.[7]

An issue that would scramble state politics in coming years—the legalization of abortion—made an initial appearance at the 1969 legislature. It was a Republican, Senator Kelly Gage of Mankato, who sponsored a bill that would have allowed the termination of a pregnancy in cases of rape or incest or if the mother's life was in danger. The bill cleared the Judiciary Committee on a recorded voice vote that included chairman Rosenmeier voting "aye." That was the bill's only appearance all session. Gage opted not to take it to the floor. But Rosenmeier's vote had been noticed by an ambitious young DFL attorney in Brainerd, Winston Borden. He realized that he had the issue he needed to topple the mighty Rosenmeier in the 1970 election. Thus ended Rosenmeier's thirty-year senate career. Borden was among the first to show the state's political establishment the potency of the abortion issue, particularly in rural Minnesota. Given how the parties would eventually realign over abortion, there's considerable irony in the fact that Borden won as an antiabortion DFLer.[8]

High property taxes continued to eclipse all other issues in state politics. Property taxes were levied primarily to pay for local schools and city services. The 3 percent sales tax enacted in 1967 was not sufficient to stop the rapid rise in tax bills or soothe unhappy taxpayers. The legislature did not compel cities, counties, and school districts to cut their levies in compensation for increased state aid, and many did not do so voluntarily. A 1968 analysis by two economists sponsored by the state AFL-CIO endorsed the intention and direction of the 1967 tax-reform measure but predicted that it would prove too small to live up to its promises. The law directed that sales tax proceeds be deposited in a Property Tax Relief Fund, which in turn paid a property tax credit to homeowners of up to $250 and renters up to $45 per year. The economists' projection, which would prove accurate, showed a $73 million deficit in the relief fund by 1971. "The authors feel that changes in the Minnesota revenue system with respect to the Property Tax Relief Fund will be necessary within the next two years," they advised.[9]

Conservative legislators evidently thought so, too. They created a commission to study further tax changes. But other than enlarging a credit for low-income senior citizens, LeVander and the 1969 legislature stuck with the tax policy changes that had been made two years earlier. The *Minneapolis Tribune* reported, "The Legislature mostly left the major taxes alone, although admitting that their impact is inequitable, that the income tax is high and the property tax is going out of sight." By 1970, property taxes for homeowners across the state had climbed 65 percent on average in just three years. There was no doubt about what issue would dominate state political campaigns that year.[10]

Widespread unhappiness about property taxes helped attract an unusually large number of credible DFL candidates into the 1970 governor's race. By the end of 1969, that array included two charismatic DFL state senators from St. Paul, Wendell Anderson from the city's blue-collar East Side and Nicholas Coleman from the economically mixed Summit-University area west of the city's center. Also running: Minneapolis law professor and former southern Minnesota congressional candidate David Graven; former state agriculture commissioner Russell Schwandt; Hennepin County Attorney George Scott; DFL state party chairman Warren Spannaus (who would soon shift his sights to the attorney general's office); and wealthy businessman Robert Short, an undeclared candidate who let it be known that while he would not be bothered with an endorsement fight at the DFL convention, he would mount a primary challenge to any endorsee not to his liking.

The strength of that lineup reflected DFLers' sense that Harold LeVander was vulnerable and their expectation that he would seek a second term. Inside the LeVander administration, we privately questioned both of those assumptions. The governor's poll numbers weren't great, but Harold was an effective campaigner. We had little doubt that he could be reelected.

But I was increasingly convinced that LeVander did not enjoy being governor. He was an upright traditionalist in a leadership role at a time of disruptive social change. He was distraught over antiwar protests, a sit-in by black students at the University of Minnesota in 1969, a teacher's strike in Minneapolis in 1970. He gave voice to his worry at the 1968 Republican state convention, which met days after Robert Kennedy's assassination. "All is not well in America when assassinations are compounded with riots and wars, when crime runs rampant, when hunger cries out, when groups prey upon groups, urban pitted against rural, business versus labor, students versus administration, black versus white. Then there is something desperately wrong with the spirit of our people," he said.

When LeVander went to Sweden the next month to attend a meeting of the World Council of Churches, his daughter Jean had to twist his arm hard to get him to meet with a nineteen-year-old draft dodger from Minnesota, Mark Alan Shapiro. Shapiro was on the staff of the American Deserters Committee in Stockholm, which was a destination for a growing number of young Americans unwilling to fight in Vietnam. Jean considered it important for her father to hear Shapiro's perspective, and for Minnesotans to know that their governor was willing to listen. The *Minneapolis Star*'s religion reporter Willmar Thorkelson got the story. But I don't think the meeting opened Harold's mind.[11]

It was difficult for me as his chief of staff to convey to others what drove LeVander's decision-making process. Though we had worked together for years in the law firm, the governor's office was a new environment for both of us. I was often left to guess about what he wanted the staff to do, or why. I would occasionally ask him, "What

LeVander leaves for Sweden, 1968. *Courtesy of MNHS Collections*

do you want to accomplish here? To what end? What's the mission?" Or even, as we neared the final year of his term, "Why did you want to be governor?" The answers often weren't clear.

I was so conscious of the passage of valuable time. Increasingly, my focus was at home. My wife, Judy, was first diagnosed with breast cancer in May 1967, not long after the birth of our fourth son, Daniel. The cancer had metastasized, and the treatment was radiation. I enlisted University of Minnesota oncologist Dr. B. J. Kennedy, who was experimenting with chemotherapy, to visit her. I remember Judy's answer to his question, "Are you afraid of dying?"

"Not at all," she said quite clearly. "God's will be done."

At that point I knew why she meant for me to stop thinking about leaving my position to "help her with the boys." "This was meant to be, and you were meant to be prepared for whatever the consequence is for each of us," she said so often.

In the healthy times between the cancer showing up somewhere new, I involved her in almost everything I could, including several National Governors Association conferences. The most enjoyable was a cruise to the Virgin Islands, during which a member of California governor Reagan's staff intercepted a call from President Lyndon Johnson to NGA chair John Connolly of Texas with instructions to "deep six" a Republican proposal on the conduct of the Vietnam War. Judy met and was photographed with nearly every governor.

Judy was active in the Mrs. Jaycees club in South St. Paul; its members were exceedingly helpful with childcare, errands, meals, and the like. But it was clear in early 1970 that I needed to stay close to her and the boys. I knew I could not spend the summer and fall stumping the state for LeVander's reelection; I doubted that I could stay in the governor's office during a second term. I don't recall that Harold and I discussed Judy's health in connection with his decision, though he was well aware of her situation. It went without saying.

LeVander and I were close, but our relationship was that of mentor/mentee. We were not confidants. Yet I sensed that his heart was telling him it was time to yield the governor's office to the next generation. I did not learn his decision about a second term until a few hours before he announced it publicly on January 26, 1970. I was not surprised when he said he would not run again. He spoke for many of the Republican officeholders of that era when he said, "I have never considered myself a career politician. . . . I believe the strength of our system is to be found in the citizen-politician who recognized a duty and gives of himself for some period of time and then is willing to retire from the scene and let others assume the responsibilities of the office." As he cited his record of accomplishment, he prominently mentioned his willingness to employ state government as a tool for environmental protection, orderly urban growth, public education, consumer protection, and racial justice. Those were matters of Republican pride.[12]

I was well aware that two younger Republicans were in the wings, eager to jump into the governor's race. It is to the credit of both attorney general Doug Head, then thirty-nine, and lieutenant governor James Goetz, just thirty-three, that they had done nothing publicly to appear to push the fifty-nine-year-old LeVander aside. Head had launched a campaign for the US Senate seat being vacated by Eugene McCarthy, who seemed to lose interest in the Senate after his presidential foray in 1968. That was not the case with the other Minnesotan who had vied for the presidency in 1968. As soon as Hubert Humphrey began to hint that he would ask the voters to send him back to the US Senate in 1970, Republican desire to seek the seat lessened considerably. Two weeks after LeVander said he would leave the governor's office, the attorney general announced that he had abandoned his Senate campaign in favor of a bid to move across the state capitol hallway.[13]

Head was a strong candidate. Goetz sought to make the customary rural/urban division in state politics work to his advantage, as LeVander had in 1966. Goetz owned KAGE radio and was an on-air personality in Winona. But Head's four years in the attorney general's office had shown Minnesotans that there was more to him than his Hennepin County base. And four years in the governor's office had shown me that his backers, the Young Turks of Hennepin County, were talented and sincere public servants with the whole state's interests in mind. I came to admire them and considered many of them friends.

The rural/urban divide that has become painfully stark in twenty-first-century state politics has been present since statehood. But it was narrower in the 1960s than it is today, in part because both of the state's major political parties had a stake in both regions. Neither party saw an advantage in fanning regional resentments. Republicans controlled the Minneapolis City Council in the 1960s and elected several legislators in St. Paul. DFLers had an iron grip on the Iron Range, yet Elmer L. Andersen showed in 1960 that a Republican could make inroads in that stronghold to good effect.

The notion of Minnesota as a singular economic unit with a distinctive culture jelled during the mid-twentieth century. Since the state's earliest days, the industries of the Twin Cities were tied to the natural resources of Greater Minnesota, and agriculture's diminishing need for human input in the twentieth century created a flow of human capital from farms to the cities. But a Minnesota identity was promoted in a new way in the 1960s when a new Major League Baseball team, NFL football team, and NHL hockey franchise invited their fans to root for Minnesota, not a particular city. In 1968, at the urging of board member Elmer Andersen, the Minneapolis Symphony became the Minnesota Orchestra. The *Minneapolis Tribune* positioned itself as a state newspaper—which it had long been on Sundays—and TV and radio stations in the Twin Cities expanded their reach to serve more of the state. In 1967, an upstart radio station with a commercial-free, listener-supported funding model was born at my alma mater, St. John's University. It took the name Minnesota Public Radio and set to work building a statewide network that became a national public broadcasting model.

That "One Minnesota" backdrop made Head's claim to statewide appeal an advantage. But the younger Goetz was more telegenic and dynamic on the stump. It took five ballots at the June 19 convention for Head to secure the endorsement. With that defeat, Goetz opted not to seek another term as lieutenant governor—something he still could have done independently in 1970. By 1974, governors and lieutenant governors in Minnesota would be obliged by constitutional change to run together as a ticket.[14]

The DFL Party endorsed St. Paul senator Wendell Anderson for governor the following weekend—and Bob Short opted not to run in the DFL primary. Anderson was just thirty-seven, but he had already served twelve years in the legislature, where he stood out less for lawmaking acumen than for youthful good looks and athleticism. (He had been a hockey star for the University of Minnesota and a member of the 1956 US Olympic hockey team.) Though no policy wonk, Anderson was an effective communicator and hard worker who out-hustled the rest of the DFL field to win his party's nod. He was also the beneficiary of the DFL's lingering wounds from 1966 and 1968. Nicholas Coleman, who ran second to Anderson in the endorsement fight, had the stronger legislative record and more evident intellectual gifts. But Coleman had backed A. M. "Sandy" Keith over Governor Karl Rolvaag in 1966 and McCarthy over Humphrey in 1968. With Humphrey seeking a Senate comeback in 1970, the "Party That Hubert Built" was keen to show a united face once more.[15]

Thus, the players were in place by the end of June for a gubernatorial contest remembered nearly fifty years later as one of the state's finest. While the Anderson-Head battle lacked the pathos and colorful personalities that would make other races memorable, it featured two uncommonly able politicians, both solidly backed by a broad-based political party—one slightly left of ideological center, one slightly right. Coming just as the baby boomer generation reached voting age, the Anderson-Head race would make a lasting impression on the electorate. It set a high bar.

Policy-rich campaign fodder was readily available in 1970. Federalism was under fresh scrutiny both in Washington and in St. Paul. The United States had struggled since its founding—and shed blood during the Civil War—over the rightful role of the federal versus state governments. Similarly, state government clashed periodically with cities, counties, and school districts over control of both policy and purse strings. Those relationships were under renewed discussion in the 1960s in high-level policy circles, where "revenue sharing" was the new buzz word. It had many variations around one central concept: Larger governments should collect taxes—a task at which they excel—then distribute the proceeds to local governments for use with some degree of local discretion.[16]

Revenue sharing had high-level backers in both of Minnesota's parties. My boss gained appreciation for the idea through participation in the National Governors Association, where Governor Nelson Rockefeller championed the idea. But he found plenty of company among the unusually strong cadre of Republican governors serving in the late 1960s. LeVander joined GOP gubernatorial peers that included George Romney of Michigan, Mark Hatfield of Oregon, Jim Rhodes of Ohio, Winthrop Rockefeller of Arkansas, Spiro Agnew of Maryland, and John Volpe of Massachusetts. They all saw revenue sharing as the right Republican response to Lyndon Johnson's Great Society, which created a host of well-intentioned domestic initiatives that were orchestrated in Washington and ran roughshod over regional differences and local preferences. The governors also saw revenue sharing as an appealing remedy for ailing state budgets. Cutting government services at a time of rising demand was not responsible; continuing to raise taxes, as Minnesota had done, was not politically feasible. A third way—enlisting the entire nation to help pay for local services—sounded good to governors.

Revenue sharing aligned with something fundamental in Minnesota Republican notions about government. As Elmer Andersen once explained, his kind of Republican was not enamored of government for its own sake. "I believe government's role should be limited," Andersen said in his 2004 book, *I Trust to Be Believed: Speeches and Reflections*. Government's role was to help people be self-supporting, not to support them, he said. That work could best be done by local government, the government closest to the people. At least in theory, revenue sharing would allow local governments considerable freedom in deciding how best to strike the goal Elmer described as "a good balance between personal responsibility, private sector and community responsibility, and government."

In Minnesota, revenue sharing quickly found favor with the Citizens League. It came under new leadership in 1967 when *Minneapolis Star and Tribune* editorial writer Ted Kolderie succeeded Verne Johnson as its executive director. But the league's real direction came from its thousands of members and a core group of several hundred active participants. Both DFLers and Republicans were part of that group. Because its focus was on municipal, metropolitan, and state government—and perhaps because the legislature was still at least officially nonpartisan—efforts to gain partisan advantage were largely set aside when Citizens League members gathered to prepare their periodic recommendations for better government.[17]

That's what the league did just as the 1970 gubernatorial campaign shifted into high gear. On September 1, the league issued what may qualify as the most impactful report in its history, *New Formulas for Revenue Sharing in Minnesota*. It was controversial, so much so that it took three meetings for task force chair Bill Hempel to win the approval of the league's own board. It called for "re-equalization" of funding for school districts and local governments on a formula-driven basis, "using a state fiscal policy that aims gradually at enlarging the proportion of local government revenues derived from state-collected sources." The word "gradually" was likely intended to soften the implication of that recommendation. The Citizens League—a bipartisan group with a Republican bent—was calling for a major increase in the state income and/or sales tax for the sake of property tax restraint and improved local government services.[18]

The league's annual dinner, a major event among the civic-minded crowd in the Twin Cities, came one month later, on October 1. The evening's headliners were gubernatorial candidates Head and Anderson, debating the league's revenue-sharing recommendations and other topics chosen by Minneapolis attorney John Mooty, the moderator. The two gubernatorial candidates had schooled themselves on the report and were ready when Mooty launched into a series of questions about the optimal relationship between state and local governments in providing and paying for services. Head spoke in general terms about allocating resources on a statewide level and holding down property taxes to the extent possible. He allowed that he had "misgivings" about the league's proposal.

Anderson did not: "The Citizens League proposal is for the state to assume the full operating cost of education. I feel very strongly this should be our goal, and if elected governor I would support it enthusiastically."[19]

The difference in those responses would define the remainder of the campaign. The day after the debate, Head hardened his resistance to the league's idea of a state surge in education spending. He argued that it would erode local control and lead to undesirably high state taxes. Head believed Anderson had blundered politically by endorsing such a major change. But voters who wanted their property tax bills to stop climbing were paying attention. So were parents whose children were being shortchanged by a school funding system too dependent on a community's property wealth. Even as it endorsed Head, largely on the strength of his superior record in previous public service, the *Minneapolis Tribune*'s editorial board acknowledged that Anderson "could become a governor with high capacity for public leadership."[20]

The voters evidently saw that, too. Anderson won on November 3 with a solid 54 percent of the vote. He claimed a mandate to pick up the league's report and run with it in the Republican-controlled 1971 legislature—while grousing privately about the league's posture during the campaign's final weeks. League leaders had fallen silent as Anderson defended its report and Head attacked it. That was at the advice of John Mooty, Kolderie reported years later. "Let the report speak for itself," Mooty had urged. Kolderie told an unhappy Anderson: "Those of us working with ideas can't be taking sides in a political fight." That may have been a prudent position for the league. But it also may have been a case of the partisan loyalty of some league leaders trumping ideas—and if so, it would be a harbinger of things to come.[21]

My heart was heavy in the weeks after the election, but not because of Anderson's victory. By Election Day, Judy was rapidly failing. She died on November 14. One of my most precious memories of Harold and Iantha LeVander are of them sitting patiently outside her room at St. Joseph's Hospital in St. Paul the night she died, waiting to say good-bye to her and to comfort me. They might have chosen to stay in seclusion that evening, since the day's news had been about police foiling a serious plot to kidnap the governor and a St. Paul City Council member. Instead, they were stalwarts at my side at a dark time.[22]

I don't think the governor was just trying to console me a few days later when he said that while he would welcome me back at his South St. Paul law firm, he thought I should seek bigger opportunities. "You'd make a great governor someday. . . . If only you'd gone to Gustavus, you'd be a shoo-in!" he said with a teasing smile and a typical twist of his cigar. Perhaps he saw in me something of his brother Pete, who had so desired to hold statewide office.

I soon had my sights on something else. Former governor Elmer Andersen had been an occasional visitor to our office—as would be his wont with all the governors that succeeded him. His visits were usually unexpected, but always at a time when instinct told him that the governor might welcome a chat with a sympathetic elder statesman. I had long admired Elmer; on those visits, I came to view him with awed respect. I knew few other people who cared as much about Minnesota.

On one of those visits, Elmer asked to "have a few minutes" of my time. He told me his H. B. Fuller Company was growing in size and beginning to acquire interests in companies outside the United States. It had become a publicly traded company in 1968. Elmer said he was hoping I might consider "helping him out" by becoming an in-house legal counsel to work with the company's longtime outside counsel in St. Paul and an international firm he planned to hire in Chicago. His corporate leadership role required a good deal of travel in those years, he explained. One of the roles he envisioned for me was serving in his stead in local civic activities. It was an easy offer to accept.[23]

As Governor Wendell Anderson turned his campaign promises about revenue sharing into a proposal for the 1971 legislature, I was watching from my new office across from Elmer's at H. B. Fuller's headquarters, about five miles west of the capitol. It didn't take me long to realize that I was in a very special place. I had considerable freedom to shape my role and to build on Elmer's long-held notion of the purpose of any corporation: service to customers, employees, shareholders, and the community, in that order. I created a community affairs council within the company that included representatives of each of those four stakeholder groups, with the aim of enhancing our company's impact for good.

That made me a detached but very interested observer as Anderson struggled to sell the conservative-controlled legislature on a major income tax increase for the sake of fairer school funding and lower property taxes. The new state budget also had to close a $400 million forecasted deficit for the 1972–73 biennium that appeared in the final weeks of LeVander's administration. Anderson's mission wouldn't be called "the Minnesota Miracle" until the following year. But it looked from the start as if the new governor would need something akin to supernatural intervention to succeed. He was asking Republican legislators to embrace a major change in state policy that the Republican candidate for governor had rejected and that included a hefty increase in a tax that Republicans had long considered a drag on economic growth. The governor's proposal was producing the kind of headlines that strike fear in politicians' hearts, such as "Gov. Anderson Asks Tax Increase of $762 Million" in the January 28, 1971, *Minneapolis Tribune*.[24]

It was soon apparent that this would not be a typical DFL-versus-Republican dispute. Conservative legislators were aligning on both sides. The split in GOP ranks was a testament to the progressive Republican roots of the DFL governor's proposal. It particularly appealed to Senator Stanley Holmquist. The Grove City school superintendent and businessman who was key to increasing state school funding as a freshman house member in 1947 had by 1971 become senate majority leader—though with a razor-thin 34–33 majority. Holmquist's DFL counterpart, minority leader Nicholas Coleman, teasingly called him the "barely majority leader." Holmquist knew he was serving his last term in 1971. He had one more chance to improve education funding in Minnesota—and he was convinced that could only happen if a smaller share of school funds was raised with the unpopular property tax.[25]

Early in the session, Holmquist stayed noncommittal and advised his caucus members to keep an open mind. He quietly assigned Young Turk leader Wayne Popham, also serving his final term, to carry his preferred version of the school/tax overhaul. It closely paralleled the Citizens League's recommendations. The governor's own version of the school aid plan had been introduced in the senate by DFLer Gene Mammenga, a professor at Bemidji State College; Coleman carried the governor's tax bill. A rare joint house/senate tax committee hearing in April that drew a large, loud crowd protesting high property taxes appeared to pull Holmquist off the fence. At that meeting, Holmquist had been booed when he attempted to tell the crowd that the legislature does not set property taxes. The crowd knew better—that in fact, state policy plays a strong albeit indirect role in determining how much school districts, cities, counties, and special taxing districts levy. Days later, on May 4, Anderson summoned reporters to a press conference that was akin to a rally for his proposal. Conspicuously seated amid other supporters was Stan Holmquist.[26]

Resistance came primarily from the Minnesota house and was led most visibly by its gifted conservative majority leader, Ernie Lindstrom of Richfield. Lindstrom, an attorney and certified public accountant who grew up in poverty in North Dakota, was a vigorous forty years old in 1971. He went so far as to designate himself a one-man "truth squad" and to follow Anderson and Christenson around the state, disputing the governor's case for his reform proposal. In Lindstrom's view, shifting school funding from the property tax to the income tax was unlikely to hold property taxes down for long. He said Minnesotans should opt instead for stricter spending restraint. "The real dollar saved is the one not spent," he said. But as he explained decades later, he was not as much anti-tax as he was opposed to a state income tax that he believed was too susceptible to manipulation by wealthy people and disproportionately burdensome for the middle class. Neither was he against state takeover of all services then financed by local governments. But he didn't want to start with schools. Rather, he favored state takeover of welfare costs that he argued—correctly—were excessively borne by his home county, Hennepin.[27]

Not all house Republicans shared Lindstrom's disdain for Anderson's reform plan. For example, the conservative assistant majority leader, Tom Newcome of White Bear Lake, was a supporter, largely because the school property tax burden was unusually high in his district. At Christenson's urging, Anderson shored up that support by conducting a gubernatorial town hall meeting in White Bear Lake to explain how his proposal would benefit that district. But the governor couldn't go everywhere. Opposition from Lindstrom and Speaker Aubrey Dirlam of Redwood Falls was enough to scuttle the Popham bill in the house, even though it had prevailed in the senate with bipartisan support. When that bill was sent to the house on the last day of business in the regular session, the house refused to concur. The session ended with no action.

That could have been the end of the story that year. A similar result in today's legislature would almost certainly be declared a bust by two parties each more eager to accuse the other of obstruction than to reach a compromise that would leave some in each party dissatisfied. But in 1971, Anderson called a special session to begin the day after adjournment and pick up the work where it left off. All the spending bills needed for government to operate had been enacted—another difference from today's lawmaking pattern in St. Paul. No threat of a government shutdown could be used to extract concessions from the other side.

Thus began the longest special session in state history. It produced one notable bill in the early going, a "fiscal disparities" bill that allowed for metro area local governments to share in the growth of their respective commercial-industrial property tax bases. It created a regional pool to which 40 percent of tax-base growth would be "contributed" by each municipality, then redistributed on a need-based formula basis. That way, the benefits of new development would accrue to more than one municipality. It was the first of its kind in the nation and—naturally—its origin was a Citizens League study, issued in 1969. That study had been prompted by the ideas of the progressive Republican legislator from Anoka who was among the fathers of the Metropolitan Council, Representative Chuck Weaver. He was enamored of revenue sharing; tax-base sharing evolved from it and proved quite durable. The Fiscal Disparities Program continues largely unchanged today, having worked for nearly fifty years to tamp down rivalries over development and pressure for annexation and consolidation among metro municipalities.[28]

The rest of the Minnesota Miracle was slower in coming. The first tax bill didn't arrive on the governor's desk until August 4. It was promptly vetoed. Its $600 million tax increase was too small to suit Anderson. But the governor from St. Paul's blue-collar East Side objected more to the way the bill's taxes were structured. "Business receives nearly half of the relief, while homeowners, farmers, and working people pay nearly two-thirds . . . of the [tax] increase," Anderson complained in his veto message. The bill had been a product of an all-conservative conference committee and had passed on a nearly party-line vote. No veto override was possible with such narrow margins.[29]

That too could have been the end of the year's reform effort. But working in close collaboration, Anderson and Holmquist devised a way to keep at it. Holmquist made the unusual motion for a recess in the special session until October 12. Then, at Anderson's request, the legislature appointed a ten-person committee, five from the senate, five from the house, to meet at the governor's residence in closed-door conversations to work out a bill. Among the ten conferees were three liberals, senate leader Coleman, house leader Martin Sabo, and Senator Harold Kalina from a blue-collar Minneapolis district. Their presence signaled that the final deal would need to be more generous to Minneapolis and St. Paul than the vetoed bill had been, as well as more generous to lower-income taxpayers. When the liberals pushed for those changes, they found an ally in Holmquist. Years later, Jerry Christenson, the educator who headed the State Planning Agency in the Anderson administration, recalled Holmquist's reply to Republican senators who did not want to make provision for the disproportionately large population of special-needs students in the core cities: "I was superintendent of schools some years ago in Grove City, and when we had a special-needs kid who had a learning disability and we didn't have the capacity to take care of him, that kid ended up in Minneapolis. That's why we have to do it. Those kids are coming from all over." Christenson called that speech "an act of courage. . . . Stan Holmquist was really some kind of hero."

When the legislature came back on October 12, a deal was nearly done. It involved a 25 percent increase in the income tax and boost in the sales tax from 3 to 4 cents on the dollar, producing a total tax increase of $581 million. The state's share of school costs rose from 43 to 65 percent. A uniform statewide school levy was set; no district could tax its property owners beyond that amount without first obtaining their permission via a referendum. Spending disparities around the state did not disappear, but the new restrictions did not allow them to widen further. The bill also beefed up state aid to cities and counties and created a "circuit breaker" tax relief program for homeowners of modest means whose property tax bills were deemed disproportionate to their incomes. "What developed was a sense of the state at a huge control board, manipulating the switches and dials to make the tax-and-finance system run," the Citizens League's Kolderie said. "It was the only case in America of [school funding] equalization being accomplished through the political process rather than through the courts." The bill passed with broad bipartisan support and was signed into law on October 30.[30]

In the intervening decades, Lindstrom has been proven right in one respect: The 1971 reform bill was not a permanent remedy to rising property taxes. In subsequent years, legislators have felt compelled again and again to move their control-board levers to restrain what is still the least popular and most regressive tax in Minnesota. But they've been tweaking the fiscal structure established in 1971, not junking it in favor of a different design. The progressive Republican principle that the quality of a child's education should not depend on the property wealth of his or her community has held fast, even when the state has fallen short in its implementation.

The 1971 session was a breakthrough year in policy. It was also the end of a legislative era. The 1972 election would usher in the first DFL-controlled legislature in state history. With it would come a host of changes in the legislative institution itself. Women legislators began arriving in larger numbers, starting with six elected to the house in 1972—two Republicans and four DFLers. Open, recorded meetings came with a commitment to more citizen participation that has served the institution well. But more participation created demand for separate offices for all legislators so they could more conveniently meet with visiting constituents. To create space for legislative offices, state agencies were moved from the capitol into quarters scattered throughout St. Paul, triggering a building boom that culminated in the controversial construction of the Minnesota Senate Office

Building in 2015. With more constituent involvement also came the need for more staff and more professionalization in staff ranks. That was a push Republicans had started in the 1960s with the creation of House Research. But credit must be given to DFL house speaker Martin Olav Sabo, a future congressman and exceptional leader whose vision of the modern legislature guided changes in Minnesota and many other states through his leadership of the National Conference of State Legislatures.

Those were needed and welcome changes. I can't say the same about other institutional adjustments. I agree with Robert Brown, a state senator as well as GOP state chairman in the 1970s, who holds that the move to annual sessions that began in 1974 may have done more to deprive the legislature of talent than any other single change. Up-and-coming community leaders who were willing to set their professional pursuits aside for a few months every other year were less willing to do so every year. Candidate recruitment became far more difficult.

At the same time, the legislature's veneer of nonpartisanship fell away. The liberal and conservative caucus names gave way in 1973 to the party labels DFL and Republican. A harsher partisanship was not felt immediately. But it would come all too soon.

6 BUST AND BOOM

The TICKET-SPLITTING PROPENSITY of Minnesota voters in the mid-twentieth century was on vivid display in 1972. As they were installing the first DFL-controlled legislature in state history and returning Democrat Walter Mondale to the US Senate with 57 percent of the vote, Minnesotans also helped give Republican president Richard Nixon one of the biggest margins of victory in the nation's history. Nixon clobbered South Dakota senator George McGovern by 18 million votes nationally, carrying every state save for Massachusetts and the District of Columbia. He topped McGovern in Minnesota by nearly 100,000 votes and even carried the state's urban core, Hennepin County. That presidential result eased the sting of losing the legislature's majorities and allowed progressive Republicans like me to think that our dominance in state politics would return soon enough.

We didn't see Watergate coming.

It's hard to overstate the blow that my party sustained when in 1973 and 1974 the story unfolded of presidential involvement in both a politically motivated break-in at the Democratic national headquarters in the Watergate Hotel and the cover-up that ensued. Thanks to aggressive journalism, particularly at the *Washington Post,* the dark underbelly of American politics was put on more vivid display than ever before in the nation's history. Nixon's caught-on-tape words and deeds were unsavory enough in the eyes of seasoned politicians like Minnesota's Republican national committeeman Rudy Boschwitz, who seethed to state party officials, "That SOB lied to us!" To average Americans, they were shocking. And because Nixon had become inextricably tied to the Republican Party in the public mind after being its presidential nominee three times, offended Americans turned on my party, too.

When Nixon resigned on August 9, 1974, he turned the presidency over to Gerald Ford, a nice guy and longtime House member from Michigan whom Nixon (and the sins of former vice president Spiro Agnew) had made vice president the year before. The beating that the GOP took in the 1974 congressional elections a few months later is now the stuff of legend. The 1975 US House of Representatives convened with the largest Democratic majorities since the peak years of the New Deal, far larger than either party's majorities in that body have been since then.

What may be less well remembered is how far down the ballot the Watergate contagion spread. In 1974, DFL governor Wendell Anderson carried all eighty-seven counties in his bid for a second term, despite having signed into law the biggest tax increase in Minnesota history three years earlier. His Republican opponent John Johnson was a Minneapolis state representative with a trust-inspiring Scandinavian name but a low profile. Stronger potential Republican candidates, including Boschwitz, the telegenic head of a Twin Cities home improvements retail firm as well as the party's national committeeman, and investment banker Wheelock Whitney, had prudently opted not to run in Watergate's wake, despite the pleading of the party's able chairman, state senator Bob Brown of Stillwater.

The Watergate wave swelled the DFL majority in the Minnesota house to 104 of 134 seats, the biggest majority either party had seen before or has seen since. It was twenty-seven more seats than DFLers controlled two years earlier—and that majority had already been swollen by the 1972 redistricting plan, drawn by a three-judge federal panel dominated by US circuit judge Gerald Heaney, an active DFLer before his appointment to the federal bench. Republicans could count it a blessing that the state senate was not on the ballot that year, or the carnage for the party at the state capitol may have been worse. Not long after the 1974 election, several GOP-commissioned polls measured the share of Minnesota voters who called themselves "active Republicans." At the low point, the result was in the single digits.[1]

A wave election like 1974 hits political parties with hurricane force. For the losing party, it ends scores of careers, alters the reputations and standing of those who survive, and invites the kind of soul-searching that allows new or previously discarded ideas a chance to flourish. For Republicans in Minnesota, the Watergate wave came when other forces were already producing change.

The legislature's shift to annual sessions likely would have made candidate recruitment difficult for Republicans regardless of Watergate. The business and professional men (the legislature was still a male bastion) to whom Republicans had long turned for talent were less willing to sign on when the time required was four or five months every year rather than every two years. Many people believed that legislative service would soon require a full-time, year-round commitment. Their fears were only partially exaggerated.

The move to party designation turned off some potential candidates, too. Some legislators had campaigned for years without attaching themselves to a political party. Senator Gordon Rosenmeier, for one, liked to boast that he had never attended a Republican precinct caucus or convention. He evidently wanted his Little Falls constituents to think he operated above the partisan fray. That stance was no longer possible after 1973, and it took some talented people out of the candidate pool.[2]

A desire to reclaim a bit of nonpartisanship figured into the decision of a few Republican legislators to be labeled "independent-Republicans" in the Minnesota legislative manual for 1975. They did so for their own sakes, not intending to launch the rebranding of the entire party. But a new state party chairman in 1975, Chuck Slocum, was ready to try something bold to signal to Minnesotans a break with the party of Nixon. At age twenty-eight, Slocum was the youngest party chairman in the country. But his youth belied his already extensive experience running campaigns for the state party under chairman Dave Krogseng, managing legislative operations as an aide to senate majority leader Stan Holmquist, and working for a major Minnesota employer, Dayton Hudson Corporation.

Slocum commissioned a poll to test the appeal of a change in the party's name to Independent-Republican. He employed Bill Morris, a University of Minnesota political scientist who would go on to be the state party chairman in the 1980s. Morris found that in a general election, 3 percent more voters would opt for a nameless generic candidate labeled "Independent-Republican" than labeled simply "Republican." When Morris presented those results to the party's executive committee that fall, someone asked for his recommendation. "I'd change the name in a nanosecond," he advised. "Look at how many elections are won by 3 percent of the vote or less." The executive committee backed the idea with a near-unanimous vote. The only opposition came from four committee members who had already signed on with the presidential campaign of Ronald Reagan, the Republican governor of California who was challenging the sitting GOP president, Gerald Ford. It was an early sign of dissention to come.[3]

DFLers and some editorial writers ridiculed the name change idea in the weeks before the November 15 party convention that adopted it. But Slocum, state chairwoman Carolyn Ring, and the party's two national committee members, Rudy Boschwitz and Iantha LeVander, pushed back with a response published by the *Minneapolis Star* on the day of the convention. They argued that something more than cosmetics motivated the change. The party was also committing itself to representing and involving independent voters in matters such as ensuring the openness of precinct caucuses, supporting a presidential primary with no requirement of prior registration, and sponsoring outreach efforts to groups including young voters, women, and organized labor. Further, the leaders argued, independents and Republicans think and often vote alike on matters such as economics and law and order. The name change "more accurately reflects the vote base of the present Republican Party," they said. With the parties' bases in flux, there was some wishful thinking in that claim. But it could be made with a straight face.[4]

The change that would prove the most transformative to Minnesota's two major political parties in the 1970s and beyond originated not in Minnesota but at the US Supreme Court. On January 22, 1973, the landmark decision legalizing abortion in the first two trimesters of pregnancy—*Roe v. Wade*—was issued by a 7–2 court majority. Writing for that majority was a Minnesotan in the Stassen Republican line, Harry Blackmun. He had grown up in the Dayton's Bluff neighborhood of St. Paul as a schoolmate of Chief Justice Warren Burger and got to the high court via an appointment by President Nixon after a long stint as resident legal counsel for the Mayo Clinic in Rochester, Minnesota. It's worth noting that Burger also joined the seven-justice majority on the case. Burger persuaded his colleagues not to issue the opinion until after the 1972 presidential election. But it would be Blackmun, not Burger, who would suffer the abiding enmity of abortion opponents, and as a result be denied a bust outside the historic Minnesota Supreme Court chamber in the state capitol three decades later.[5]

Blackmun's ruling ruptured a political hornets' nest. The resulting furor would last for decades and would reshape both major parties in Minnesota.

As the positions of the two Supreme Court justices who were sometimes called "the Minnesota twins" indicate, some Republicans in 1973 were at least open to Blackmun's argument that abortion early in pregnancy is a matter beyond the reach of government because of an implicit right to privacy embedded in the US Constitution's Bill of

Rights. In the Minnesota legislature, for example, an effort to ease restrictions on abortion was mounted in 1971 and spearheaded by freshman Republican senator George Pillsbury, whose family members had been early supporters and volunteers for Planned Parenthood. The burgeoning women's movement was felt in both parties in the early 1970s, with Republican feminists joining DFLers in pushing ratification of the Equal Rights Amendment through the legislature early in the 1973 session. An active Republican in Albert Lea in those years, my friend and future US Senate staffer Lois West Duffy, relates that she and a number of other women in her political circle wanted the government to stay out of abortion entirely. On that basis, they would be labeled "pro-choice."[6]

But the supporters of Blackmun's decision in Minnesota Republican ranks were likely outnumbered from the start by people like me. I saw the abortion issue through the lens of my Roman Catholic faith. The church held that a fetus is a soul-bearing person and that ending a pregnancy is murder. I did not like government allowing anyone the choice to kill a fetus. Roman Catholics were not a large contingent within the state GOP in the 1970s. The party's long-standing strength among the state's mainline Protestants, particularly Lutherans, still prevailed. But many Republican Lutherans in Minnesota belonged to conservative synods that preached a fundamentalist theology on matters like abortion. And abortion was a galvanizing issue for the state's small but rapidly growing evangelical Christian population. That segment of churchgoing Minnesotans was not much associated with either political party—yet.

The first test of state Republican sentiment on abortion came at the 1974 state convention in Duluth. A platform plank calling for a constitutional amendment "to establish a uniform national law on the issue of protection of life" was approved by a 586–339 vote. That carefully vague language was described as "moderately pro-life" by *Minneapolis Star* political reporter Peter Vaughn. With worry about Nixon's worsening situation dominating the convention, that language was as divisive as the delegates cared to make it.[7]

The same platform called on the legislature to rescind the ratification of the Equal Rights Amendment it had bestowed only the year before. That move was a blow to the newly created GOP Women for Political Effectiveness, which would later take the name the GOP Feminist Caucus. One of its founders who had served on the 1974 platform committee, Emily Anne Staples (later Emily Anne Tuttle), was so offended that she switched parties in response and filed her candidacy for a state house seat as a DFLer. She didn't win that year, but two years later she would become the first DFL woman elected in her own right to the state senate. Her departure from the GOP was a harbinger of more to come.[8]

The DFL Party, which included a larger Roman Catholic constituency, was likewise split over abortion. At its state convention that same month in Minneapolis, a proposed platform plank backing the *Roe v. Wade* decision did not achieve the 60 percent vote needed under that party's rules to adopt it. The vote revealed a very divided party: 607.9 for, 577.1 against.[9]

With both parties split on abortion, few foresaw in the mid-1970s that the issue would be the single biggest driver of a coming realignment. But a rules change within the Democratic Party nationally and in the DFL in Minnesota was frustrating abortion opponents, foiling their dream of controlling Democratic platforms and securing the allegiance of its candidates. New rules for electing delegates to party conventions had come into play in 1972. They bore a strong Minnesota stamp, arising in the wake of the bruising presidential battle in 1968 between Minnesotans Hubert Humphrey and Eugene McCarthy. Embittered McCarthy backers were furious that Humphrey had been nominated despite not entering or winning any primaries. The unhappy Democrats in 1968 included women, members of racial and ethnic minorities, and the young people who had dominated McCarthy's insurgent campaign. They faulted a nomination process too much controlled by party bosses and officeholders, not rank-and-file voters. After Humphrey's defeat, a commission headed by South Dakota senator George McGovern was empaneled by the Democratic National Committee to recommend changes that would better assure those groups of representation. When McGovern left the commission in 1971 to run for president, he was succeeded by Minnesota's US representative Don Fraser—hence the name attached to the changes they wrought: the McGovern-Fraser rules.

The new rules eliminated winner-take-all election of delegates in the Democratic Party. No longer could a caucus or convention's majority control an entire delegate slate. Proportional representation was assured to minority groups that reached a mathematically determined threshold of "viability." In Minnesota, that rule was combined with a voting method for caucuses developed by a McCarthy backer who would go on to win a Nobel Prize in economics, Leonid Hurwicz of the University of Minnesota. He called it the "walking subcaucus." It's a method of proportional representation that allows subgroups within a body to choose their own representation at next-level conventions. It sounded feasible on paper. In practice, it proved chaotic and confusing. DFLers were open to using the new method in 1972. But by the next presidential election, walking subcaucuses were out of favor with any faction that wanted not just to be represented but to control the decisions the party made. Abortion opponents did not want to be a perpetual minority in a political party. They wanted to take charge, so that they could one day change the law.[10]

Minnesotans motivated by a desire to end legal abortion began moving into the Republican Party in bigger numbers after 1976. The first wave was dominated by former DFLers. Their arrival coincided with the departure of Republicans who had been discouraged or defeated by Watergate. That made the mid- and late-1970s a time of rapid turnover in my party. Those years saw the start of a disconcerting shift away from broad-based parties to parties that defined and organized themselves around divisive single issues and cultural identity. Those changes presented a challenge to those who sought party endorsement to run for office in 1978—including me.

I had decided in early 1977 that I would run the next year for the office I believed best suited my experience, governor of Minnesota. That's not a customary way for one to begin a political quest that ends with election to the US Senate. But there was a good deal that was unconventional in Minnesota politics in 1978, the year Republicans remember as "the Minnesota Massacre." It was the boom that followed the bust of the three previous elections.

I had not completely left public life when I departed the governor's staff in January 1971. But for a number of years I stifled any thought of running for office. I concentrated instead on my family and on the interesting mix of public service opportunities then afforded to a Republican during a DFL-dominated time.

Quickly—perhaps too quickly—I found a new wife and mother for my four boys. Penny Baran Thuet and I were married in the chapel at St. John's University on September 11, 1971. *Minneapolis Tribune* society columnist Margaret Morris made note of our wedding's bipartisanship: Penny was an assistant press secretary to DFL governor Wendell Anderson, and she was the widow of Marine captain Stephen Thuet, the son of former DFL state senate majority leader Paul Thuet, whom I had worked to defeat in 1966. Steve Thuet was killed in Vietnam in 1968; he and Penny had no children. My four boys were between the ages of eight and four when we married. Penny was suddenly immersed in motherhood, with both of us naïve about the challenges that presented. As I would confess to a reporter years later, the sadness of so many losses made bonding difficult in our family.[11]

I found myself thinking often about something Elmer Andersen said to me as he recruited me to H. B. Fuller: "Dave, you don't need a job. You need a purpose." That rang true to me, as did something else Elmer often said: "The purpose of life is service." That's something I had first learned growing up on the campus of St. John's University and the largest Benedictine monastery in the world. I came to believe deeply that my purpose is service to others. When my sons were young, that purpose had a family focus. I needed to provide for them and be involved in their activities. The family moved to Minneapolis, where I was soon president of the Burroughs Elementary School PTA. All four of my sons swam competitively, so I agreed to chair the state Amateur Athletic Union (AAU) swim meet in St. Louis Park.

Public service never fully left my sights while I worked at H. B. Fuller. Thanks to Elmer, it didn't need to. He encouraged me to devote ample time to public work, either on my own or as his staffer and/or surrogate. For example, the St. Paul Chamber of Commerce had a corporate social responsibility committee composed of CEOs and their designees. I served as staff director for that committee when Elmer headed it.

Elmer's relationship with Wendell Anderson plus my own with the new governor (we'd been near-contemporaries at the University of Minnesota Law School) and with Anderson's chief of staff, my fellow St. John's alumnus Tom Kelm, got me involved in several projects that needed a bipartisan push. Kelm called me a few times in 1971 and 1973 when he needed to round up conservative/Republican votes for something worthwhile, like the new Minnesota Zoo. Many of the new DFL governor's initiatives were in fact projects started during the LeVander administration. During the 1971 session, some of Anderson's bills had conservative chief authors.

The legislature created a constitutional study commission in 1973 to consider how to finally give Minnesota one unified state constitution, not two, as had been the case since the 1858 Congress blessed both the Democratic and the Republican versions of constitutions submitted by the Territorial Legislature in advance of statehood. Elmer was its chair; I was its executive director. Elmer was also asked to head a panel to write a judicial code of ethics. I staffed that, too.

Some of my activities didn't involve Elmer. I was seen as a "good government Republican," an extension of sorts of the Andersen and LeVander administrations, willing to contribute to bipartisan, committee-based problem solving. That's why in 1975, Wendell Anderson named me vice chair of the first Minnesota Ethical Practices Board, a body created in the wake of Watergate to administer the state's new public campaign financing system. That same year, Wendy also appointed me to the Governor's Commission on the Arts, chaired by Minneapolis attorney Stephen Pflaum. My title was executive vice chairman, implying that much of the work of the commission would be mine to oversee. I think I was tapped because I could be helpful in both raising private donations and securing money from the 1977 legislature. That work brought me much-valued connections with Linda Hoeschler, then the arts grants coordinator for the Dayton Hudson Foundation, and Jimmie Powell, a recent Macalester College graduate and a social research powerhouse who would go on to a distinguished career as a US Senate staffer. Together, we prepared a 278-page report, "Minnesota: State of the Arts," that showed that the investment Minnesota made in arts education in public schools was an important contributor to the state's quality of life. It laid out a rationale for taxpayer support of the arts that thirty years later would be applied to a successful campaign to dedicate a small percentage of the state's sales tax to arts and culture.[12]

The preservation of open space also captured my attention during the early and mid-1970s. Serving on the South St. Paul city parks and recreation commission brought me to the attention of Al Hofstede, a future Minneapolis mayor whom Wendy had appointed to be the second chair of the Metropolitan Council. Hofstede recruited me to chair the new Metropolitan Parks and Open Space Commission, a planning body. There, I caught the vision of a region-wide, regionally funded network of parks and undeveloped open spaces connected by recreational trails. It would build on the work done in the nineteenth and early twentieth centuries to give Minneapolis and St. Paul the most acclaimed urban park systems in the nation. A few years later, after our family had moved to Minneapolis, I was tapped to be the chairman of the governing board of the Hennepin County Park Reserve District. Though its main mission was the oversight of Hennepin County parks, it also helped similar bodies in suburban Anoka and Scott Counties establish the parks that would help make a regional park system a reality. I was part of a push at the 1975 legislature to get a $40 million appropriation for Twin Cities area parks. Our notion was to apply to parks the same funding concept that had been applied to public education: employ the powerful money-raising engines of federal and state governments, then distribute the proceeds via a regionally designed process for spending by local administrators.

For me, those ideas about the rightful roles of federal, state, and local governments had taken shape during the LeVander years. They were reinforced by my involvement in the Citizens League, Minnesota's homegrown, citizen-driven public policy think tank. In 1972, I was part of a Citizens League task force that produced a report whose recommendations would affect Minnesota progressive Republican thinking for years to come. "Why Not Buy Service?" asked the title of the report that the league board approved in September 1972. Its argument: government services need to be made more efficient if they are to remain available and affordable, and that can best happen if government functions as the purchaser of those services from independent providers, either for-profit or nonprofit, rather than as the provider of services itself. As did all Citizens League recommendations in that era, this report had a bipartisan stamp. Among the DFLers involved in the task force were former Minneapolis mayor Arthur Naftalin and future state senator John Brandl. But the report's recommendations particularly resonated with Republicans like me. We weren't small-government advocates. We wanted government to respond vigorously and effectively to solve societal problems. But we were willing to tap the private sector and unleash the power of competition to achieve government's goals. Serving on that task force reinforced my own thinking and provided a springboard for new ideas, particularly about health-care financing and education reform.[13]

When Chuck Slocum in early 1977 called a meeting of Republicans he thought should consider running for statewide office, I was on his invitation list. I gladly attended. In the 1976 election, with Minnesota's Walter Mondale running for vice president, we Republicans had taken another drubbing. But a few weeks later, Governor Wendell Anderson committed a political blunder for the ages: he arranged for his own appointment to Mondale's unfinished US Senate term. He resigned as governor, allowing lieutenant governor Rudy Perpich to take the office—breaking the long run of governors with Scandinavian heritage. Then Perpich immediately appointed Anderson to the Senate. It smacked of self-dealing, which is a political sin in Minnesota. Public disapproval of the move was immediately clear. By a 4–1 margin, those polled by the *Minneapolis Tribune*'s Minnesota Poll said in mid-December that they wanted Mondale's seat filled by special election, not by an Anderson-Perpich self-appointment scheme. Suddenly both Anderson and Perpich looked vulnerable in the 1978 election. Then on February 22, 1977, a special election for a congressional seat in northwestern Minnesota flipped what had been Democrat Robert Berglund's seat to Republican Arlan Stangeland. That outcome fueled the optimism of those Slocum summoned to the Decathlon Club. I let myself dream that 1978 could be my year to return to the governor's office, this time as governor.[14]

I made my candidacy official on June 18, 1977, and started stumping the state in much the same way that I had campaigned for Harold LeVander eleven years earlier. I reconnected with people I knew through St. John's University, the Knights of Columbus, the Jaycees, Republican politics, and the other civic work I'd done that brought me in touch with Minnesotans. It was a distinguished but small segment of the population. "Durenberger Is Known, but Not by Public" read a headline in the July 31 *Minneapolis Tribune*.

But that wasn't my campaign's biggest problem. Rather, it was the sense by party insiders—and particularly party donors—that a better candidate was in the wings. US representative Al Quie was hinting that after twenty years in Congress, he was ready to come home and make the governorship the capstone to his political career. His name was much better known than mine. "I have a lot of respect for Al

Quie," I said on June 18, when I was asked by a reporter about the possible Quie candidacy. "I would not have made up my mind to get into this if I really thought he wanted to run for governor." I hoped I was right.[15]

When Quie made his candidacy official at the state fair in late August, it was page-one news around the state. I was mentioned in those stories as "also running." But by then, I was not inclined to step aside. I had the advantage of being steeped in state rather than federal issues for the past dozen years. At a series of joint appearances with Quie that fall before Republican audiences, I believed that I had outperformed him. He evidently thought so, too. At one point, he paid me a visit at home to confess that one of our encounters left him with negative feelings about me. A devout Lutheran, Quie asked me to pray with him as he sought forgiveness. I did.

It was an encounter both awkward and touching, at a spiritually significant time for me. At a suggestion from a totally unexpected quarter—DFL state senator and physician John Salchert of north Minneapolis—I spent a weekend in November 1977 at Cursillo, a lay-led retreat experience aimed at intensifying one's Christian faith. For me, it was life changing. Raised among priests and monks at St. John's, I assumed I knew it all. But I had not yet developed a personal relationship with the man Jesus of Nazareth. Cursillo sparked that relationship. To this day, that relationship has never failed me, even though on many occasions I failed it.

Then US senator Hubert Humphrey died. Minnesotans knew that the cancer that had been found in Humphrey's abdomen in August 1977 was inoperable and that the man who had dominated DFL politics for thirty years was dying. Still, when the end came on January 13, 1978, it was a grievous loss to many Minnesotans and a cyclone altering the state's political landscape. I was in Morrison County, driving to Prinsburg to speak at the inauguration of a new Jaycees chapter, when I heard the news on my car radio. I, too, felt a pang of grief. I'd had a sweet encounter with Senator Humphrey only a few months earlier, in August 1977, at a gas station in Delano when he was on his way to a Vikings game. As I gave him my campaign literature, he kindly told me that many of his friends said I would be a good governor—which he repeated to a state fair audience the following week! It was a politically generous gesture by a great Minnesotan.

I wondered how the election year would change as a result of his death. The answer unfolded in the ensuing weeks. Governor Rudy Perpich appointed Humphrey's widow, Muriel, to his Senate seat, which could be filled by appointment until the next general election. That meant that for the first time in state history, the governorship and both US Senate seats would be on the same ballot. (The 2018 election presented the state's voters with the second such lineup.) Minneapolis US representative Don Fraser announced that he would run for the Humphrey seat, regardless of whether Muriel Humphrey sought the seat in her own right. Republicans were pleased. We saw Fraser as too liberal for average Minnesota voters, and a comparatively easy mark.

I was at the Hunt Hotel in Montevideo in west-central Minnesota on April 8 at a fundraising dinner for the party's Sixth Congressional District when word came that Muriel Humphrey had made an announcement. She would not run for "the Humphrey seat" that fall. Rudy Boschwitz, by then running against the politically wounded US senator Wendell Anderson, called me out of the ballroom to a small area where a TV was broadcasting Muriel's announcement. We listened, then Rudy turned to me and said, "You've got to run for that seat! You can win it!"

I'd been getting the same word from high-level messengers for some weeks. After the precinct caucuses, rumors starting flying that I was considering dropping out of the governor's race to run for another office, say attorney general, or that I wanted to run as Al Quie's lieutenant governor. Ray Plank, the CEO of the Apache Corporation and a major Republican donor, went so far as to broadly hint that if I left the governor's race for the Senate race my existing campaign debt would be "taken care of." I had resisted such entreaties until then. I was clearly struggling to keep pace with the First

District congressman both in winning delegate support and in raising money. But I had a sense that I was gaining on Quie. My message—government should be both compassionate and effective, and to do so it must operate as close to the people as possible and function as a purchaser rather than a provider of services—was catching on.

The pressure for me to switch to the Senate race cranked much higher in the days after Muriel Humphrey's decision. The party's Washington brain trust got into the act, dispatching Republican National Committee leaders Chuck Bailey and Charlie Black to Minnesota to meet with me and make the case that the Humphrey seat was winnable, especially by a candidate like me. They arranged a trip for me to Washington to meet with US senator Robert Packwood of Oregon, then head of the Senate Republican campaign committee and a moderate-minded politician whose views on issues were compatible with my own. Also on the agenda: a conversation with Senator Chuck Percy of Illinois, a former governor and a friend of Elmer Andersen. They helped me see that I could help change the role of government in Washington as well as at the state capitol. I wanted more decisions made at the state and local level, but I wanted resources raised in a fair manner to match the policy commitments government made. They said, "Then you have to come to Washington. That's where the money is." In particular, they mentioned their colleague Senator Howard Baker of Tennessee was championing revenue sharing with the states, a LeVander "hot-button" I loved. They also said health care was something they believed would need federal policy reform. The comment stuck in my mind.

When a national campaign consultant named Roger Ailes came to assess my chances, I must have been in full "sell" mode. An hour into our conversation, Ailes looked at me and said, "I'm going to get you elected to the US Senate." I asked him why he wanted to work for me. He replied, "A competitor of mine has the Boschwitz campaign, and you and I are going to whip his ass." Outperforming another Republican wasn't a big motivator for me. But I decided to hire the future founder of Fox News, who would go on to become one of the most successful and most hated men in the public affairs arena. Ailes was forced out of Fox in 2016 because of a sexual harassment scandal. Despite his besmirched reputation today, I've never regretted my decision to employ him. Ailes worked on each of my three campaigns. He taught me that in the modern campaign era, in-person, on-screen issue presentations won elections. I needed to learn the new norm in campaigns—to communicate directly with the voters, not with detail-laden speeches but in pithy sound bites.

The calculus for Republican success in the race for Humphrey's Senate seat improved again when a new DFL candidate entered the field to run against Fraser. Businessman and DFL maverick Robert Short, a conservative figure who had run unsuccessfully for Congress and lieutenant governor in the past, jumped in. Short was a wealthy man who owned—and moved—two professional sports teams, the Minneapolis/Los Angeles Lakers of the NBA and the Washington Senators/Texas Rangers of Major League Baseball. He had the means and personality to make himself a force to reckon with in the DFL primary election. As soon as he was in the running, it was apparent that the DFL could be in for another of its periodic civil wars. Independent-Republican insiders were keen to avoid that kind of conflict in our party. Staying united was seen as crucial to seizing the opportunity at hand.

With my wife Penny's encouragement—she said she would love to live in Washington—and a vow of support from someone I much admired, Third District US representative Bill Frenzel, I yielded. At several Republican congressional district conventions on April 22, I announced that I was switching to the US Senate race. My announcement was met with standing ovations from victory-hungry Republicans and page-one stories in Twin Cities newspapers. I did my best to make my own enthusiasm match theirs.[16]

I spent the summer contrasting myself with the man I considered the likely DFL nominee, Don Fraser. "I am going to be mainstream and

As a candidate, 1978. *Courtesy of the author*

he's going to be elitist. He believes government can do more for you than you can do for yourself," I said. I subscribed to the optimistic view of humanity that Elmer Andersen often expressed: If government can create the conditions for success by assuring equal opportunity, people will take care of the rest themselves. Put people in an environment in which they can be at their best, and they will be. I thought I was describing a stark contrast with the activist government that Fraser had stood for during eight years in the state senate and sixteen years in Congress. But voters evidently didn't perceive a night-and-day difference in our thinking. And that turned out to be to my advantage.[17]

Minnesotans awoke on September 13, the day after the primary election, to shocking news: maverick Bob Short had a few-thousand-vote lead over establishment favorite Don Fraser. Short's lead held and grew through the day as the last votes trickled in from remote northern precincts, in the part of the state where Short's positions against legal abortion, gun control, and motorboat restrictions in the Boundary Waters Canoe Area were a winning combination. His "Dump Fraser" bumper sticker had become a popular vehicle ornament on the Iron Range, to the irritation of Twin Cities DFLers. I was told years later that as DFLers in Minneapolis's tonier precincts—

Governor Al Quie delivers the State of the State Address, 1981. *Courtesy of MNHS Collections*

Fraser's stronghold—absorbed the blow of his defeat with their morning coffee, they turned to each other and said, "Let's take a look at Durenberger." They evidently liked what they saw. And they definitely did not like Bob Short.[18]

Those sentiments—plus my improved campaign operation, headed from late July forward by former legislator and LeVander campaign veteran Paul Overgaard of Albert Lea—propelled me into an enviable position. The fellow who would be remembered as "the reluctant US Senate candidate" led the Republican ballot on November 7. I wound up with 61.5 percent of the vote, compared with Short's 34 percent. Republicans did well up and down the ballot: Boschwitz knocked Wendell Anderson out of the US Senate, winning 56.6 percent of the vote, and Al Quie unseated Rudy Perpich to win the governorship with a solid 52 percent majority. The Minnesota house's big DFL majority evaporated, producing an unwieldy 67–67 tie. Those results proved the prescience of a Republican billboard posted around the state earlier in the year: "Something scary is going to happen to the DFL in November. It's called an election."[19]

The results in my race stand today as a marker of a less partisan era. I bested Short by nearly 3–1 in Hennepin County and 2–1 in Ramsey County, the core metro counties that typically are DFL strongholds. Short's primary campaign had pandered to populist thinking on the Iron Range, a vote-rich region in a DFL primary but an area whose sentiments about guns, abortion, and the environment were increasingly out of step with metro DFLers. That difference would prove persistent and important in coming decades, as the DFL's hold on Greater Minnesota in general and the Iron Range in particular would loosen. The voting pattern in the Durenberger-Short contest might be deemed a harbinger of that change. It also demonstrated that in 1978, a Republican in the Stassen-Youngdahl-Andersen-LeVander progressive line could appeal not only to Republicans but to tens of thousands of DFLers as well.

7 WHEN EVERY STATE IS HEARD FROM

Two Minnesotans stood out in the large class of nineteen new US senators elected in 1978. Rudy Boschwitz and I took seats that had been occupied by Democrats for decades. National trend-watchers took our victory in Vice President Walter Mondale's home state as a sign of weakness for Democrats and a portent of trouble for the Carter-Mondale ticket in 1980. Minnesota provided two of the three-seat Republican gain that year in a Senate that was still firmly in Democratic hands, 58–41–1.

Among the nineteen Senate newcomers, I had an advantage. Mine had been a special election to fill Hubert Humphrey's unexpired term. A new state law called for the term of his appointed successor, his widow Muriel, to expire at midnight the day after the election. I was sworn into office on November 9 in a cozy ceremony attended by several notable Senate Republicans, including Minority Leader Howard Baker of Tennessee. My early arrival made me eighty-second in seniority in the Senate as a whole, right behind Don Stewart of Alabama, the other newcomer who had won a special election for a partial term. But I was the first Republican to take office and that helped me land a plum assignment: the Finance Committee, controller of the federal purse.[1]

Minnesota's 1979 congressional delegation included five Republicans and five Democrats. *Back row:* Jim Oberstar (DFL), Tom Hagedorn (IR), Arlan Stangeland (IR), Bill Frenzel (DFL), Rick Nolan (DFL), Martin Sabo (DFL). *Front row:* Rudy Boschwitz (IR), Dave Durenberger (IR), Bruce Vento (DFL), Arlen Erdahl (IR). *Courtesy of the author*

That brought me into the orbit of a Senate titan, Democratic finance chairman Russell Long. The son of a Louisiana political legend, Huey Long Jr., who had been assassinated inside his state's capitol in 1935, Russell Long had already been chairman of the Finance Committee for a dozen years when I arrived and knew how to make a rookie senator of the opposite party feel welcome. He sent me an endearing handwritten letter tracing the shared histories of our states at opposite ends of the Mississippi River, both part of territory acquired for the United States in the Louisiana Purchase of 1803. He invited me to pay him a visit. When I did, he gave me a one-on-one orientation session. We discussed some of the issues before the committee. One during that period of rapidly rising oil prices was President Jimmy Carter's proposal for a windfall profits tax on the oil and gas industry—a major industry in Long's home state—to pay for home heating assistance for low-income Americans, including Minnesotans. The wily Long then informed the neophyte, "What my constituents do is produce the stuff and what yours do is burn it." Easily reading my noncommittal reaction, he burst out laughing. I noted that on that issue, the thinking of a Republican from Minnesota might be closer to the Democratic president's than that of a Democrat from Louisiana.

What Long said next made a lasting impression on me. He launched into a discourse on Senate history that focused on the reasons for the upper chamber's creation nearly two centuries earlier. The nation's founders did not want large population centers to control national policy. Neither did they want one region to have dominion. They knew well the distinct differences between the colonies that sprang from the diverse places settlers came from, the reasons they emigrated to North America, and the values they brought with them. Each state had a measure of sovereignty, the founders believed. Each state deserved an equal voice in one of the two lawmaking chambers. That wasn't just a matter of fairness. It was the founders' recipe for sound national policy. "So, son," he concluded, "the good news is that when every state is heard from, we get national policy that's good for your constituents and for mine."

When every state is heard from, the result is sound policy. Those words stuck. Russell Long encouraged me to bring the best Minnesota Republican ideas to the Senate—not because he necessarily agreed with those ideas, but because he believed that a good outcome would be achieved if every senator represented his or her state in that way. More than that: he had no doubt that the Senate's lawmaking process was capable of combining fifty states' perspectives into coherent policy. He believed deeply that compromise was not just possible but was the essential work of the Senate and duty of a senator.[2]

Those were guiding values in the Senate that I came to know and love in the ensuing sixteen years. I had initially aimed for a different office. But it didn't take me long to discover that my second choice was the right one. The Senate allowed me considerable latitude to go deep on matters especially important to Minnesota, while also developing the working knowledge and relationships necessary to make a contribution on a wide range of topics. Policy, more than politics, held my interest. Getting policies right improved people's lives. With Long's encouragement ringing in my ears, I looked for ways to bring Minnesota's progressive Republican thinking to the Senate.

I made it a point to get to know as many senators as possible and learned that people go to the Senate for many different reasons. I found people who had already made substantial contributions to their country. They had succeeded by earning the trust of their constituents, even constituents who disagreed with them on particular issues. Among them were war heroes like Bob Dole of Kansas and Danny Inouye of Hawaii, who coincidentally had spent months in the same army rehabilitation hospital in Michigan at the end of World War II. There were former astronauts John Glenn of Ohio and Harrison "Jack" Schmitt of New Mexico; successful businessmen Chuck Percy of Illinois, the former CEO of Bell and Howell, and my fellow Minnesotan Rudy Boschwitz, the founder of Plywood Minnesota; and former governors, state attorneys general, and mayors, like Dick Lugar of Indiana, who as mayor of Indianapolis set in motion changes that would make it a destination city in the twenty-first century.

On hand, too, were world-class intellectuals like Pat Moynihan of New York, who became one of my best friends. He was a genuine expert on foreign relations and national security. His ideas about public policy, which his fellow Democrats called "neoconservative," were a lot like mine. The "neocons" agreed with me that a change in the role of government was often necessary to cure what ailed big policy-driven systems such as health care, housing, and welfare. I also became close to Democrat Henry "Scoop" Jackson of Washington, who greeted me with an offer to help me better understand my Scandinavian constituents. "The best of them kept going west to Washington and became mine," he told me. The idea registered with me: migration patterns help explain national politics and underscore the need for "every state to be heard from."

These senators had acquired all the acclaim their egos needed before they arrived in Washington. Their aim in the Senate was not more fame. It was to do more good for more people in America and abroad. One of my great joys was getting to know so many national treasures.

If you go to the Senate for the right reasons, the work is demanding. A senator is expected to be in at least two places at once, both traveling the back roads of one's state and sitting in one or more committee chairs in Washington. It wasn't unusual for three committees on which I served to meet at the same hour. Further, learning subjects as complicated as health care, environmental protection, taxation, or national security well enough to speak about them with confidence requires a good deal more study than is needed to simply know how to vote. Still more work—and nerve—are required to sell ideas to colleagues, knowing that powerful interest groups are paying lobbyists and political organizers handsomely to counter your argument.

In those years, most members of Congress moved their families to new homes in the Washington area and their children to schools there. Three of my four sons enrolled in Langley High School in Virginia. I got to enjoy their baseball games and saw the Army-Navy

Club swim team go from last to first place in the metro DC league with the addition of the Durenberger boys. My eldest son accompanied Scoop Jackson's daughter to her cotillion ball in Seattle. The youngest did childcare for Dan Quayle's sons, the oldest of whom went on to election to the US House from Arizona. I well remember the Saturday session of the Senate in which Ted Kennedy was working to pass a bill which Republicans opposed. That same afternoon, Dick Lugar and I had sons who were graduating from Langley High School. To accommodate us—his opponents!—Kennedy moved to delay the votes on issues we opposed until we returned from the graduation ceremony.

That gracious gesture spoke well not only of Kennedy but of a Senate that allowed any member from either party to make a difference. I sought to take full advantage of the opportunity. The best way to build trust, I learned, is by finding and sticking to the truth, and the best place to find that was in the middle, among progressive senators from both parties, rather than among special-interest or partisan extremes. Not that members weren't partisans. But the numbers compiled by political scientists who analyze congressional voting records illustrate how partisanship changed during my Senate tenure. In 1973–74, a few years before I arrived, twenty-nine of one hundred senators scored as either conservative Democrats or liberal Republicans. In other words, they frequently voted with members of the opposite party. By my final two years in the Senate, only three senators' voting records set them apart from their parties' respective ideological orientation. According to that same scale, Congress today is more polarized than at any point since Reconstruction.[3]

Each party in the 1979 Senate had an ideological left, middle, and right. Intraparty divisions were often on display. For example: conservative Democrat Russell Long refused to invite liberal Democrat Ted Kennedy to testify on a health reform bill in Long's Finance Committee until the year I arrived, when some of us Republicans persuaded him to do so. Republican Jesse Helms of North Carolina was a right-wing ideologue and former radio talk-show host who constantly hassled the cabinet members of Republican presidents and irritated his Republican colleagues by offering hot-button amendments to "get us on the record" on single issues. That way, Richard Viguerie, who had founded *Conservative Digest* magazine a few years before, could feed news of the vote to Helms's mailing list of 25 million. Regional ties mattered as much as partisan ones: Republican Thad Cochran of Mississippi and Democrat David Pryor of Arkansas, both members of my class of 1978, voted more often in concert with each other than with me.

The standing Senate committees and subcommittees were where, week by week, members revealed to each other the foundations on which they based their policy notions, allowing each other to judge whether those foundations were solid. My choice of the Finance Committee was lucky. There, I could put to good use my Minnesota experience with intergovernmental relations and my immersion in "changing the role of government." That interest made my next committee choice clear. I asked to serve on Government Affairs and its Intergovernmental Relations (IGR) subcommittee. In 1978, the subcommittee was chaired by the "father of IGR," Senator Edmund Muskie, the Maine Democrat who had run for vice president with Hubert Humphrey in 1968.

Those committees afforded me a fine opportunity to bring Minnesota thinking to the fore. The work done in Minnesota in the 1960s and 1970s on such things as state aid to schools, cities, and counties; regional tax-base sharing; and human services administration gave me a vision of what was possible at the federal level. Muskie and his successor, Jim Sasser of Tennessee, shared that vision. They invited their subcommittee to think about how to build more problem-solving capacity within state governments.

Serving the Government Affairs Committee was an education in itself. For example, it afforded me an early understanding of what would become the most serious environmental issue of our time—climate change. Committee chair Abe Ribicoff, a Democrat from Connecticut, scheduled a daylong hearing in 1980 on what scientists were calling the "ozone hole" in the earth's atmosphere. It was my first detailed exposure to the notion that human activity was altering the planet's atmosphere with highly disruptive and undesirable consequences. There was no orthodoxy of climate change denial among Republicans—yet. For this Republican, the compelling information I heard that day convinced me that the United States has a responsibility to reduce or eliminate the environment-altering pollutants that respect no state or national border. To Ribicoff's credit, and to that of our relationship, he invited my wife and me to accompany him and his wife on a special trip to Egypt and to Israel at which we introduced President Carter's new peace emissary, Robert Strauss, to the leaders of those two countries.

Republican minority leader Howard Baker (rather than seniority) controlled GOP appointments to the so-called select committees, including the Select Committee on Intelligence, for which he tapped me. It was work I took very seriously. I arrived in the Senate a year after the committee had been made permanent. That was a response to the excesses of the Vietnam War, when a nation disgusted by what had been done in its name sought more accountability from the CIA and the defense establishment. Nowhere was bipartisanship more obvious than on the intelligence committee, chaired by the likes of Democrat Birch Bayh from Indiana and Republican Barry Goldwater of Arizona. Nowhere was it more possible for a new senator to school himself in foreign policy and national security. The committee members themselves were scholars. I was amazed when Scoop Jackson once interrupted a briefing on Iran to offer a detailed history of one of the oldest countries in the world, including its origins and our past relationship. I had knowledge to contribute about Central America, where I knew every country from my work at H. B. Fuller. Beyond that region, I had a lot to learn.

I wanted very much to get involved in energy and natural resource policy. The committee that controlled it was dominated by southern and western mineral and public land states. I thought a Minnesota perspective was in order. I was well aware that my 1978 election was secured in part by support from Minnesota environmentalists who were appalled that Don Fraser had lost the DFL primary in part because of his work to secure the Boundary Waters Canoe Area as a federally protected wilderness. But my interest in nature was personal as well as political. The outdoors had been my playground growing up in Collegeville. And I'd seen as a member of the Metropolitan Parks and Open Space Commission how important green space is to urban vitality.

In the House, my friend Jim Oberstar, a Democrat from the Eighth District, was vigorously supplying Minnesota input on these issues. He was eager to guide me if I could arrange to do as much in the Senate. But I had to bide my time and settle for securing appropriations for Minnesota's federally protected zones—the BWCA, Voyageurs National Park, the Minnesota Valley National Wildlife Refuge. It would be four years before I landed a seat on the Environment and Public Works Committee. It was worth the wait: Environment and Public Works proved to be the most productive and progressive policy-making committee in Congress in the 1980s.

My committee assignments guided me as I decided how best to staff my offices in Washington and Minnesota. I wanted staff that could help me acquire the kind of expertise that inspired trust in other senators. For example, on the intelligence committee I inherited Ed Levine from retired Senator Cliff Case (R-NJ) and as my foreign policy adviser Bruce Jentleson, who went on to become an internationally recognized foreign policy expert, author, and director of the Sanford School of Public Policy at Duke University. I also wanted top-notch constituent services, knowing that they would help me build trust at home, particularly among Minnesotans who did not agree with me on every issue. I decided to build a policy and constituent service staff in Minnesota nearly equivalent in size and experience to that of my Washington staff.

I had first-rate assistance, starting with my chief of staff, George

Thiss. Thiss had been the Minnesota Republican Party chair from
1965 to 1971 and built a stellar reputation for personal warmth, integrity, and ability. After chairing the party, Thiss took charge of the Upper Midwest Council, a regional economic organization that would
have been called a think tank if that term had been in vogue in the
1970s. Thiss was willing to work for me, but he and his wife, Joyce,
did not want to move their two young sons to Washington. I decided
that keeping my chief of staff based in Minnesota wasn't a bad idea
for a senator whose name would be on a ballot again in four years.
It's a decision I never regretted. George was assisted in Minnesota
by two very able retired mayors, Phil Cohen of Brooklyn Center and
Alex Smetka of Rochester. They were soon joined by Citizens League
staffer Jon Schroeder to work on policy matters. Jon and his wife,
Dana, became dear friends, and to this day they are involved in civic
affairs and public policy reform.[4]

Also with me from the start was my campaign press aide, Tom
Horner. The son of pioneering Twin Cities sports-news broadcaster
Jack Horner, Tom had been a journalist with the suburban Sun
Newspapers chain when I convinced him to join my campaign staff.
He was at my side when we walked into what had been Muriel Humphrey's office in the Dirksen Building and found that Senator Humphrey had left us a bouquet of chrysanthemums, a kind personal
note, and a friendly young staffer, Libby Shelton. I was delighted to
learn that Libby was willing to stay on the job. I eventually made Tom
my administrative assistant—and in 1980, Tom made Libby his wife.
Tom likes to say that "Libby and I discovered bipartisanship before it
was cool."

Another Humphrey holdover was legislative assistant Danny
McNamara, whose knowledge of the appropriations process ran
deep. His Humphrey connection was strong; his father had worked
for Hubert Humphrey from the start of Humphrey's Senate career in
1949. Danny was willing to take a chance on a Republican, as I was
on him. It was a decision that paid huge dividends for my constituents. For example, Don Loeslie, a farmer from Warren, Minnesota,

was president of the National Association of Wheat Growers in 1980 when President Carter imposed a boycott on US sales of any kind to the USSR in response to its invasion of Afghanistan. Don sought me out and explained the negative economic consequences to our state. I put McNamara on the case, and soon the 1980 Budget Act had an amendment excluding US agricultural products from international sanctions or boycotts. Another time, "Danny Mac" and I used a budget bill to remove the last barrier to St. Lawrence Seaway access to the port of Duluth. His work on "my" achievements in federal infrastructure financing in Minnesota was better than most members of the Appropriations Committee, and to me a source of great pride.

One key hire showed me that the progressive Republican tradition was not unique to Minnesota. Ralph Neas came to work for me as legislative director. He had held that same position with Massachusetts senator Edward Brooke, a rare African American in the US Senate and a Republican who lost his 1978 reelection campaign to Democrat Paul Tsongas. Neas and I shared a Catholic background. He was a graduate of a Benedictine high school in Illinois and the University of Notre Dame. He was pleased to find that like Brooke, I was interested in using public policy to advance racial and gender justice. In later years, he would go on to a number of leadership roles in organizations promoting civil rights, environmental protection, and affordable health care.[5]

Ralph would be with me for only two years, and about half of the first year was unlike anything either of us had expected. On a trip to Minnesota in February 1979, Ralph was diagnosed with Guillain-Barré syndrome, a neurological disorder that can cause paralysis and death. When he finally left the hospital, doctors told him that his was the worst case they had seen in which the patient did not die. Under the care of spectacular nuns at St. Mary's Hospital in Minneapolis, Neas eventually made a full recovery.[6]

I like to think his rebound was spurred by his enthusiasm for an idea he brought me during my first days in the Senate—the Women's Economic Equity Act. Ralph had spent a dozen years compiling a list of statutory and regulatory discrimination against women. His idea was that those restrictions on women's rights and opportunities could be altered with one piece of landmark legislation that he would write and I would carry in the Senate. I warmed to the idea right away. It seemed like such a Minnesota thing to do.

I enlisted two able House sponsors, Maine Republican Olympia Snowe and Colorado Democrat Pat Schroeder, an alumna of the University of Minnesota. We embarked on a two-pronged strategy. We would press for action on our overarching bill. But we would also be on the lookout for opportunities to amend discriminatory language out of federal law, one instance at a time. We found that the latter strategy was more effective than the former. It was difficult for a freshman senator in the minority to get a hearing on a reform bill. But my seat on the Senate Finance Committee proved to be a fine spot for finding anti-female language and enlisting committee support to amend it. Representatives Snowe and Schroeder had good success with the same tactic. Within ten years we had passed nearly every part of our bill into law. We didn't have the satisfaction of a White House signing ceremony because we did it one section at a time. But the work got done. (Olympia Snowe and I had a celebratory moment of our own not long ago, when I ran into the now-former senator from Maine at an airport baggage carousel. She spotted me first, pointed, and shouted, "Women's Economic Equity Act!")

Ralph Neas left my staff in 1980 to take the executive director's job at the Leadership Conference on Civil Rights. With his encouragement and Minnesota inspiration, I continued to look for ways to take down as many barriers for women and minorities in federal law as I could. It pleased me to be seen as the go-to Republican senator by advocates for equal rights and social justice. For example, it was a privilege to be asked by former battlefield nurses in Minnesota to carry the fight to add a Vietnam Women's Memorial to the planned Vietnam Memorial on the Capitol Mall.

On that and other gender justice issues, I worked with an outstanding group of Minnesota women from both political parties, often led by the spirited Kathleen Ridder of St. Paul. Ridder's interest in bringing more women into the ranks of the judiciary, including the US Supreme Court, became my passion as well. I didn't mind incurring the wrath of my more conservative Republican colleagues when I worked with Democrats to reauthorize the Voting Rights Act and make voter registration available to applicants for driver's licenses, a convenience known as "motor voter." I also was proud to be the Republican committee author of the Americans with Disabilities Act.

Shortly after the Ninety-Sixth Congress began in early January 1979, President Carter invited the new members of the Senate and House and their spouses to dinner at the White House. I was seated at a table with the president and First Lady Rosalyn Carter and two new Democratic House members, Geraldine Ferraro of New Jersey and Michael Barnes of Maryland. Before dessert was served, the president spoke about the responsibility each of us shared with him, representing our fellow Americans at a difficult time in the nation's history. Then he asked us to stand, hold hands, and join Arlo Guthrie and his band in singing "This Land Is Your Land." Some may have considered that a corny conclusion to the evening. I found it moving. Carter had described well the task we'd undertaken and the expectations our constituents had for us. We had a sacred duty to earn their trust.

In the room that evening was a new House member from Carter's home state of Georgia, Republican Newt Gingrich. On his third try, Gingrich had won a seat that had long been occupied by Democrats. Many legislative and congressional districts in the Deep South were still in conservative Democratic hands then. The latter-day claim that the South was lost to the Democrats as soon as Democratic president Lyndon Johnson signed the landmark 1964 civil rights bill into law is overstated. But a gradual partisan shift was in progress in the South that would continue throughout my Washington years, to palpable effect. That night, I doubt that I knew or noticed Gingrich. In a few years, everyone in Washington would.[7]

The "Gingrich Revolution" that would turn congressional Republicans to the right was still years away. But savvy observers would have already seen the Senate Republican caucus dividing into two camps, conservative/southern and western versus progressive/northern and midwestern. Early in 1979 I was invited to both of the Wednesday noon lunches the two camps conducted. These were purportedly sociable rather than strategy-setting gatherings—but it was clear that like-minded Republican senators preferred to socialize with one another rather than with those in the opposite camp. I gravitated to the moderate "No Name" group, which included my Finance Committee colleagues Bob Packwood of Oregon, Jack Danforth of Missouri, John Chafee of Rhode Island, and John Heinz of Pennsylvania. All of them, like me, would be up for reelection in 1982. That gave us a bond that grew into friendship. I noticed that my Minnesota "twin" Rudy Boschwitz showed up occasionally at both our Wednesday luncheons and the more conservative gatherings, which we No-Namers sometimes called "the Jesse Helms group" after one of its dominant personalities. I took Rudy's fence-straddling as a clue that he aspired to one day play a role in caucus leadership.

It's been said that whenever a US senator looks in the mirror, he sees a future president. That quip never applied to me. I was fully and happily engaged in Senate service, unperturbed by presidential ambition. But like everyone in Washington, I was gripped by the dramas that weakened the Carter presidency in 1979 and 1980.

The economy was already slow and inflation running high when in early 1979 oil prices spiked in the wake of a coup against the US–backed Shah of Iran, Mohammad Reza Pahlavi. Americans soon found themselves waiting in long lines to purchase gas and grumbling about an ineffective federal government response. Inflation and interest rates climbed at a double-digit rate. Then in November, fifty-two Americans were taken hostage in their embassy in Tehran. A Minnesotan, L. Bruce Laingen, was the chief US diplomat at the embassy, heightening Minnesota anxiety as the hostages remained in captivity through all of 1980.

Rather than inspiring Americans to rally behind their president as some other foreign threats have done, the Iran hostage crisis dragged Carter down as it dragged on. An aborted rescue attempt in April that resulted in the deaths of eight servicemen added a whiff of incompetence to Americans' growing impression that their president was ineffective. Of course, that impression was amplified by the Republican who was challenging Carter in the November election, former actor and two-term California governor Ronald Reagan.

In hindsight, some analysts see the rise of Ronald Reagan as a major shift in a conservative direction for both the Republican Party and the nation. I don't fully subscribe to that thinking. To be sure, his campaign rhetoric was laden with anti-government slogans like "Government is not the solution to our problems; government *is* the problem." He professed unquestioning faith in the free enterprise system and said that federal interference in that system was to blame for the nation's economic malaise. His reluctance to acknowledge that government is also a problem-solving tool likely contributed to his tepid initial reception among Minnesota Republicans, who had seen state and local government serve them well. A *Minneapolis Star*–CBS News survey at the state's February 26, 1980, precinct caucuses found a dead heat between Reagan and his more moderate-minded opponent (and future running mate), George H. W. Bush.[8]

I opted not to take sides in their contest. But after Reagan won the nomination, I had no qualms about backing him. My sense, then and now, is that Reagan's appeal was based on more than issues. Unlike the Republican candidate in 2016 who campaigned to "make America great again," Reagan never doubted America's greatness. He saw this nation as "a shining city on a hill" and conveyed an optimism that Americans craved. Government needed to be limited, in Reagan's view, but with leadership and focus it could get things done. That can-do sense was a tonic to a nation that was "all too mindful of the disappointments of the past, but seeking hope in the future," as described by *Time* magazine less than two months before the election, drawing from a Daniel Yankelovich poll. Voters, the poll found, were "caring about issues, although much more concerned about character." Reagan's leading backers in Minnesota were concerned most about winning the election. His most vigorous Minnesota organizer was Marsie Leier, a powerhouse party activist from Roseville who emphatically told anyone who asked why she supported Reagan: "Because he can win!"[9]

Win he did, by a whopping 489–49 in the Electoral College—though Minnesota stayed loyal to its native son, Walter Mondale, and gave its ten electoral votes to the Democratic ticket. President Reagan was the first president to take the oath of office on the west front of the Capitol, the side facing most of America. I loved the symbolism of that choice and the accountability it represented. He confirmed our understanding of the enormity of the problems the nation faced and said of taking them head on, "If not now, when; if not us, who?"

A new Senate majority—the first Republican majority since the 1950s—was sworn in the same day. New majority leader Howard Baker took us to the old Senate chamber in the Capitol for a ceremony that included a reading by Senate historian Richard Baker of the history of the body, including the critical responsibility of the "two members from every state." Thus were the thirteen progressive Republicans from northern, midwestern, and West Coast states encouraged to work with like-minded Democrats as we tackled the nation's problems.

President Reagan announced a set of principles and recommendations for change, then left it to Congress to work out the details of implementation. He had the confidence to accept that success in some areas sometimes came with failure in others. There was no public castigation when occasionally Senate Republican leaders would report that they just didn't have the votes for a Reagan initiative. Instead, he'd console Howard Baker, or later his successor as Republican majority leader, Bob Dole. "Well gosh, you win some and you lose some," the president would say. Or, in Yogi Berra style, "You know, 70 percent success isn't half bad."

Reagan was also willing to give his cabinet members the authority to do their jobs as they saw fit, even when they displeased the right wing of the Republican Party. For example, as the death toll from HIV/AIDS mounted, President Reagan's surgeon general, C. Everett "Chick" Koop, asked me to gather four of my most conservative Republican colleagues so he could listen to their complaints about the moral consequences of federal prevention policy, which I did, and he did, patiently. Then he said firmly, "Gentlemen, we have a million ministers, priests, and rabbis in this country, but only one surgeon general, and I'm it. I take the back seat to no one as a political conservative, but we've a big job to do." "We" did it. Koop joined me on a visit to Minneapolis and Willmar in 1982 to meet gay men and their families.

Presidential grace during adversity was welcome during Reagan's first two years in office because the economy was producing a great deal of the latter. The recession of 1981–82, brought on by the Federal Reserve's efforts to control inflation, was the sharpest downturn the nation had experienced since the Great Depression. Reagan's approval rating in public opinion polls, which began in the politically robust 65 percent range in early 1981, started a skid later that year that bottomed out in January 1983 at 35 percent. (Notably, that's about where President Donald Trump's approval rating hovered through most of his first year in office.)[10]

Nationally, the unemployment rate climbed to nearly 11 percent, higher than seen during the Great Recession of 2008–10. Construction and manufacturing—jobs that paid mortgages and supported families—were particularly hard hit. I'd venture that no region suffered more than Minnesota's Iron Range. Seven of the range's eight taconite plants closed, driving the unemployment rate in parts of northeastern Minnesota above 50 percent. Its distress in turn made the bottom fall out of state coffers and put Governor Al Quie in a tight spot. Minnesota governors are obliged by law to act to keep the state budget in the black at the end of each two-year fiscal cycle. When a deficit is forecast after a budget has been enacted, a governor can either call the legislature into session to amend the budget or can act unilaterally to "unallot" by executive order. Either path is fraught with political peril.

Quie chose the latter option when the downturn first hit. On August 19, 1980, he lopped 8.3 percent off spending commitments the state had made through the following June 30. The chief beneficiaries of that spending—school districts, cities, and counties—howled in protest. The cuts' timing gave those entities little choice but to cut spending themselves. Quie deemed unallotment politically preferable to calling a special legislative session weeks before the election. He was in the middle of his four-year term. To the extent that there was a political price to pay, he was willing to pay it, convinced that it would be a temporary hit.[11]

About that, he was wrong. The state budget's bleeding worsened in 1981. Legislators raised the sales tax in June, only to have the red ink return in July. By December, legislators were back in St. Paul for their third special session of the year, with a gaping $600 million hole to plug in a $7.7 billion two-year budget. Throughout Minnesota, families were making plans for a bleak holiday season. Churches in the Twin Cities were collecting food and clothing for people on the Iron Range. Quie's approval rating had been below 40 percent since summer; a Minnesota Poll in late October found only about one in four voters saying they would vote for Quie in 1982 over his two most likely DFL opponents, attorney general Warren Spannaus and former governor Rudy Perpich.[12]

Quie had never taken a "no new taxes" pledge. Grover Norquist and his Americans for Tax Reform would not arrive on the political scene until 1985 to coerce Republican elected officials into denying themselves access to one of government's most effective problem-solving tools. Instead, Quie's proudest accomplishment as governor was income tax restraint via indexing, the automatic adjustment of income tax brackets so that inflation alone did not increase the state income tax burden on taxpayers. He had struggled to push indexing through the 1979 legislature, where DFLers were in firm control of the senate and the house was locked in a 67–67 tie. Quie was loath to change course so soon thereafter and raise income taxes to balance the state budget. But he had been a champion for public education throughout his career. K–12 education accounts for about 40 percent of the state budget. It had already seen several rounds of cuts; the governor did not want to inflict more. As he would explain years later with an emotion-laden metaphor: "When your child is seriously ill, you throw away the family budget, and spend whatever you need to spend to save your child."[13]

On January 14, 1982, Quie allowed a 10 percent income tax surcharge to go into effect without his signature. Less than two weeks later, he made good on a campaign promise. He had said in 1978: "If this man can't improve state government and cut taxes at the same time, he won't make excuses. He simply won't run again." On January 25, Quie announced that he would not seek reelection.[14]

Three more times in 1982, Quie had to call the legislature into special session to fix the leaky budget. But as a lame duck, he developed a strong working relationship with DFLers, chief among them the senate majority leader, Roger Moe. The decisions they made that year to both cut spending and raise taxes may have been politically painful in the short run. But they were credited for Minnesota's quick fiscal rebound as the economy improved in 1983 and for the relative financial stability the state enjoyed during the next two decades. Quie's service to Minnesota has continued in a variety of ways as an elder statesman, now age ninety-four.

Minnesota voters returned DFLer Rudy Perpich to the governor's office in 1982; he would go on to become Minnesota's longest-serving governor. That year, the state's voters did two other things pertinent to this story. In the September 14 Republican gubernatorial primary, they rejected lieutenant governor Lou Wangberg, a conservative former Bemidji school superintendent, in favor of the more progressive (and pro-choice) Wheelock Whitney, the former CEO of a large investment banking firm. The party convention had preferred Wangberg over two former DFL legislators who had converted to the Republican Party because of the abortion issue, Marion "Mike" Menning of Edgerton and Glen Sherwood of Pine River. Whitney had opted to bypass the convention, which he knew would not be friendly territory, despite his long involvement with the party and the debt owed to him because of his willingness to run for the US Senate in 1964, a tough year for the GOP. His primary win was followed by a drubbing in the general election; Perpich returned to office with nearly 59 percent of the vote. But the primary had demonstrated that the state's Republican voters still liked the Stassen progressive line.[15]

The other notable move by 1982's voters was to reelect me. I defeated Mark Dayton—a future Minnesota governor—by six percentage points.

That's a margin observers sometimes call "comfortable." But there wasn't much comfort for me in that fall's campaign. Throughout the country, Republican senators were in tough battles for reelection, the consequence of a sour economy and President Reagan's sliding popularity. Like me, most of them had voted for the Economic Recovery Tax Act of 1981. It slashed federal income tax rates for both individuals and businesses, with the aim of stimulating the economy. Instead, its impact on the federal debt pushed interest rates up. Dow Jones averages fell by more than 20 percent in response, and Americans became familiar with the term "double-dip recession." A corrective tax bill was enacted in September 1982, but by then considerable political damage had been done. Progressive Republicans like me were vulnerable because we tended to represent states with potent Democratic parties, which Minnesota's DFL most certainly was.

But in Dayton, I had a young and relatively inexperienced challenger whose family ties proved to be both a political asset and a liability. Dayton is one of Minnesota's best-known and trusted business names, thanks to the reach and reputation of Dayton's Department Store and its business successor, Target Corporation. Mark's great-grandfather founded the company; his father, Bruce, was a leader among five brothers who oversaw its expansion in the mid-twentieth century. Mark's then-wife, Alida, hailed from the well-known and wealthy Rockefeller family. Their combined fortunes made it possible for thirty-five-year-old Mark to largely self-finance a $5 million campaign against me. But it also created a narrative that worked against Dayton: here's a youngster with little real-world experience, trying to buy himself a seat in the US Senate.

On Labor Day weekend, my pollster Bob Teeter called with stunning news: the Durenberger-Dayton race was effectively neck and neck. My adviser Roger Ailes told me to "kick it into high gear." He urged me to talk about not only what I was doing right in the Senate but also what Dayton would do wrong. We decided to tally the cost of Dayton's proposals for new federal spending and came up with $241 billion—a figure that sounded astronomical in 1982 and that planted worries about financial trouble if Dayton were elected. That became the basis of a TV ad about the "Dayton's bill" Mark proposed to send to taxpayers. That mild stuff was called negative campaigning in those years and left Dayton crying foul.[16]

Meanwhile, I made sure Minnesotans knew that I was not walking in lockstep with President Reagan. For example, the Associated Press reported on October 6 that I considered Reagan's energy policies "worse than Jimmy Carter's." I emphasized that I had been named senator of the year in 1981 by the Sierra Club, which was no fan of Reagan or his interior secretary James Watt. My campaign got wind that James Baker, Reagan's politically astute chief of staff, had raised money for a special ad buy the Sunday night before the election in every state in which a Republican senator was in a close reelection campaign. It was to be a message to that state's voters from the president himself, on behalf of that senator. My campaign chair and good friend Gene Holderness and I debated how to respond, knowing that

Reagan was not a popular figure in Minnesota. We decided to ask Baker and his people to let us use the spot instead for a direct message from me to the voters. That was in keeping with the good advice Roger Ailes was giving in those years: A candidate should look people in the eye and make a connection with emotion as well as ideas.[17]

Who knows whether that late ad made a difference. But something did. The tight polls of early September gave way to that "comfortable" win on November 2. I have to admire the prescience of the *Star Tribune*'s editorial board, which said as it endorsed me, "Perhaps Mark Dayton will prove to be the right politician for a later time." At the end of 2018, he is due to complete two strong terms as governor.[18]

———————

The same editorial praised me for "exploring ways to make health care more cost effective." It said I was willing to "force more decisions on health care consumers accustomed to comprehensive coverage" for the sake of both better care and lower costs. That was a very abbreviated description of my thinking. I had decided to devote considerable time and energy to one of the most complicated and vexing issues in American life, health care and its financing. I wanted to go national with ideas I had acquired in Minnesota, where health costs are among the lowest in the nation and the population's health ranks high.

Minnesota might be deemed the birthplace of health maintenance organizations—medical insurance systems that provide services for a fixed annual fee. I first heard about the concept when I met its modern-era father, Dr. Paul Ellwood, soon after becoming Governor LeVander's chief of staff. The executive director of the American Rehabilitation Foundation (formerly known as the Sister Kenny Institute, founded to treat polio victims), Ellwood was also a physical medicine professor and health policy scholar at the University of Minnesota. He paid a visit to the governor's office soon after LeVander and I arrived. That was also soon after Congress and President Lyndon Johnson enacted Medicare, health insurance for the elderly, and Medicaid, which covered the disabled and families with children who were poor enough to qualify for Aid to Families with Dependent Children, aka welfare. Medicaid required a state funding match but allowed states considerable discretion in deciding what share of the population would be eligible and what would be covered. Ellwood supported federal involvement in bringing the benefits of health insurance to underserved populations. But he wanted us to know that he detected a flaw in Medicaid's design: doctors and hospitals were given too much power to set the payments that would flow to them. The federal willingness to pay reasonable and customary fees for services put providers in charge of costs, he said, and that meant that Medicaid costs were sure to grow at a pace that would soon become uncomfortable for state governments and employers.

Ellwood's prediction was spot-on. I connected with him again around 1973, when the Citizens League task force on which I served sought him out. By then, he and Walt McClure had founded Interstudy, a health policy think tank based in Minnesota, and had coined the term "health maintenance organization." The concept was not unheard of; a number of small prepaid health coverage plans had operated in various parts of the country for several decades, and Kaiser Permanente in California had made a name for itself with the approach. But it took the post-Medicare inflation in health-care costs to pique wider interest in the idea. Ellwood had advised President Nixon and others in Washington in 1972–73 as they put together legislation that offered start-up HMOs federal grants and loans and required employers of twenty-five or more people to offer an HMO option if a federally certified HMO was available nearby. When the federal government finally established a certification procedure in 1977, HMOs began to pop up all over the country. Minnesota was in the vanguard, as usual. Group Health, a nonprofit, consumer-directed health plan, had been created in the Twin Cities in 1957.

I brought enthusiasm for this approach with me to Washington and asked to be appointed to the Senate Finance Committee's health subcommittee. I had plenty to do right from the start. President Carter was pushing for Congress to authorize the federal government to set annual budgets for hospitals and doctors, based on formulas developed in Maryland. That sounded like federal overreach and a step toward "socialized medicine" to us Republicans and even to some Democrats. We beat back that idea.

I was eager to do more than stop bad ideas. In 1980, with the advice of Paul Ellwood and Alain Enthoven at Stanford University, I assembled my first reform bill, the Consumer Choice Health Reform Act of 1980. Among other things, it put some teeth into the Nixon-era bill, saying that employers would lose their federal tax exemption on health-care premiums if they did not offer their employees access to the services of a federally qualified HMO in their areas. The Government Research Corporation/North America praised the bill and summarized my approach: "Government should expand choices to the individual, not limit them; the price of a good or service should be a true measure of its cost; government should not facilitate hidden costs or cross-subsidization; and the government role in stimulating competition should be to ensure fair market conditions, not to provide services or to regulate a particular brand of competition."

Not long after the election of a can-do Republican president and a Senate Republican majority, I had an important conversation with my colleague John Heinz of Pennsylvania. He remarked that the GOP class of 1976 would be up for reelection during President Reagan's midterm. If that midterm election followed the usual pattern, the party of the sitting president would face a stiff political headwind. Although I arrived in office in 1978, he knew that I too was up for election in 1982. He suggested that I should put myself in the thick of important work that would showcase my contributions. Why not take the chair of the health subcommittee?

I liked the idea, and warmed to it even more when my McLean, Virginia, neighbor, Senator Richard Schweiker of Pennsylvania, was named the new Health and Human Services secretary. I was in the health subcommittee chair when Schweiker came to promise the president's support for major systemic changes in health-care "markets." We talked about using Medicare financing authorization via the biennial Budget Resolutions Act as the means to that end. I immediately strategized with other subcommittee members about how we might alter Medicare reimbursement to provide incentives for slower cost growth. Some of the states represented on the committee had been trying new approaches, as HMOs and multi-specialty group practices were becoming more common around the country.

Addressing the Group Health Association of America, 1990s. *Courtesy of the author*

The result of our brainstorming was a provision in the Budget Resolution Act of 1982, sponsored by Heinz. It authorized a demonstration in which Medicare would pay HMOs 95 percent of what it paid for traditional coverage, while freeing participating HMOs of some requirements concerning benefits so that they could compete on that basis.

Before that demonstration could be launched, we took another major step. In 1983, we determined that Medicare should no longer pay hospitals for every bandage, cotton swab, and aspirin administered to every Medicare patient. Instead, we decided, the federal government should pay hospitals and doctors a fee based on each patient's diagnosis, severity of disorder, age, and gender. If surgery were involved in a patient's treatment, more should be paid, of course. But hospitals would no longer have an incentive to keep a patient longer or administer more tests or drugs than necessary to treat the patient's illness. Hospital profits would be squeezed, but hospital practices would also be standardized, improving care overall—at least, in theory. As chair of the Finance Committee's health subcommittee, I was the chief sponsor of the legislation, which was signed into law in midsummer.

Weeks later, I found myself in front of the board of directors, officers, and top surgical staff of the Texas Medical Center in Houston, Texas, explaining the new Medicare Part A payment system. Texas Medical is one of the nation's largest and most renowned medical networks, with 65,000 employees. After my presentation, I was asked many questions, the last one from an older man in blue scrubs who had come in late and found a seat right in front of me. I stared down at the name Michael DeBakey over his pocket and listened to the most distinguished heart surgeon in the world telling me he knew as much about health care as anyone, was in demand around the world for his opinion, and in this case, his opinion was that the new funding scheme Congress had devised was going to fail. As he spoke, I wondered what a guy from Collegeville, Minnesota, would come up with to say in response. It came out something like this: "Dr. DeBakey, like everyone from Minnesota who takes pride in our nation's medical achievements, I recognize the value of your opinion on medical matters. But in the case of how hospitals should be paid, the US Congress believes differently."

My reception wasn't a lot better a couple of weeks later, when I was invited to speak to the board and leadership at the St. Cloud Hospital in Minnesota. I gave them the same talk I gave in Texas. Afterward, the kindly Benedictine nun who was president of the hospital looked at me and chided, "David, you should know better than to do this to us. You were born in this hospital!"

The hospital reimbursement system my bill created became known by the acronym DRG, for diagnostic related grouping. It's still in use today. But I was on notice: on health care—and a good deal more—resistance to the progressive Minnesota Republican ideas I had brought to Washington was strong and growing, even in Minnesota.

8 THE CENTER SLIPS

INNESOTA'S REPUTATION as a reliable blue patch on red-and-blue presidential election maps traces to 1984. My state stayed loyal to its native son, Walter Mondale, in his futile quest to unseat President Ronald Reagan. The nation's economy had rebounded nicely by 1984, and so had Reagan's popularity. Minnesota was the only state Mondale won, and he did so just barely, with less than a four-thousand-vote margin.

That was weak solace for Democrats, made weaker still by other contests that year. My Senate colleague Rudy Boschwitz waltzed to an easy victory over DFL secretary of state Joan Growe. (It would take twenty-two more years for Minnesotans to finally send a woman to the US Senate.) And Independent-Republicans took back control of the Minnesota house for the first time since 1971, albeit with a narrow 69–65 majority.

Like other Republicans, I cheered those results. But I was aware of something the numbers alone did not reveal. Reagan's resurgence had attracted a wave of evangelical Christians to my Independent-Republican Party. These were not the former DFLers, many of them Catholics, who had left that party over the abortion issue five or ten years earlier. These were people who had not been politically active before but were made to feel welcome in the GOP by a president who in 1980 had appeared before fifteen thousand people at an evangelical Christian rally in Texas and said, "I know you can't endorse me. But I endorse you and what you are doing."[1]

Opposition to legal abortion was their marquee issue, and by 1984 they found ample support for that cause within the Independent-Republican Party. By the mid-1980s, support for abortion rights disqualified one from party positions in much of the state. Litmus tests over abortion were employed to elect even lowly precinct caucus chairs and county convention delegates. (DFLers would soon come to apply the same test in reverse.) Many Republican veterans, including me, opposed legal abortion but considered the issue less pressing than others confronting the state and nation. That made us objects of suspicion in evangelical eyes.

But the 1984 newcomers were motivated by more than abortion. They were antiestablishment people with views on a number of issues that ran counter to the thinking that characterized Minnesota's Stassen line. Many mistrusted and rejected public education. They were skeptical about science and hostile toward the teaching of evolution. The women's movement struck some as a threat to traditional family values, and the budding gay rights movement was sinful in their eyes. They were wary of government activism, fearing encroachment on religious liberty. Like most Republicans, they favored strong American support for Israel. But their interest in Israel was apocalyptic. They saw the creation of the Jewish state as the fulfillment of end-times prophecies.

Encouraged by the Reagan presidency, evangelical leaders in Minnesota and around the country encouraged their flocks to sign on with the Republican Party. They could do so with relative ease in a year when Republican caucuses and conventions were placid affairs. The lack of a contest at the top of the ticket in 1984 kept less-engaged Republican "regulars" at home. It was a year of opportunity for newcomers to climb party ranks.

The new IR majority in the Minnesota house included a sizable faction allied with these newcomers. Most visible in that camp were state representatives Allen Quist of St. Peter and Ralph Kiffmeyer of Big Lake; they spoke for perhaps a quarter of the majority caucus.

That cohort was one of at least three distinct philosophical camps in house IR ranks. A second group were the political heirs of Stassen, Andersen, and LeVander. They were the problem solvers who were unafraid to employ state government as their tool. This group's priorities aligned with mine: high-quality public education, affordable health care, environmental protection, accountable government, and a fair, business-friendly tax code to pay for it all. This camp's leading lights included Bill Schreiber of Brooklyn Center, a former IR minority leader and the chair of the house tax committee; Dave Bishop of Rochester; John Rose of Roseville; and John Himle and Kathleen Blatz of Bloomington.

A third house IR subset might today be called Tea Partiers, though no one in the mid-1980s would have recognized that label. They were younger, brasher, and more motivated by ideology than religion as they pursued smaller government. Their base resided in Greater Minnesota, reflecting a shift in focus for the party that twenty years earlier had developed Minnesota's policy response to urban growth. Some in this group had been first elected in the 1978 "Minnesota Massacre." By 1981–82, they were giving Governor Al Quie and other IR elders fits, refusing to go along with the tax increases included in proposed bipartisan remedies for recurring state budget shortfalls. It might be fairly claimed that their resistance to Quie's deals with the legislature's DFLers contributed to his decision not to run for a second term in 1982. This libertarian-minded group was on the ascendency in the Minnesota house after the 1984 election. They installed one of their own, David Jennings of Truman, near the Iowa border, as speaker of the house.

Jennings rallied the new majority behind his camp's top agenda item, a tax cut of at least $1 billion. When first proposed, such a large tax cut seemed to be a fiscally risky reach. But Minnesota's economy was running hot in 1984–85, and the state treasury was accumulating impressive surpluses. In January, when the state's forecasted surplus reached $1.2 billion, DFL governor Rudy Perpich proposed a $600 million tax cut geared primarily to middle-earning income tax payers. By May, tax receipts were up and Perpich was happily going along with a tax cut just short of $1 billion. It would be structured to his specifications. In the name of "simplification" and a better competitive position for Minnesota, Perpich had pushed for ending federal income tax deductibility for state tax purposes in exchange for reducing state income tax rates into single digits. Perpich was governing as a centrist, pro-business DFLer. At least on tax policy, he could be met in the middle by Independent-Republicans.

But on other matters, the new IR house majority clashed with Perpich and the DFL and, to a lesser extent, with Republicans in the Minnesota senate. With its four-year terms, geographically larger districts, and pattern of longer tenure among members, the Minnesota senate is slower than the house to bend in the political wind. The IR senate caucus in 1985 numbered just twenty-five out of sixty-seven members. Most could have been called progressive Republicans. (One of them, Dean Johnson of Willmar, would serve as both Republican minority leader in the 1990s and, after defecting to the DFL in 2000, as DFL majority leader from 2004 to 2006.)

The political pedigree of the senator chosen as minority leader in January 1985 illustrates some of the reasons progressive Republican thinking had such staying power in the state senate. Glen Taylor of North Mankato was a farm kid from Comfrey, Minnesota, a wedding stationery company employee who seized a chance to buy the company in 1975. It would become the foundation of a large business network that ultimately would include the multifaceted Taylor Corporation, the Minnesota Timberwolves and Lynx basketball franchises, and the *Star Tribune* newspaper. In the late 1970s, Taylor was an ambitious local businessman whose civic work included leadership of the Mankato-area chapter of the Jaycees. The Jaycees was for Glen a principled, development-oriented leadership training and proving ground, as it was for me. While he was his chapter's president, it was ranked number one in the state.

When the area's state senate seat became vacant in 1980, it was not the IR or the DFL Party that sought out Glen as a candidate. It was a delegation of his fellow Jaycees. "You'd be so much better" than the candidates the two parties had found, they said. He was persuaded to enter the contest not by ambition to pursue a political career or advance a political cause, but by the chance to engage more seriously in public service. "It was a way to help others and the community," he recalled decades later.[2]

Only when Taylor filed for office did he decide whether to enter the Republican or the DFL primary. He opted for Republican, he recalled, not so much because he was in tune with the party's philosophy but because "it gave me a better chance to win." He ran with the support of his local teachers' union, something few if any Republican legislators can claim today. Soon after taking office in 1981, he was assigned a leadership post within the minority caucus by his newfound mentor, minority leader Robert Ashbach of Arden Hills. Ashbach was a construction company owner and banker who appreciated having another entrepreneur on his leadership team. Ashbach's legislative service began a decade before legislators ran with party designation. He was a loyal Republican, but—like Taylor—not a fierce one. Ashbach left the senate in 1982 and was succeeded as minority leader by Jim Ulland, an economist by training whose legislative biography identified him as a "tree farmer" from the Duluth area. Taylor took charge of the caucus in 1985 after Ulland resigned to take an executive position with First Bank System, today's US Bancorp.

Senators like Taylor, Johnson, Dennis Frederickson of Morgan, Bill Belanger of Bloomington, Howard Knutson (and later, his son Dave) of Burnsville, and Gary Laidig of Stillwater gave the Senate IR caucus a solid progressive core, larger than its house counterpart. The difference was evident when the state budget that seemed so healthy in 1985 took a turn for the worse in 1986. The $1 billion tax cut the legislature and governor had deemed affordable just a year earlier suddenly looked reckless in the face of a forecasted deficit in excess of $700 million. The house Republicans' preferred remedy looked heartless in many eyes: they sought a 30 percent cut in the already modest monthly cash benefits supplied to recipients of Aid to Families with Dependent Children, otherwise known as welfare.

The proposal was met with a torrent of criticism, and not just from DFLers. Sermons were preached against the proposal in churches. Protestant and Catholic bishops issued statements condemning the plan. Protesting welfare recipients and their young children regularly filled the capitol rotunda, where they were only too happy to share their personal stories with capitol journalists. The IR chair of a key appropriations subcommittee announced he could not support the AFDC cut. "I strongly feel I was put here for something important, and I doubt I was put here to reduce the bread and milk money for a thousand children in Minnesota," said Representative Bob Anderson, IR-Ottertail.[3]

But speaker Jennings held firm for several bruising weeks before finally yielding to the governor and senate. He was convinced that a majority of Minnesotans wanted less spent on welfare and that they would much prefer an AFDC cut to a tax increase. The position house Republicans took "allows us to clearly define, for the first time in a long time, the differences between the two parties in this state," Jennings said. "We'll be able to clearly see who wants to prevent tax increases and who doesn't."[4]

That was the position IR gubernatorial candidate Cal Ludeman—a former house member with a decided libertarian streak—and many house IR members took into the 1986 general election. It didn't serve them well. Perpich won a third term with more than 56 percent of the vote, and Independent-Republicans lost eighteen seats and the majority in the Minnesota house. It would be a dozen years before they would take back house control.

Minnesota wasn't the only state in which Republicans suffered reversals in Ronald Reagan's second midterm election. In eight states, US Senate seats flipped from Republican to Democratic control. Few in

Washington were surprised. Some of the Republicans who had been swept into the Senate with the Reagan victory in 1980 were not strong enough after one term to hold their seats in a presidential midterm election year. After six years in the majority, I was back in the minority in 1987. There I'd stay for the remainder of my Senate career.

Reagan's ebbing political strength in his second term contributed to those 1986 Republican defeats, and what came just days after the election weakened his influence further. News broke that an American military transport aircraft bearing US weapons intended for the right-wing rebels in Nicaragua—the Contras—had been shot down in October by a surface-to-air missile. The rest of the story gradually emerged. The weapons intended for the Contras were but one part of a covert, extralegal scheme by the Reagan administration to supply weapons to both Iran and the Contras in exchange for the release of US hostages held in Lebanon by Hezbollah, a paramilitary group tied to Iran. Supplying weapons to Iran violated an arms embargo that had been in place since the hostage-crisis years of 1978 and 1979. Supplying the Contras was another violation of US law, a law that I had a hand in drafting and strongly supported. My business experience in Central America and all I had learned since 1979 as a member of the Senate Select Committee on Intelligence convinced me of the futility of attempting to overthrow the revolutionary government in Nicaragua with a ragtag force like the Contras. I made that argument whenever I could. But President Reagan was listening to CIA director William Casey, not me.

I played a role in the events that ensued. In 1985, I had become chairman of the intelligence committee. It was the first time in thirty years that a Minnesotan had headed a major US Senate committee. This one had a mission and a style of operation unlike any other committee in Congress. Its charge was to provide legislative-branch oversight of executive-branch covert operations while preserving a shield from public view. Hence, the committee operates behind closed doors. Its value is to serve notice to any president intent on extralegal adventurism that a bipartisan panel in the Senate is watching. Because the intelligence committee's contribution to national security lies in the confidentiality of its work, we did not go public ourselves with our investigations. But the president knew that if we deemed it necessary, we could divulge what we knew to others who were free to call the executive branch to account.

When news broke about the downed plane bearing guns to Nicaragua, an alarm went off for me. A few weeks earlier, the president's national security adviser had assured the committee's ranking Democratic member, Vermont senator Patrick Leahy, and me that no such assistance was being offered. I knew that delaying the committee's investigation would increase the likelihood that people who knew the truth would not share it, or that they would concoct a shared version of what had happened that would be sold as the truth. Though the results of the election made me a lame-duck chairman, I quickly convened the committee for a series of closed-door interviews with key administration figures in late November and early December. President Reagan offered to be one of them. After consulting with Bob Dole, who was still majority leader for a few more weeks, I spurned the overture. I reasoned that Reagan's arrival on Capitol Hill would blow the cover off our work and undercut the reputation for independence that I was keen to maintain.

Rather than having Reagan come to us, I went to him at the White House a few weeks later, accompanied by the committee's staff director, retired Navy captain Bernie McMahon. We were so intent on maintaining a low profile that we entered the White House via a tunnel we accessed at the nearby US Treasury Building. We spelled out to the president what we knew. He took in our story without visible reaction until we had finished, when he turned to his chief of staff Donald Regan and said, "Well, Don, that's about the way we remember it too, isn't it?" He registered no dismay and offered no rebuttal, even though we were telling him that we knew he had not been truthful when he told the nation on November 13 that the United States had not attempted to trade arms for hostages. I sensed that day that he didn't have much political fight left in him.[5]

Long before the Iran-Contra investigation, I had been trying to clarify just what the Reagan administration was doing in Nicaragua. Jerry Fearing, the *St. Paul Pioneer Press*'s political cartoonist, noted my efforts in March 1985. *Courtesy of the author*

Since he left office and particularly since his death in 2004, Reagan has become almost a cult figure for Republicans who favor less taxation and smaller government. His "government is the problem" campaign speeches from 1980 became akin to sacred writs for the twenty-first-century conservative movement. What that movement does not care to recall is the extent to which Reagan governed as a pragmatic and, by today's lights, moderate conservative. To be sure, he promoted a tax cut in 1981, but he also signed tax increases into law in 1982 and reordered taxes in a revenue-neutral way in 1986. The latter bill stands out as a historic achievement, both for the bipartisanship that produced it and for the sound tax policy it delivered. It broadened the tax base by closing loopholes in order to reduce the top marginal individual income tax rate to 28 percent.[6]

On other policy matters, too, Reagan often worked in concert with a Democratic-controlled House and a Senate that operated in bipartisan fashion. The result was progress on touchy issues that elude compromise today—immigration, US–Soviet relations, tax policy, health policy reform, and Social Security's solvency among them. It's a shame that Reagan was not able to speak for himself for long after he left office. His post-presidency public appearances were infrequent. They ended in 1994 with his announcement that he was suffering from Alzheimer's disease, which took his life in 2004.[7]

There were signs aplenty as the Reagan presidency wound down that the nation's political climate was changing, and my party was in the vanguard of change. A new nonprofit advocacy organization, Americans for Tax Reform, was founded in 1985 by a Harvard-educated libertarian economist named Grover Norquist. It immediately made its presence felt by promulgating what it called a Taxpayer Protection Pledge, better known as the "no new taxes" pledge. Candidates for office were asked to take the pledge; those who did not were in for opprobrium from conservative media and grassroots activists affiliated with Norquist's group. At the start, they were deemed upstarts and an irritation by many in the GOP establishment. By the George W. Bush presidency, Norquist and his leadership team were the party's establishment, so valued that they met weekly at an office in the White House.

Conservative media emerged in those years, too. Actually, "exploded" would better describe what happened after the Federal Communications Commission dropped its thirty-eight-year-old requirement that licensed broadcasters present both sides of controversial issues—the Fairness Doctrine. FCC chair Mark Fowler, an attorney who had worked on Reagan's presidential campaign and was appointed to the FCC post in 1981, had been gunning for the Fairness Doctrine on First Amendment grounds for years. He finally succeeded in taking it down in 1987 when the supposedly bipartisan FCC was composed completely of Republican presidential appointees. The argument that carried the day was that the broadcast media had become as diverse as print and thus deserved the same freedom that print media enjoyed. At about the same time, AM radio stations around the country were looking for a lifeline as music broadcasting shifted to FM stations, which offered better high-fidelity sound quality. AM talk radio was cheap to produce with sufficient voice recognition and good at generating a loyal audience.

Almost overnight, it seemed, AM stations began airing a daily diet of conservative talk radio. Weeks before the 1988 Republican National Convention, a little-known talk-radio jock from Sacramento named Rush Limbaugh moved to WABC in New York and launched "The Rush Limbaugh Show," offering three hours of daily diatribe against anyone he deemed insufficiently committed to conservative American values as he defined them. His usual targets were liberals, feminists, and Democrats, but he wasn't constrained in turning his rhetorical heat on moderate Republicans. Limbaugh's broadcasts soon attracted such a following that other conservative radio jocks got on the same horse all over the country. A notable example: Jason Lewis, Minnesota's self-styled "Mr. Right," who is now a Republican congressman from Minnesota. I well recall going to the White House one day and seeing about fifty of Limbaugh's right-wing media counterparts camped out on the front lawn, in line for pre-arranged interviews. Their success would serve as inspiration in subsequent years as the cable TV era dawned. Among those watching radio's rush to the right with keen interest: my campaign consultant Roger Ailes, the future CEO of Fox News.

That said, it would be inaccurate to blame Republican conservatives alone for the pulling apart of the American body politic that occurred as the Reagan presidency wound down. One often overlooked episode in Senate annals—the Democratic majority's rejection of US circuit judge Robert Bork's nomination for the US Supreme Court in 1987—was a key dividing point. It injected a new level of partisanship into appointments to the nation's courts, initiating a tit-for-tat between the two parties that has ill served this country ever since.

I brought to the Senate a keen appreciation for the judiciary, acquired both as a practicing lawyer and as a governor's chief of staff. I had seen the financial sacrifice required of any good lawyer who was willing to accept appointment to the bench. As a new senator in 1978, I was also a beneficiary of the Senate's tradition of bipartisanship in federal judicial nominations and confirmations. When two federal district court vacancies occurred in Minnesota early in my tenure, the Democratic vice president offered me the chance to make one of the recommendations for nomination to President Carter. Mondale's gesture was a courtesy, to be sure. But it also was a way to assure that I would not take advantage of a senator's "blue slip" privilege to block their appointment of a Minnesotan to the federal bench, a prerogative customarily afforded to senators regarding home-state appointees—a Senate tradition that I knew nothing about at the time. I eagerly sent the president the name of fellow St. John's University grad Robert Renner of Walker, who had been among the outstanding members of the Minnesota house during the heyday period of Republican progress. Carter followed through with that nomination without hesitation.

From that point forward, I made it my policy not to question the nomination of any potential judge for purely partisan reasons. The Senate's "advise and consent" role, in my view, was to provide a final check on a nominee's character and competence, and nothing more. I was satisfied if a nominee was deemed qualified by his professional peers and had a record of integrity and responsible public service.

Early in the Reagan presidency, I pressed that very point with the new Republican administration. It came to my attention that my next two proposed judicial nominees from Minnesota, my former law partner Paul Magnuson and David Doty of Minneapolis, were being questioned on behalf of Attorney General Ed Meese about their positions on issues like abortion and gun control. Asking how someone might rule in a specific case was out of bounds in my book. I said as much to Meese. I was told that the practice would stop. I'm not convinced that it did in every case. (Both Magnuson and Doty were nominated and went on to brilliant careers on the bench and remain active as senior judges today.)

The Bork appointment in July 1987 to a seat that had been held by retiring justice Lewis Powell, a Nixon appointee, gave the Senate's new Democratic majority a chance to take this game to a new level. The appointment was politically charged for several reasons. Robert Bork had been solicitor general of the United States during the Nixon and Ford administrations. At one point during the Watergate saga he demonstrated a degree of loyalty to Nixon that Democrats found questionable. When Nixon set out to fire special prosecutor Archibald Cox in October 1973 because Cox was seeking the release of Nixon's Oval Office audio recordings, both the attorney general and the deputy attorney general resigned rather than carry out the president's order. That left Bork as acting attorney general, and he willingly complied.

Bork was also a leading proponent of "originalism," the idea that judges should adhere as nearly as possible to the original intent of language in the US Constitution. In his view, more modern rereadings of the Constitution amounted to "legislating from the bench," an inappropriate usurpation of the rightful roles of the legislative and executive branches. During two stints as a law professor at Yale University, Bork touted that philosophy to criticize the Warren and Burger courts in rulings on abortion and civil rights. That made him popular with the increasingly powerful southern and Christian conservative elements in the Republican Party—and anathema to liberal Democrats.

Well aware that they were increasingly dependent on a liberal urban base to win elections, Democrats brought out their biggest guns to defeat the Bork nomination. Senator Joe Biden of Delaware, the new chair of the Judiciary Committee, led the charge. He was joined by Edward Kennedy of Massachusetts, who railed that "Robert Bork's America is a land in which women would be forced into back-alley abortions, blacks would sit at segregated lunch counters, rogue police could break down citizens' doors in midnight raids, children could not be taught about evolution." The onslaught worked. Bork's nomination went down to defeat on a 42–58 Senate vote that, by to-day's standards, was somewhat bipartisan: two Democrats voted with us, while six Republicans voted no. I was not among them. Bork easily passed my test. He was clearly a person of integrity and competence, respected within his profession. What's more, I felt some empathy for the distinguished lawyer. He had been treated so shabbily during the run-up to his nomination hearings that when I met with him after one unpleasant encounter, he had difficulty lifting a cup of coffee to his lips without shaking.[8]

Bork's rejection triggered intense conservative anger. Republicans routinely described Bork as having been "savaged" by Democrats. They vowed revenge. The strong feelings even targeted the Reagan White House. Some on the right blamed Reagan's chief of staff Howard Baker—the former Senate majority leader—for an ineffective defense of the judge. "The next nominee had better be somebody as conservative as Bork, or else life at the White House is going to be very unpleasant," threatened Richard Viguerie, the founder of *Conservative Digest* magazine and an increasingly influential figure on the libertarian right. They were barely mollified when circuit judge Anthony Kennedy was finally confirmed for the Powell seat on the high court in early 1988.[9]

Hostility toward other Republicans was a clear violation of Reagan's oft-cited Eleventh Commandment: "Thou shalt not speak ill of thy fellow Republican." But as 1988 approached and the campaign to succeed him quickened, the president was no longer in a position to enforce that rule. And many Republicans were in no mood to heed it.[10]

Even though I'd been in the Senate for nearly ten years as the 1988 election approached, I was aware that in some eyes I was still the occupant of "the Humphrey seat"—and as a Republican an interloper, at that. Hence, it caused me some concern when state attorney general Hubert H. Humphrey III, the late senator's eldest son, emerged as the leading DFL candidate to unseat me. He had been attorney general since 1982 and had won reelection in 1986 with more than 70 percent of the vote. "Skip" Humphrey would be no pushover.

But I had won my first race with considerable support from people who had been Humphrey voters, largely on the strength of one issue: natural resource conservation. Bob Short's willingness to allow motorboats and other modern human intrusions in the Boundary Waters Canoe Area helped him defeat Don Fraser in the 1978 DFL primary. In turn, my record and positions on environmental protection made me acceptable to some Fraser voters and boosted me against Short. I believe my environmental record in the Senate helped keep those voters in my corner.

Even in the 1980s, it wasn't politically easy for a Republican in Washington to favor more governmental action to keep the air and water clean and wholesome. That meant spending more money, at a time when most Republicans wanted government to spend less. It was telling that the first Reagan-era budget resulted in a 40 percent cut in federal funds directed to environment-related purposes. It would take nearly twenty years for that funding to be restored.[11]

But the opposition I encountered seemed more regionally than ideologically based. And it was often bipartisan. For example, both Democrats and Republicans from coal-dependent states resisted my push to do something about acid rain, a byproduct of burning high-sulfur coal. Acid rain damages both forests and lakes, making it a particular threat in Minnesota. I started working on policies to minimize acid rain as a new member of the Senate Environment and Public Works Committee in 1983 and found a willing ally in a future Democratic majority leader, George Mitchell of Maine. Our idea was to require electricity generators to reduce sulfur emissions over a period of years and to tax utilities based on the amount of sulfur dioxide they emit. The proceeds of the tax would be used to develop and install "scrubber" technology on the smokestacks of coal-fired power plants. I could not get enough traction while Republicans controlled the Senate to advance that idea. When Democrats took control in 1987, Mitchell and I tried again. But it took three more years, a new president, and a worsening problem before we landed an acid rain amendment in the revision of the Clean Air Act in 1990.[12]

From 1983 until Republicans lost the majority, I chaired the environment committee's subcommittee on toxic substances; thereafter, I was its ranking Republican member. That committee had jurisdiction over federal efforts to keep drinking water safe for consumption. The last congressional move in that direction had been made in 1974, and it had not been very effective. It ignored nonpoint groundwater contamination, even though groundwater was the source of a large share of the water dispensed by the nation's household taps. What's more, the Environmental Protection Agency (EPA) had set safe-consumption levels for fewer than two dozen of the scores of pollutants commonly found in drinking water, though the 1974 law had authorized the agency to do more. States were unhappy with the confusion the 1974 law had created. They wanted more definitive answers than they were getting to the question, "How clean does water have to be to be safe?"[13]

I got busy with the help of a superlative staffer I had brought with me to Washington from Minnesota, Jimmie Powell. In my first term Jimmie did an impressive job helping my Intergovernmental Relations subcommittee make the case for the policy design I favored—setting federal standards, then empowering state and local governments to meet those standards and improve on them as they saw fit. He was a whiz at finding examples of that approach's effectiveness. Jimmie and I worked together to assemble the Safe Drinking Water Act of 1986. It directed the EPA to set maximum contaminant levels for eighty-three substances "known or anticipated to occur" in drinking water. It pushed the agency to be more aggressive in enforcing

I held a news conference on acid rain on October 25, 1983, but my initial efforts to pass legislation addressing the problem were not successful. Jerry Fearing, the *St. Paul Pioneer Press*'s political cartoonist, depicted the country's response in August 1985. *Courtesy of the author*

the law. And it offered states a carrot and a stick to protect ground-water. It said they must develop wellhead protection programs to keep contaminants away from the areas around wells that supply their drinking water, and it provided federal cleanup grants to com-munities that rely solely on aquifers experiencing pollution. Presi-dent Reagan signed this bill into law on June 19, 1986.[14]

That success buoyed me as my toxins subcommittee turned next to improving the Clean Water Act of 1972. It was riddled with loop-holes that I believed should be closed. Two years of persistence and a lot of bargaining finally produced a bipartisan bill in the fall of 1986 that passed both chambers unanimously. But President Reagan used his pocket veto power to stop it. He objected to the cost of one of my favorite features in the bill, an $18 billion revolving loan fund—known today as the Clean Water State Revolving Loan Fund—to help the cities that needed the most support to construct and upgrade sewage treatment plants. It was a version of the Minnesota revenue-sharing model—federal funding sent via needs-based formulas to state and local governments, which controlled how it was spent. It relied on partnerships between the EPA and state governments that were geared to building more vigorous water protection programs at the state level.

That design did not bother the president, but the bill's cost did. I vented my displeasure to reporters after the pocket veto. "This ad-ministration has broken a pledge to state and local governments," I sputtered. Early in 1987, the new Democratic majority in the Senate sent nearly the same bill to Reagan, who vetoed it a second time. This time, there was no Republican majority to block a veto override. The bill became law over Reagan's veto on February 4, 1987.[15]

I was at work on my next major water bill as the 1988 campaign season arrived. Called the Groundwater Research, Management, and Education Act of 1988, it asserted for the first time a federal interest in keeping groundwater free of contamination. The bill included fund-ing for grants to states, to be used for pollution abatement projects as states saw fit. Though it was a small start, I still consider that kind of federal-state partnership the right approach for dealing with a problem that remains with us, particularly in agricultural regions of the country.[16]

My record on the environment was strong enough to win me the endorsement of both the Sierra Club and the League of Conservation Voters. By that time both organizations more often backed Democrats than Republicans. But I can attest that as late as 1988, it was possible to be an environmentalist and a Republican in good standing, at least in the polls. Marlene Fluharty, chair of the Sierra Club's national political action committee, praised me for having the third-best pro-environment voting record in the Senate in 1985–86. And in an April 1988 Star Tribune Minnesota Poll, I had a 12 percentage point lead over Skip Humphrey.[17]

The Minnesota Independent-Republican Party was still quite tolerant of its "middle-of-the-road" and occasionally contrarian US senator. I had taken occasional heat from conservatives in the party when, for example, I had refused to support cuts in income-related social programs without first enacting a replacement for them. (My motto was "replace before repeal," the reverse of the now-infamous anti–Affordable Care Act slogan.) But there was nary a whiff of any serious effort to challenge me in the 1988 primary.

Nevertheless, the Republican presidential contest in Minnesota that year provided a marker of how far the party of Stassen had shifted to the right during my years in Washington. During the weeks preceding the nonbinding presidential straw poll conducted at Minnesota's February 23 precinct caucuses, the national press was covering the GOP contest as if it were already a two-man race between vice president George H. W. Bush and Senate majority leader Bob Dole. The 56,000 Minnesotans who cast ballots at their Tuesday night caucuses evidently didn't see it that way. They put Dole in the lead, with 42 percent of the vote. In second place was television evangelist Pat Robertson, with 28 percent. Robertson had never held elective office, yet was seen as qualified for the post on the strength of his television presence—a harbinger of things to come. His stridently antiabortion, "family values" campaign had particular appeal among Republicans in the northern Twin Cities suburbs and northeastern Minnesota—the latter result previewing a shift in voting habits in what had long been a DFL stronghold. In third place with 15 percent of the vote was New York US representative Jack Kemp, a former professional football player who advocated for lower taxes in the name of supply-side economics, which held that the economic stimulus that tax cuts provide can generate enough growth to make the tax cuts pay for themselves. That idea has remarkable staying power, despite little evidence at either the federal or state levels that the trick actually works. Though Kemp didn't rack up a large vote total, he had some of the state party's most prominent conservative voices on his side, including US representative Vin Weber from southwestern Minnesota, an ally and confidant of House GOP rising star Newt Gingrich. Vice President Bush—who would go on to be the party's nominee and President Reagan's successor—came in fourth in Minnesota, with a meager 11 percent of the straw vote.[18]

I had an early sense that Bush wasn't going to sell well among Minnesota Republicans. What's more, my Senate effectiveness depended on maintaining a good relationship with my caucus leader, Bob Dole. For those reasons, both my colleague Rudy Boschwitz and I decided we were not going to take sides in our party's presidential nomination fight. We resolved to stay neutral until the nomination was decided.

One day on the Senate floor, during a close vote that required the vice president to preside and cast a vote in the case of a tie, Bush called the two of us up to the dais. In as accusing a voice as I'd ever heard from George Bush, he told us he felt betrayed by our support for Dole's presidential bid. "The least you could do is stay out of it," he said angrily. We assured him that he had been misinformed. "No way would we even think about doing that!" we said. We reminded him that I was up for election in 1988, which gave me particular incentive to stay neutral in the presidential race. "We want people to know we'll support either of you when endorsed," we said. I'm not sure we convinced him.

Bush would have been entirely acceptable to the Republican Party that Harold Stassen built in Minnesota. He even had Minnesota ties that included a training assignment at Fort Snelling during World War II and abiding friendships with his Phillips Academy schoolmate Wheelock Whitney, Wheelock's sister Sally Pillsbury, and his fellow Yalie George Pillsbury—all prominent Minnesota Republicans. But blue-blooded Bush, the son of a Wall Street banker and US senator from Connecticut, was not conservative enough for the people who had come to dominate the party that still used the name Independent-Republican. Some of those people were not satisfied by what I thought were hugely important accomplishments during the Reagan presidency, and others refused to extend any credit for those accomplishments to the vice president.

Dole's Minnesota appeal was another sign that my party had withered in the urban centers of Minneapolis, St. Paul, and Duluth but had gained strength in Greater Minnesota—particularly in farm country. A Kansas senator who took a back seat to no one in farm policy expertise, Dole performed best in the straw poll in the agriculture-dominated counties along the state's western and southern borders. It mattered that his Minnesota campaign chairman was Cal Ludeman, the farmer from Tracy who had been the Independent-Republican nominee for governor in 1986.

Dole was an old-line Republican conservative, a philosophical vein that included Robert Taft and Richard Nixon. Yet as a Senate leader, he had the ability to put his foot into any number of camps and make things happen. His great skill was in knowing his Senate colleagues and their political circumstances very well. He knew when to rein people in and when to let go. That kind of leadership is very effective in a legislative body and would have been an asset in the White House, too. But in a presidential contest, it didn't suit the party activists who were motivated by single-issue causes and crusades.

That was the mindset of the Robertson supporters, for whom the abortion issue was at the pinnacle of politics, and to a lesser degree the Kemp backers who wanted candidates to take Grover Norquist's "no new taxes" pledge. And it didn't work on the national level. Dole was soon overwhelmed by the better-financed and better-organized Bush operation. Bush went on the attack after a weak start in the 1988 primaries, with ads accusing Dole of occasionally voting to raise taxes—a record shared by nearly every senator who had served as long as had Dole, a senator since 1969. Those messages were crafted by the consultant who had been my own campaign's guru, Roger Ailes. They didn't make me proud, but they turned the tide. Bush carried all sixteen primaries on Super Tuesday, March 8, and left Dole in the dust after that. Not for the first time—and certainly not for the last—the presidential preferences of Minnesota's Republicans differed from the nation's.

Having sidled up to the Norquist/Kemp libertarians in order to clinch the nomination, Bush wasn't about to turn back until he had won the White House. Anti-tax rhetoric became a prominent part of every Bush speech during the run-up to the national convention. On August 18 as the nation watched, he accepted the nomination with words written by Peggy Noonan: "Read my lips: No new taxes!" Every subsequent news summary of the convention included that moment. It would be better remembered, for both good and ill, than any of the kinder, gentler things he uttered at other times. That pledge from a Republican with Bush's pedigree—and the fierce resolve of party activists to hold him to it—made clear to me that a new day had dawned in Republican politics. And Republicans like me were going to have to watch out.

9 RELATIONSHIPS

T HE SKEPTICISM George H. W. Bush and I faced on our party's right flank didn't perturb either of us much during the remainder of the 1988 campaign. We both cruised to victory. Bush won 426 of 537 Electoral College votes and—with the help of some memorably nasty attack ads designed by Roger Ailes—topped Democrat Michael Dukakis by almost 8 percentage points in the popular vote. I had an even easier time with Skip Humphrey, winning with a margin of more than 15 percentage points. The state house (the senate and governor were not on the ballot) stayed in DFL control, but Independent-Republicans gained two seats.[1]

By the numbers, not much changed in Congress either. The Democrats' 55–45 advantage in the Senate held firm, and Democrats actually picked up two seats for a 260–175 majority in the House. But with the third straight election of a Republican president, Democrats in the Senate brought to the 1989 session a heightened awareness that bipartisan compromise is what makes representative government work. Many Americans had just shown with ticket-splitting votes that they liked the productive government they had seen in the last half of the Reagan years. Democratic senators chose a new majority leader with that in mind. George Mitchell of Maine—a state with a political orientation similar to Minnesota's—replaced Robert Byrd of

West Virginia, who had been the Democrats' leader for the previous dozen years.

Mitchell's office was next to mine in the Russell Senate Office Building. When the news of his election arrived, I headed to his office and wrapped him in a big hug that came right from my heart. George had been my friend since he came to the Senate a year after I did, replacing Senator Edmund Muskie, who had been appointed secretary of state. George became my ally on environmental legislation, health reform, and more. He consistently sought to set sound policy rather than score political advantage. With Mitchell in the lead on the Democratic side and Bob Dole on ours, I trusted that "every state would be heard from," regardless of its senators' party affiliation, and progressive policy would result.

Early in his tenure, Mitchell reached out to the new Republican president and signaled a willingness to cooperate to get things done. He also gave Dole an assurance that sounds quaint today: "I would never, ever surprise him, in a procedural or other way. . . . I had no desire or interest in embarrassing him in any way." Mitchell and I were already at work on a renewal of the Clean Air Act and better accommodations for the nation's disabled citizens via what would become the Americans with Disabilities Act.[2]

More generally, I knew Mitchell shared my thinking about the importance of designing national policy to pay for access to services that meet essential human needs—health care, clean air and water, higher education, housing, transportation, and support for the disadvantaged and disabled. We agreed about the need to bring out the best in private markets, and to give states and local governments the flexibility to deliver services in ways that maximize efficiency and individual choices wherever possible. We shared a conviction that if we could do all that well, we would deliver the progress the word "progressive" implies.

As the Senate's majority leader, George's role was determining the Senate's agenda. But he was also eager to work with President Bush to secure a lasting peace as the Soviet Union's long-expected collapse became imminent. He was uniquely skilled in diplomacy. In fact, historians may better remember Mitchell as an international peace-maker than as a Senate leader. After leaving the Senate in 1994, he represented this nation well as subsequent presidents sought to end chronic conflict in Northern Ireland and the Middle East.

Bush's willingness to play his part in bipartisan policy making with a Democratic Congress qualifies him as a progressive Republican. So does the political sacrifice he made in 1990 for the sake of federal fiscal stability in the face of a weak economy and a drop in expected tax revenue. He broke his "read my lips" pledge and agreed to a budget that raised the top-bracket individual income tax rate from 28 percent to 31 percent and made several other revenue-raising modifications to the federal tax code. He faced a ferocious howl from the Republican right (including from his own vice president, Dan Quayle) after he announced his intentions in June. But he stuck to a position that Harold Stassen—by then an elder statesman living again in Minnesota—and my old boss Harold LeVander likely cheered: government must operate within its means.

That was very much the position that the dean of Minnesota's congressional delegation, Bill Frenzel, brought to Washington in 1970 and was still stressing in 1990 as ranking Republican member of the House Ways and Means Committee. Bill was the lead House Republican in the joint House-Senate-administration budget talks that summer and fall. It was his last year in office. After twenty-eight years of every-other-year elections—eight years in the Minnesota house and twenty in Congress—Bill and his wife, Ruthie, were ready for a slower pace. But lame-duck status did not diminish his responsibilities in 1990, or alter his influence as one of the most respected fiscal watchdogs on the Hill. Neither did it change his view that, over time, budget deficits inflict serious damage on the nation. He was on a mission that summer to set the nation on a sounder fiscal course without harming either the economy or people in need of government support. He argued that minimizing the federal deficit was so important that it warranted a modest increase in federal taxes.

Bill explained his position in an essay in the *Star Tribune* a few days before the 1990 election. The essay's aim was to boost my colleague Rudy Boschwitz, who was in an unexpectedly close reelection race with DFLer Paul Wellstone. But Frenzel also explained his own vote a few days before in favor of the second-largest deficit reduction bill in US history—the one that Bush would sign in violation of his "read my lips" promise. It had become "essential for Congress to make some progress in meaningful long-term reduction of the federal deficit," he wrote. He had convinced me weeks earlier. Both Boschwitz and I voted yes for the tax increases in the budget bill.[3]

In Minnesota's southwest-suburban Third District, Frenzel was succeeded in 1990 by state senator Jim Ramstad, a moderate who assured voters in each of his nine congressional campaigns that he shared the values of Bill Frenzel. Both of their good names are still sometimes invoked during campaigns by the seat's current occupant, Republican representative Erik Paulsen, though the parallel is harder to detect. In 2017, Paulsen voted for a tax bill that is forecast to raise the federal deficit by at least $1 trillion over the next ten years, in order to deliver a tax cut that is skewed dramatically and permanently in favor of wealthy Americans, while offering temporary relief to everyone else. I doubt Frenzel would approve.

"Republicans used to be interested in not running continual rivers of red ink," Bill told the *New York Times* in 2012. "If that meant raising taxes a little bit, we always raised taxes a little bit. Nowadays taxes are like leprosy, and they can't be used for anything, and so Republicans have denied themselves any bargaining power." I miss that sensible voice. Bill died in 2014 at age eighty-six.[4]

In an economic sense, the 1990 tax increases came at an inopportune time. The nation was sliding into a modest recession. But that argument wasn't what drove the red-hot anger over the budget bill in my party's right wing. A sense that Bush had lied to them was part of their fury. So was their desire to convince an increasingly demanding group of libertarian-minded donors that they could count on Republicans to lighten government's impact on high-income individuals and corporations. An increasingly vocal cohort among congressional Republicans argued that only if they swore that they would never, ever raise taxes and then made good on that promise could the party move into the majority. Ending Democratic rule in Congress had in their minds become an end so desirable that it justified norm-busting means.

No one was more intent on breaking the Democrats' nearly forty-year hold on the US House, or more certain about how to do it, than Representative Newt Gingrich. A former college professor, Newt was first elected to Congress in 1978. He had been the first Republican elected in decades from his suburban Atlanta district, and he believed he knew how to work that same political magic around the country. We were both considered at the time to be progressive. But I saw a key difference between us. My aim was to be effective for my state. Newt's ambition was to rise within the ranks of the US House and work his will on the body as he climbed.

Gingrich began cultivating a subcaucus of younger conservative House Republicans that took the name the Conservative Opportunity Society when it was formally announced in 1983. With strategic help from one of his closest allies, Representative Vin Weber from southwestern Minnesota's Second District, and Wyoming representative Dick Cheney, Gingrich used that group as his springboard to election as House minority whip in 1989.[5]

From an institutional standpoint, the distinction between Gingrich's and Mitchell's thinking about what the American system of governance requires could not have been clearer. Mitchell respected the leadership role the Republican president was constitutionally obliged to play. He held that his job as Senate majority leader was to cooperate with Bush whenever possible. Gingrich had a much different view. He faulted Bush and his own party's leaders in Congress for failing to challenge Democrats whenever and however possible. He saw House Republican leader Bob Michel of Illinois as an impediment to his goals. Michel was a practitioner of civility who believed that professional courtesy aided the effectiveness of all members, whether in the majority or minority. Gingrich saw the House's norm of civility as its Achilles' heel, one he could target. He started by charging House Democratic leaders with violations of ethical practices.

I could not have disagreed more with that tactic. Since my days working in the Minnesota governor's office, I have seen repeatedly that effective policy making depends on strong personal relationships. In the US Senate, those relationships are key to assuring that "every state is heard from." Effective House members would have said the same. By seeking to damage interparty relationships, Gingrich was targeting something fundamental to an institution on which America and the world had relied for two hundred years.

Gingrich aimed high. His target was the Democratic Speaker of the House, Texan Jim Wright. Wright had written a book, *Reflections of a Public Man,* in 1986 and sold copies to trade associations and other groups in lieu of accepting speaking fees. In April 1989, the House Ethics Committee reported that it had found "probable cause" to charge Wright with using book sales to evade House limits on the acceptance of honorariums from interest groups. It also accused him of improperly accepting gifts from a Fort Worth developer. Wright denied that he knowingly violated any rules. But after six weeks of pummeling in the press, he had had enough. Decrying the spirit of "mindless cannibalism" that had infested the House, Wright resigned from office on May 31.[6]

Gingrich's strategy would lead to trouble for me for which I was totally unprepared. I, too, had written a book—two of them, in fact, published by Piranha Press of St. Louis Park, Minnesota. *Prescription for Change,* published in 1986, was a six-year summary of my public speeches that emphasized how consumer choice could be the key to better results and lower costs in health care. *Neither Madmen nor Messiahs* was a book on national security policy written in 1984, before I became chair of the Senate Intelligence Committee. Relying on a Senate Ethics Committee ruling issued to Maine senator Bill Cohen that he could receive honorariums for appearances to speak on his books without violating the Senate's rules on outside income, I did the same. As a result, I, too, came under investigation by a committee of my peers.

The first inkling of trouble came in the last weeks of my 1988 campaign, when a group of DFL lawyers filed a complaint with the Senate Ethics Committee. The initial charge: taking my son Mike with me on a trip to Puerto Rico at the expense of a Minnesota-based company that manufactured medical devices and drugs on the island. I thought the public purpose of that trip was clear. I was gathering facts concerning a federal tax break granted to companies that manufacture goods in Puerto Rico, a matter that would come before the Senate Finance Committee on which I served. I wasn't much concerned until, in February 1989 at a reception hosted by the American Israeli Political Action Committee, Robert Squier, the Democratic Party's presidential campaign guru and a consultant to Skip Humphrey's campaign, came up to me, put his finger on my chest, and said, "Don't get too comfortable in this job, Durenberger. We're going to get you yet."

In March 1989, mine became the first of a half dozen cases that would be filed that year against senators from both parties, including two national heroes, Democrat and former astronaut John Glenn of Ohio and Republican and former prisoner of war John McCain of Arizona. The Senate Ethics Committee decided it needed outside counsel, and chose Bob Bennett, a brother of Reagan-era secretary of education Bill Bennett, to do fact-finding normally done by staff. Bob made a point of telling me apologetically years later that he decided he had to make the first case on his docket count. I was confident that I had done nothing intentionally wrong, and that if I had erred, my mistakes would be understood and could be corrected. Hence, I gave the ethics committee unfettered access to my files, both personal and official. That meant that more than my expensing of a trip to

Puerto Rico would come under scrutiny. Bennett took full advantage of my naïveté.

Bennett's recommendations to the committee concerning me were agonizingly slow in coming. But come they did on June 12, 1990. He functioned as a de facto prosecutor. Without even a pretense of input from my side, he charged me with wrongfully padding my $98,400 annual Senate income through a book marketing deal, reimbursement for the use of a friend's condominium in downtown Minneapolis, and acceptance of free limo rides in Boston in 1985 and 1986. He recommended that the Senate formally denounce me for "knowingly engaging in unethical conduct" which "brought dishonor and disrepute to this institution." Denunciation is a seldom-employed official scolding. It stings personally and politically. But it allows a senator to publicly ask for forgiveness and continue to serve.[7]

Once again, I was too trusting of colleagues. My attorney and I negotiated a plea agreement with New Hampshire senator Warren Rudman, the ethics committee's ranking Republican. I agreed to the word "denouncement" and that I would ask the full Senate to vote in the affirmative on that motion. That 96–0 vote (Boschwitz and I both voted "present") happened on July 25 after two hours of remarks by colleagues on both sides of the aisle that sought to ease my pain with praise for my character and contributions. In exchange, I received Rudman's pledge that none of the office and personal files the ethics committee had obtained would be turned over to the Justice Department, where they might be used for purposes of criminal prosecution. I held up my end of the deal, even though it meant denying me the opportunity to demonstrate in court the honest intentions surrounding both the condo deal and the publication of *Neither Madmen nor Messiahs.* My nemesis on the committee, arch-conservative Republican senator Jesse Helms of North Carolina, did not.[8]

That betrayal led to nearly three years of federal court proceedings that finally ended in a plea bargain in August 1995. I pled guilty to five misdemeanor charges of converting public funds to private use, totaling $425. In exchange, prosecutors dropped more serious charges. Judge Stanley Harris said I was "a fine human being" who "had accomplished a lot" and added that after reading my case, he did not understand why it was even before him for trial or disposition. He sentenced me to a $1,000 fine and a year on probation. Along the way, I also lost my license to practice law in Minnesota. And I repaid the Senate more than $40,000 for improper reimbursement for staying in the Minneapolis condo between 1983 and 1988.[9]

Nearly three decades later, this story is still painful and embarrassing to tell. I was a man of modest means in a rich man's club. If anything, I was guilty of pushing too hard to maximize my income by taking advantage of what I believed were legitimate expensing maneuvers. I was doing so at a time of personal distress. My wife Penny and I separated in 1985 and divorced some years later. I say that not to make excuses but to explain the context of my actions.

I now see this episode as part of a larger story—the end of bipartisan comity, a crucial institutional norm, in the US Congress. Instead, "ethical practices politics," a rough game of partisan "gotcha," has taken its place and done lasting damage. Less than two years after my censure, the same search-and-destroy mentality that targeted me would end the elective careers of two talented Minnesota congressmen, Republican Vin Weber and Democrat Gerry Sikorski, both accused of writing overdrafts on their House bank accounts worth tens of thousands of dollars. They too said they were following what they understood to be accepted practice, but norms and customs were no longer a defense. Weber declined to run again in 1992; Sikorski was defeated by former TV anchorman Rod Grams, a Republican who stood well to the right of the state's Stassen line. The House bank scandal was a theme pounded by Gingrich and his allies in campaigns around the country that year and in 1994. They argued that under Democratic majorities, Congress had lost its ethical mooring, and only a Republican majority could restore it. Ironically, Gingrich himself was censured by the House for an ethics violation only a few years later.

More ironic is this: The years in which the House and Senate ethics committees have been zealously seeking to punish activities that "bring discredit" to those bodies are the same period in which public approval of Congress has dropped, at one point in 2013 reaching a low of 9 percent.[10]

To be sure, some members of Congress have breached the public trust in significant ways and deserved to lose their standing or their seats. But today, those who serve in the US House or Senate are subjected to such exceedingly harsh scrutiny that one mistake is sufficient to rain down partisan hellfire. Campaign rivals often seek to build themselves up by tearing the other person down. Under those conditions, many good people choose not to run. The public questions the capacity of its institutions to accomplish anything. And the nation is not well served.

Politics being a human activity, it's prone to occasional episodes of chaos and drama. Had it not been for one such outbreak, the 1990 election might be remembered as the Independent-Republican Party's decisive departure from the progressive tradition that began with Harold Stassen. Instead, that election gave the Stassen line a brief new lease on life.

In 1990, DFL governor Rudy Perpich decided to seek an unprecedented fourth term, despite a rocky third term that had eroded his popularity. One midsummer poll showed him with a politically perilous 60 percent disapproval rating. He faced a serious primary election challenge from a member of his own administration, commerce commissioner and future state attorney general Mike Hatch. Though Perpich outpolled Hatch by nearly fifty thousand votes in the September 11 DFL primary, he was vulnerable.[11]

It was a situation that might have tempted Republican voters to cast DFL ballots in the primary for the candidate they deemed easier to defeat, as some GOP voters had done in storied primaries decades earlier. But in 1990, Republican voters had their own contest to decide. The Independent-Republican Party had endorsed Jon Grunseth, an Ecolab corporate executive who had been a party insider since losing a congressional bid to DFLer Rick Nolan in southwestern Minnesota's Sixth District in 1974. But in Minnesota, party endorsement does not decide the nomination. The primary does, and Grunseth had two serious challengers: Arne Carlson, a former Minneapolis legislator then serving his twelfth year as state auditor, and Doug Kelley, a Twin Cities attorney and my former chief of staff. Kelley had my support.

I had a connection to the other candidates as well. Grunseth had been my 1982 campaign's finance director. He met his future wife, Vicki, during that campaign; she served as my finance director in 1988. Grunseth's campaign manager Leon Oistad had managed my 1988 campaign. My ties to Carlson were less personal but still important. Carlson had been a Democrat as a young man, employed as an organizer by Hubert Humphrey's 1960 presidential campaign. By 1962, he had become an independent, sufficiently attracted to then-governor Elmer L. Andersen to volunteer on Elmer's reelection campaign.

Elmer had a good eye for talent. As he related in his autobiography, Elmer took Arne aside and said, "I think you ought to be a Republican." He went on to explain, "Republicans would rather do things independently and privately. Liberal Republicans are fully willing to use the government when it is the only agent that can accomplish something, or when it can perform a task better or more to people's liking than the private sector could. But Republicans do not turn to government first."[12]

That sums up Carlson's philosophy, and mine, too. I'm not sure Grunseth would have concurred in 1990. He courted both the evangelicals and the libertarians that had come to dominate the Independent-Republican organization. Both Kelley and Carlson were pro-choice on abortion. Grunseth had once told the *Star Tribune*'s Betty Wilson that he might consider severe fetal deformity as an exception to an abortion ban. But that position wouldn't do in a convention endorsement contest against a fervent abortion opponent, David Printy, a former state agency head. To dispatch Printy, Grunseth made a mantra of his opposition to abortion "except in cases of rape and incest

Governor Arne Carlson with schoolchildren, about 1997. *Courtesy of Arne Carlson*

and to save the life of the mother." He uttered that line repeatedly during the primary campaign. For many IR voters, that was all they needed to know. Grunseth easily won the primary, garnering 70 percent of the vote.[13]

Then a trickle of stories began to appear about Grunseth's personal life, including his spotty record of paying child support after a 1983 divorce. Grunseth complained bitterly that he was a victim of a Perpich smear, though he had no evidence of Perpich's involvement in the stories. Then on October 14 came a bombshell: The *Star Tribune* reported that at a July 4 party at his rural Hastings home in 1981,

Grunseth had swum naked with his fourteen-year-old daughter and several of her friends, then ages thirteen to sixteen, and had tried to remove the bathing suit of one of them. He had also served the girls alcohol, two of them said in a sworn affidavit. Others present corroborated their story. Grunseth insisted, again without evidence, that the stories were lies orchestrated by the DFL governor.

The newspaper pressed on with aggressive reporting. On October 28, the *Star Tribune* reported that another woman, Tamara Taylor, had made a sworn statement about Grunseth. She said that she had been his mistress for nine years, a period that included both of Grunseth's marriages.[14]

Later that day—nine days before the election—Grunseth dropped out of the race. A legal skirmish ensued about whose name would appear as the Republican candidates for governor and lieutenant governor on the paper ballots Minnesota uses at the polls. On November 1, the Minnesota Supreme Court settled the question with a 5–2 decision. The names would be the candidates who finished second in the primary, Arne Carlson and his running mate, Joanell Dyrstad.[15]

Two days later, more damaging news broke for Republicans. Rudy Boschwitz, seeking a third term and facing an unexpectedly stiff challenge from DFL political science professor Paul Wellstone, was said to be behind a campaign letter addressed to "the Minnesota Jewish Community" that faulted Wellstone for not being active in a synagogue and for raising his children as non-Jews. Wellstone's wife, Sheila, was Christian. Interdenominational and interfaith marriages are common in Minnesota. Boschwitz's letter struck many as an attack on such unions. It more than backfired.[16]

The upshot: the two Rudys who had been leading Minnesota political figures in the 1980s both were defeated on November 6, 1990. Though Boschwitz had led in the polls all year, he lost to Wellstone by nearly fifty thousand votes. Perpich came in sixty thousand votes behind Arne Carlson—a man who ten days earlier had been attempting a write-in campaign to keep his political career alive. Minnesotans themselves could scarcely believe what their votes had wrought. A

Democrat more liberal than anyone since Hubert Humphrey would inspire the next generation of DFLers as the state's next US senator. That party would shift to the urban left without the moderating pro-business, pro-life, and Greater Minnesota influence that Perpich had supplied. Meanwhile, my Independent-Republican Party would again have a governor who embraced that unique party name and all it stood for. Carlson was determined to govern in the style of Stassen, Youngdahl, Andersen, LeVander, and Quie—whether our party's activists liked it or not.

Carlson had his hands full in 1991 with a state budget that was again awash in red ink and a DFL-controlled legislature only too eager to make the new "accidental governor" look bad. That may be why he wasn't a prime mover of what may have been the 1991 legislature's most significant accomplishment. It made Minnesota the first state in the nation to authorize "chartered" schools—that is, government-funded schools that are established by contract (or charter) with authorizing entities and operate independently of conventional public school districts. Allowing groups of teachers or other interested entities to charter new schools was hailed as a way to bring market forces to bear on public education. It would spur innovation and, over time, improvement across the board, its leading advocates said.

At the head of that national parade was Minnesota's Ted Kolderie. The former executive director of the Citizens League, by 1991 an independent public policy consultant, had become convinced that public education as it had developed in the nineteenth and twentieth centuries would not meet the nation's need for a well-educated citizenry in the twenty-first century. Empowering teachers as professionals, allowing them to compete via a proliferation of new schools under their control, and holding them accountable for the results would provide the sea change public education needed, Kolderie told anyone who would listen.

A DFL state senator from the northwestern Twin Cities suburbs,

Ember Reichgott Junge, shepherded the bill through a minefield of teachers' union opposition. She built a bipartisan coalition to do so—all the while not knowing whether the Independent-Republican governor would sign the bill if it landed on his desk. In the Minnesota house, a larger share of minority Republicans than majority DFLers supported the bill. An imbalance of that sort usually kills a bill today. To the credit of DFL house speaker Robert Vanasek, it didn't then. And when the pioneering bill reached Carlson on June 4, 1991, he indeed signed it into law.[17]

I followed the charter school developments in Minnesota with much interest. I was drawn to the idea that charter schools could free teachers to function as the true professionals they are. Public school districts should be able to "charter" their most creative teachers to test new learning techniques or programs in schools they would help create and design. Teachers should be rewarded—and held accountable—for teaching students how to learn, as well as for imparting knowledge about the subject matter at hand. They should be allowed to devote their skills to the making of new persons. It should be exciting, uplifting work. For too many, it wasn't. When I spoke with teachers about their work, I often asked, "When was the last day you recall waking up in the morning and thinking 'I just can't wait to get to school?'" The responses were never quick and often dispiriting.

In 1991–92 several of us on the Senate Committee on Health, Education, Labor, and Pensions were ready to explore education reform once again. The topic had largely slipped off congressional agendas in the late 1980s after a spurt of attention earlier in the decade, triggered by the 1983 release of "A Nation at Risk," the report of President Reagan's National Commission on Excellence in Education that was critical of public school performance. With Connecticut senator Joe Lieberman as my Democratic partner, I introduced the first federal legislation authorizing funding for charter schools. It ran into House opposition in 1992 and was dropped from the year's major education bill in the House-Senate conference committee. I voted no on that bill for that reason and vowed to bring a charter school funding provision to a vote in the next Congress. I made good on that promise in 1994, and this time, the bill passed.[18]

Unfortunately, today charter schools have become a political football. Rather than seeing them as a means to empower teachers, conservatives see the virtue of charter schools as "consumer choice." As charter schools proliferate, they reason, the public's willingness to pay for private education with public dollars will grow, and government's control over what children learn will diminish. Meanwhile, private entrepreneurs of every kind and motive saw the opportunity to go into the school business. The results have been quite mixed, with some charter schools producing remarkable success stories among at-risk students and others seeing results much less favorable than conventional public schools in the same communities. Perhaps worst of all, charter schools in many communities are the mechanism allowing for a reversal of the hard-won racial desegregation gains of the 1960s and 1970s. It's a situation that cries out for another round of charter school reform.

My eight years on the Senate Select Committee on Intelligence schooled me well in international relations. But the most valuable lesson came not in that committee but during weekly breakfasts with twenty to thirty colleagues to discuss the role that our faith in God—not our religions—played in shaping relationships with each other and with persons who bore the responsibility of national leadership. There I came to understand that the commandment to "love God and neighbor as myself" was important to international relations. It was a lesson I began to apply in earnest shortly after my reelection in 1988, when Democrat Sam Nunn of Georgia and Republican Pete Domenici of New Mexico invited me to the Four Seasons Hotel in Georgetown to meet King Hussein of Jordan, whose country they had recently visited. I was surprised when the king asked me to pray for him and for our time together. I did. That prayerful encounter launched a lasting friendship.

Since becoming king at seventeen after his father was assassinated, Hussein had been the chief broker of efforts to resolve the conflicting claims of Israelis and Palestinians to Israel. He had his own governance challenges in Jordan, whose native Arab population was substantially outnumbered by displaced Palestinians. The two of us stayed in touch as I resolved to do what I could to build more relationships in the chronically troubled Mideast. By then I understood the meaning of Mark's gospel finale: "Go into the world, and proclaim the gospel to every creature." It was not a religious conversion theme, but a mandate to be a person on the move, bringing hope and love to others.

In August 1989, I joined Democratic US representative Tony Hall of Ohio on a trip to visit the leaders of twenty nations in Asia, the Middle East, and Africa. At each stop, the leader we met would ask why we had come. My answer, recommended by my new friend King Hussein, was "to talk about Jesus of Nazareth" and the importance of the kind of relationships Jesus modeled for successful leadership.

That response led to rich conversations. Every leader conveyed a desire for unconditional relationships with their counterparts in other countries and understood how principled belief or faith contributes to such bonds. President Paul Kagame of Rwanda, who was instrumental in ending the infamous genocide in his nation, told me, "Nations of necessity have conditional relationships, but leaders of nations need real friendships." I was impressed by Burundi president Pierre Buyoya's eagerness for his successor, a political rival, to meet with me and others in Washington to establish personal relationships. If leaders from other countries understand the value of such ties, I thought, shouldn't America's leaders aim to build better relationships among themselves?

Unconditional relationships between leaders can be an enormous aid to peace, we learned. In New Delhi, India, Tony and I were able to get "five minutes" with Premier Rajiv Gandhi and wound up spending more than an hour as he described his relationship with Benazir Bhutto, his counterpart in Pakistan. "We've been at war with each other over Kashmir for years," he told us. "Whenever the shooting starts, one of us calls the other and says, 'They're at it again.'" Those calls helped quell the violence. Bhutto told me much the same story later in Washington.

Tony and I set out to create friendships of that quality with the leaders we met. I think we succeeded with Muhammad Ershad of Bangladesh, an overwhelmingly Islamic nation. We invited him to visit us in Washington and attend the National Prayer Breakfast, a Christian-organized interfaith event. He came on his sixtieth birthday, and President Bush led the crowd of 3,500 in singing "Happy Birthday." Later with a small group, Ershad broke into tears and told us that no one—not even his parents—had so clearly expressed affection to him before that day. Ershad returned to Bangladesh and informed the leaders of opposition parties that he was willing to stand for the nation's first-ever presidential election. They put him under house arrest and then in prison, from which he wrote me on a smuggled piece of toilet paper that he knew I'd been trying to get him released on my visit to his country.

Almost exactly a year after Tony and I visited Baghdad, Saddam Hussein's armies invaded Kuwait in a fit of pique involving the Kuwaiti Al-Sabah family's refusal to comply with OPEC oil-production quotas. The move upset the delicate balance of power in the region. A few weeks later, I was back in the Middle East with a much larger congressional delegation. King Hussein told me that Egyptian president Hosni Mubarak was advising President Bush that the invasion was part of a plan by the leaders of Iraq, Jordan, and Yemen to restore the old Hashemite Kingdom. It was an outright lie, the king said.

In the meantime, Bush had sent defense secretary Dick Cheney to Riyadh to persuade the Saudis that their oil fields might be invaded next. I suspected that was a pretext for obtaining long-sought permission to base US Air Force operations in Saudi Arabia, and may have been based on Mubarak's claim. When our delegation met Mubarak in Alexandria, he indeed repeated the Hashemite-plot story and told us our president had agreed to forgive a $5 billion debt Egypt owed the United States if it would participate in the ouster of Iraq from Kuwait—the mission that would be known as Desert Storm. Congressman David Obey, a Wisconsin Democrat and the House Budget Committee chair, rose to cast doubt on Mubarak's story. We were hearing this for the first time, Obey advised. The irritated Egyptian president raised his voice in reply: "I suppose next you will tell me that if he forgives our debt, he will have to forgive Poland's and everyone else's?" I came away worried about what America was getting into.

The Senate debate on January 12, 1991, before a bipartisan 52–47 decision to authorize the United States to drive the Iraqi army from Kuwait, has been praised as among the Senate's finest. Members of the foreign affairs–related committees and nearly every member of both parties spoke on each side of the question. As I listened, I hoped that the debate was being heard in Minnesota. Never before had I known my constituents to be as genuinely alarmed at what weapons "this demon" might possess, and what might happen to their loved ones in the armed forces, as they were when war with the dictator Saddam Hussein and his feared weapons of mass destruction loomed in 1991. In response, I spent every weekend for nearly four months at an Army Reserve or National Guard Armory in Minnesota, and each member of my staff was assigned as a twenty-four-hour-a-day liaison with a military family.

I had been at least somewhat persuaded by my royal friend in Jordan that he could find a way to talk his "cousin" Saddam out of Kuwait. I was hoping to avoid war. But during the Senate debate, I received a call from the US deputy chief of mission in Baghdad who had hosted me the previous year, Joe Wilson, informing me that he was on his way to the last plane out of Baghdad. Wilson reported that Saddam and his military chiefs "are all sitting around watching the Senate debate on *C-Span,* cheering every senator who opposes the resolution. We need you, Senator, to give them a kick in the ass." Which I did, voting with the majority.

The rest of the Desert Storm story is history, to which I can add

three personal notes. One: Joe Wilson married another national security officer, Valerie Plame, who became famous when President
George W. Bush decided to go back to "finish the job" and depose
Saddam Hussein. Joe was a guest at a health policy class I was
teaching in Washington in 2003. He allowed that the United States
would be sorry if it invaded Iraq then. Comments like those were
later revealed to be a reason for Bush administration officials to leak
Plame's identity as a CIA operative, thereby destroying her career and,
most likely, endangering her informants. That's how far the second
Bush administration was willing to go to silence its critics on Iraq.[19]

Two: I made it to Amman, Jordan, to see King Hussein in August
1993, but couldn't reach him until 12:30 AM because Queen Noor's
mother had been in surgery all day. The late hour did not hamper
his hospitality. He invited me and a couple of my staff members to
his house. I had a date to cross into Israel at the Allenby Bridge at
8:00 AM. Nevertheless, I accepted the invitation without hesitation.
We arrived at 1:15 AM at what looked like a split-level Edina home
with a three-car garage and lots of kids' bikes and toys scattered
around. We spent a few memorable middle-of-the-night hours listening to the best friend America will ever have in the Middle East tell
story after story about how difficult it was to help ever-changing US
officials understand his region's politics.

Three: When we left the king's home at 6 AM to make our 8 AM
entry to Israel, the king and I exchanged business cards. In Jerusa-
lem, I met Benjamin "Bibi" Netanyahu, a Knesset deputy whose party
had just lost the election. As we talked Israeli politics, I asked the
future Israeli prime minister if he knew King Hussein. He said no, so
I pulled Hussein's card from my pocket and said, "Here's his phone
and fax. Call him." Netanyahu replied, "I can't, if I want to be head of
my party." So much for peace in the Middle East, I thought as I put
the card away.

The card came out again, twice. Once was at the Mayo Clinic in
Rochester, Minnesota, where the king and queen had come to treat
the kidney disease that would end his life. I met Queen Noor first.

She reported that "when the king asked who it was from Minnesota that wanted to see him and was told it was you, he reached into his carrying case and pulled out your card." The last time was when I was introduced to his son and successor, King Abdullah, in Washington. He looked at the card and laughed. "That fax number," he said. "I know it from memory because when I was in school in Britain, my father made me fax him all of my grades when they came out." I was very fortunate to have enjoyed such a warm relationship with one of the finest men I'll ever meet.

Health care was at or near the top of lawmaking agendas in the 1990s, in both St. Paul and Washington, for one compelling reason: cost increases were out of control. Between 1983 and 1992, the cost of health care in the United States rose by an average of 9.9 percent per year. Prescription drug prices were climbing even faster, at 12.1 percent per year, and home health care—an option in increasing demand as the disabled and elderly population grew—was climbing at 18.3 percent per year. Those increases far outstripped both inflation and Americans' tolerance.[20]

From almost the start of my Senate service, I had been trying to bring both market forces and Minnesota-tested innovation to bear on this problem. This was bipartisan work. When control of the Senate reverted to the Democrats in 1987, Senator Jay Rockefeller and I exchanged the chairmanship of the Finance Committee's health subcommittee. But we continued to work as a team to carry the committee's initiatives in Medicare, Medicaid, and other tax-financed health programs. In 1986, Rockefeller and Ted Kennedy had worked with me to design a means of providing terminated employees access for eighteen months to a company's health insurance plan—the option known for the acronym of the bill in which it was included, COBRA.

My next health project would lead to an early run-in with anti-tax thinking, which then had some Democrats in its thrall, too. I worked with Reagan administration Health and Human Services secretary Otis Bowen, a former Indiana governor, and a commission to write and pass the Medicare Catastrophic Coverage Act of 1988. It was a response to the fact that, more than twenty years after the program's inception, too many Medicare-eligible Americans still could not pay all their medical bills. Medicare did not cover prescription drugs, long-term care, or some of the other costs associated with catastrophic disability. Our committee decided that Medicare needed an update, including a first step toward drug and long-term care coverage.

Our bill passed Congress by large margins in 1988. But because it paid for new benefits with a tax on beneficiaries' incomes in excess of $80,000 a year, it was soon unpopular with members of both parties. It riled a lot of military retirees in Republican John McCain's Arizona and upset AARP members in House Ways and Means chair Dan Rostenkowski's Democratic Chicago district. Those two able legislators were formidable foes. A repeal bill passed the House with surprising ease in 1989. I tried to fight it in the Senate but could not get more than forty-six votes to oppose repeal, and the first major reform of Medicare since its inception was lost.

To his credit, Rostenkowski would not let go of the matter. He felt a responsibility to find a more politically palatable way to strengthen Medicare's weak spots. He created the Commission on the Future of Health Care and Long-Term Care and announced that it would be chaired by eighty-eight-year-old Democratic US representative Claude Pepper of Florida, a nationally recognized advocate for the elderly. Not long thereafter, Pepper died in his sleep, a victim of stomach cancer. In his honor, the group was henceforth known as the Pepper Commission. Made up of six members each from the House and Senate plus three other members, the group was charged to recommend ways to improve both acute and long-term care. Rockefeller succeeded Pepper as chair; I was the commission's vice chair with Representative Bill Gradison, an Ohio Republican who had been my conference committee partner on every health-care bill.

Never before had Congress's most knowledgeable members on health care in both parties spent so much time together designing new policies rather than acting as conferees on legislation already passed by the House and Senate. We seized the opportunity and worked our way to near-unanimous agreement on an insurance approach to financing long-term care. Then Rockefeller decided to boldly attempt to expand coverage as well. He insisted on requiring all employers to either "play" by providing a basic health benefit or "pay" for a public benefit. Republicans opposed the "play-or-pay" mandate; among Democrats, all supported the idea save for Max Baucus of Montana and David Pryor of Arkansas, who objected to the burden it would impose on small employers. Rockefeller cut a deal with them to win them over. But Republicans held firm. With a Republican in the White House, that meant the chairman's idea came to naught.[21]

Almost overnight, two things had changed. A partisan divide had opened on health policy, which had until then been a realm in which bipartisan work was the norm. And health care had moved into the spotlight as a national issue, rather than one in which states had considerable sway. The national stalemate did not stop progressive health policy innovation in Minnesota. In 1991, Governor Carlson vetoed an attempt by a DFL-controlled legislature to move the state toward a single-payer system—that "single payer" being state government. It was an ill-advised if well-meaning overreach to address a problem afflicting the entire nation: an increasing share of low-income working people did not have affordable access to health insurance. Employers of part-time and/or temporary workers often did not offer health insurance, and the cost of insurance available on the individual market was out of those employees' reach.

Carlson did something akin to what Rostenkowski had done two years earlier in Washington. First, he initiated a study of alternative ways to bring health insurance to more low-income Minnesotans. Then, when the idea arose for a state-run health insurance plan with income-limited eligibility, he assembled a bipartisan working group of eight serious legislators to work with his administration's best health-care minds to hammer out the details. That approach also assured the broad political buy-in needed not only to create such a program but also to pay for it. Carlson insisted that it not be funded by the state's general fund, which was prone to falling into deficit whenever the state's economy became sluggish. He and the legislators settled on a "provider tax," essentially a state sales tax on medical bills. They also agreed that the program would require enrollees to pay a modest monthly premium, set on a sliding scale according to their income.

The result is MinnesotaCare, which after more than twenty-five years in operation is credited with producing both better health and dignity for the working poor and cost savings for everyone else. When people have insurance, they get the preventative care and early treatment that keeps their medical bills down. And health-care providers experience fewer unpaid bills of the sort that ultimately were paid by other consumers.[22]

Today, MinnesotaCare is popular with Minnesotans, so much so that DFLers regularly campaign on expanding its eligibility to people at higher income levels. Republicans resist that idea, but they have made no frontal assault on the program. MinnesotaCare is nevertheless at risk. Since 2013, it has depended on the federal government for 90 percent of its funding, through the 2010 Affordable Care Act's Basic Health Program feature. With the ACA under heavy fire from Republicans in both the White House and Congress, Minnesotans may soon have to decide anew whether they think state government ought to help make health insurance available and affordable to people at every income level.

10 LAST HURRAH

W HEN DEMOCRATS CHOSE Arkansas governor Bill Clinton as
their presidential candidate in 1992, they were also moving
health reform into the top tier of national policy issues. At Jay Rockefeller's urging, all the Democratic candidates for president had engaged on the issue, each with a slightly different approach. Clinton's
ideas were close to Rockefeller's. He said he would require private
employers to provide health insurance for their employees or to en-
roll them in a federal health-care plan and would have the federal
government supplement the cost of coverage for Americans without
jobs. His plan wasn't "single payer"–he said he wanted to preserve
the health insurance industry–but it would have greatly enlarged
the role of government by employing market-restraining tools such
as price controls.[1]

President Bush spoke less often about health care. It's a complex
subject with a long history, marked by conflicting ideas about cause
and effect. Understanding federal health policy and its impact on
care and cost requires intense and sustained effort. A successful policy maker must understand the topic in principle, become acquainted
with credible academic and professional experts in the field, and develop proposals consistent with one's own philosophy about the role
of government while staying open to ideas emerging in the other party. Among modern-era presidents, Lyndon Johnson and Bill Clinton

were the most willing and able to do this work. Johnson succeeded in creating Medicare and Medicaid because he both anticipated and mastered the politics. Clinton was unsuccessful because, though he came close to mastering the policy, he underestimated the capacity of his political rivals to turn an ill-informed public against reform.

Bush relied on Dr. Gail Wilensky, the head of the Health Care Financing Administration at the Department of Health and Human Services, to come up with a plan he could take into the campaign. Her proposal would have done little to change the health-care marketplace, save for offering low-income people tax credits or subsidies to help them pay for insurance. I advised the president and his staff to become sufficiently comfortable with the issue to hold his own in debates, but it proved a futile effort. His poor preparation and lack of evident empathy about how increasing health insurance costs were straining household budgets struck voters as an insufficient response, given that health-care costs had risen 32 percent during Bush's term.[2]

Despite Bush's weakness on what had become a central issue for the country, I had no trouble supporting his reelection. I considered his record strong on other matters critical to the United States and the world. But in part because of a lackluster Bush campaign, the voters didn't agree. Clinton won with a hundred Electoral College votes to spare.

The new president surprised us all when he announced that his wife, Yale-educated attorney Hillary Rodham Clinton, would take the lead in designing his administration's proposal to "guarantee health insurance for every American." It was an unprecedented assignment for a first lady.

Shortly after that announcement, Mrs. Clinton called to invite me to the White House to discuss the recent history of health reform and the potential for positive change. As I prepared for that first meeting, I learned that Hillary was a fan of the novels written by my St. John's University classmate Jon Hassler. That connection eventually brought Jon and his wife, Gretchen, to a couple of meetings with the first lady at the White House, at the first of which I sat in fascinated silence for forty minutes while an ardent fan quizzed Jon about his fictional characters, starting with Miss Agatha.

My personal relationship with Hillary Clinton was off to a good start. But I was skeptical about her approach to policy formation. With a wealth of experience on health reform available on both sides of the aisle in Congress, she chose Ira Magaziner, who was unknown at our end of Pennsylvania Avenue, to lead the design team. Nuala Pell, the wife of Rhode Island Democratic senator Claiborne Pell, told me she had heard Magaziner deliver a commencement speech at Brown University about how to reform the whole institution! Evidently, incrementalism was not in his nature.

Clinton and Magaziner gathered some five hundred "experts" to advise them—which isn't difficult to do when one undertakes the sweeping change they had in mind. Lots of people considered themselves worth hearing. But unless their "expertise" includes the economics of health care, the history of private and public financing policy, an understanding of the role of the states and their variations in costs, quality, and well-being, and the politics that go with all of that, all you have is a big committee. Republican senators and House members who specialized in health policy were left out of the loop. Worse yet, so were our staff members, who, like their Democratic counterparts, were authorities on the history of reform efforts and the power of special interests to make or break recommendations for change. Those were grievous omissions.

White House secrecy made the early months of 1993 a frustrating time of waiting and rumor sharing for all of the Republicans and even some of the Democrats in Congress who regularly worked on health policy. A few months into Mrs. Clinton's project, the president announced that a reform plan would not be ready in the promised hundred days from his inauguration. He then invited a representative group of us senators—Republicans included—to lunch with him and Mrs. Clinton at the White House. We received a "progress report" and were allowed two minutes each to make recommendations. I recommended that the charismatic president spend time traveling the country, speaking about the importance of health reform, and inviting suggestions from the public. "Do that," I advised, and "the public will think you are listening to them," regardless of what was in the final bill. I saw no sign that he was paying heed.

More listening to Republicans was much in order. It was becoming clear that the real threat to reform came not from the missteps of a novice president and first lady. Rather, it came from the fierce resolve among my party's conservative wing to stymie any Democratic leader, legislative or executive. In the House, Newt Gingrich was urging fellow Republicans to make the "failures" of anything "government-run," including the health-care system, a 1994 campaign theme. In the Senate, Phil Gramm of Texas, a Reagan Democrat in Congress before switching parties, dispensed the same advice as head of the Senate Republican campaign committee. Gramm and Bob Dole were already considered Republican candidates for president in 1996. Dole knew that "government-run health care" would be an issue in that campaign.

The long-awaited "Hillarycare" bill came out in mid-September. I had a call from a White House staffer the day before, allowing me a chance to preview the proposal if I would come to the Indian Treaty Room across from the White House. I was advised that I could bring a wooden pencil but no staff or notes. I declined as graciously as I could without revealing that a lobbyist had just dropped off a copy of the full proposal at my office. What I saw was gargantuan in scope. At its core was Jay Rockefeller's "play-or-pay" requirement for large employers, along with subsidies to help low-income people afford coverage. But it went well beyond that idea to include state or regional health alliances that would offer their own health plans in competition with private insurers, and would set medical fees in each region. A National Health Board would determine the benefit set that insurers were required to provide and would assess the quality of care. Long-term care, support for struggling rural hospitals, medical education subsidies, prescription drug coverage under Medicare, abortion coverage—all that and the kitchen sink were included in

Hillarycare. Senator Arlen Specter, then a Republican (and later a Democrat) from Pennsylvania, called it "government-run health care without the single payer."

The package was so complex that it seemed only Hillary Clinton could explain it. A couple of months earlier she had appeared before a sizable group of Republican senators in the Mansfield Room of the Capitol. She hit every one of their health policy questions out of the park, impressing—or stunning—most of them into silence. That may explain why after her proposal's unveiling in September, weeks went by with little public criticism from Republicans about the plan. A few days after its public release, Mrs. Clinton came to Minnesota and described the plan to a packed audience at the University of Minnesota's cavernous Northrop Auditorium, then met with me and one hundred of the top health policy thinkers in Minnesota on the Augsburg College campus. Again, she was impressive.

But in Washington the Clintons were running into a wall of opposition that impressive answers could not penetrate. Gingrich had concluded that if the Clintons succeeded with health reform, his plan to knock Democrats out of the US House majority in 1994 would be threatened. He saw the small number of progressive Republicans who were willing to work with the Clintons as impediments. I slowly came to understand that many of our fellow Republicans had been willing to go along with progressive GOP ideas about improving access to private health insurance only as long as a Republican president was in office. Bill Clinton's election changed their attitudes. Conservative Republicans were out to get him, and we were in the way.

Working with a neoconservative group led by commentator Bill Kristol, Gingrich founded the Progress and Freedom Foundation, billed as "a market-oriented think tank" that was going to "educate policy-makers, opinion leaders, and the public about issues associated with technological change." Broadly defined, that included health care. But the new organization's real purpose was revealed when Gingrich appointed Jeffrey Eisenach, the former executive director of GOPAC, his campaign fundraising committee, as its executive

director. Gingrich, Gramm, and the new foundation got busy rally-
ing the libertarian side of corporate America for a no-holds-barred
campaign against not just Hillarycare but any version of health reform that Congress might create through bipartisan give-and-take.
They preached a strategy of obstructionism. Republicans should
participate as little as possible in Democratic-led lawmaking, Gingrich urged. Cooperation only prolongs Democratic control. Don't
work with Mrs. Clinton to improve her health-care bill, Gingrich and
his allies said when they met with Senate and House health policy
Republicans. Just kill it.[3]

I fought back, going so far as to engage in a weekly "health reform
newsletter" debate with Bill Kristol. But we GOP health reformers in
Congress were getting few if any signals from the White House about
the president's willingness to deal with us. Invitations for our staff
members to go to high-level meetings at places like Princeton University turned out to be occasions at which they were expected to talk
about concessions we might make, not what the White House might
offer in exchange. The word was that Mrs. Clinton considered Republicans like me so eager to make health policy progress that she could
get the votes of three or four of us for almost any bill she might design.

If she indeed thought that way, she was making a flawed assump-
tion. A phone call from a corporate leader in Minnesota solidified
my sense that Clinton's plan was unworkable. I knew Minnesota's
major employers, all of which provided health insurance benefits for
their employees, to be open to federal changes that promised greater access to health insurance and lower medical cost. That's why it
spoke volumes to me when the CEO of General Mills, H. Brewster
"Bruce" Atwater, called me one morning with alarm in his voice. He
was calling from the Greenbrier resort in West Virginia, where Mrs.
Clinton had just described her proposal to the Business Roundtable
for Health, which he chaired. Her frequent references to "employer
mandates" had rattled her audience, Atwater related. "I can't believe
you guys would pass this," he said. He pleaded for a more reasonable
alternative.

Pleas like Atwater's grew stronger and more urgent as the Senate Finance Committee began a markup of the Hillarycare bill, mainly to allow senators more chance to hear from its proponents and opponents. Those sessions made clear that the biggest sticking point was universal coverage. The Clinton plan would require every American to purchase health insurance. Gingrich and Kristol were doing a good job convincing Americans that such a mandate would hit them in the pocketbook, hard.

That turn of public opinion created a political dilemma not only for the Clintons but also for my own caucus leader. Dole had been willing to go along with Clinton's health reform plan for his own political reasons. He thought its negatives would backfire on Clinton by 1996. Thus, he initially signaled a willingness to support Jay Rockefeller's idea that employers should be required to provide health insurance for their employees. But when the tide of public opinion shifted, Dole had to backtrack. In early June, I spent time with him on an airplane returning to Washington from Normandy, France, where we had observed the fiftieth anniversary of the D-day landing. He made clear that he'd had enough of health reform—and that he wished it would die at someone's hand other than his own.

Soon after that trip, Dole and a minority of Senate Republicans brought out a bill that looked like President Bush's 1992 election proposal. It offered modest insurance reforms and relatively small public subsidies for low-income insurance buyers. The business groups opposing Clintoncare endorsed it immediately. On June 15, I went to the White House with two other GOP health-care "moderates," John Chafee and Jack Danforth. President Clinton complained to us about Dole's shifting position. "Every time I start in the middle, Bob Dole moves the middle to the right," he said. How could I deny it? I replied, "Mr. President, with all due respect to you and to Mrs. Clinton, forget your plan. We're beyond the plan. You can chuck my plan, chuck your plan, chuck all the plans. Let's just figure out what is health reform. Let's agree. Then let's figure out how we're going to get it done."

Again, the president failed to pick up on my suggestion. Neverthe-less, several of us senators—Republican John Chafee of Rhode Island, Democrats John Breaux of Louisiana and Bob Kerry of Nebraska, and me—decided to assume he eventually would. We set out to save health reform from both Clinton and Gingrich. Along with several others, we had been meeting for breakfast every Friday in Chafee's Capitol "hideaway," accompanied by our health staff members. We decided to invite more like-minded colleagues from both sides of the aisle to join us. Before long, we were a group of twenty-seven that included some Democrats whose names we thought would be reassuring to the White House, California's Diane Feinstein and New Jersey's Bill Bradley among them. Someone gave us the name the "Mainstream Group." We elected Chafee our chair; Breaux and I were vice-chairs.

"Act quickly" was the word we heard from the Senate Finance Committee chair, Democrat Daniel Patrick Moynihan, and from the Democrats' voice of conscience on health care, Ted Kennedy. But we were aware that our work would be for naught without at least a wink and a nod from the White House indicating that, eventually, the Clintons would meet us in the middle. That signal never came. Instead, Hillary and her supporters doubled down on her position with a July bus caravan across the country. They called it the Health Security Express; Gingrich Republicans dubbed it the Phony Express.

Meanwhile, Democrats who disagreed with portions of "Hillary-care" started seeking political cover by staking out their own plans. They sensed that failure was coming and wanted to be seen standing apart from it. The longer the Clintons waited to negotiate with the Mainstream Group, the longer Moynihan said he would wait for his Republican committee colleagues Chafee and Durenberger to come up with an answer that might garner enough Republican support to avoid a filibuster and pass the Senate.

We worked all summer. Instead of celebrating my sixtieth birth-day on August 19, 1994, I appeared at a press conference with my Mainstream colleagues to announce our reform proposal. It would have both expanded coverage and controlled costs, without either an individual or an employer mandate. Princeton sociologist Paul Starr, one of the early Clintoncare architects, said it would have been "an historic advance." But he correctly diagnosed its political weakness: "There was only one problem: It didn't have much public support. It was too big for conservatives, too little for liberals."[4]

President Clinton telephoned me that night sometime after 10:00 to wish me a happy birthday—it was also his birthday, so I returned the wishes—and to vent his frustration with my party's opposition to everything he proposed. "It's like acid in your stomach," he said, referring to the Republican opposition to his health reform proposals, as well as to Bob Dole's role as both Republican leader and potential candidate for the presidency.

The Mainstreamers continued to work through the August recess. We were all the Democratic president, first lady, and Senate majority leader had going for them. But by then, a highly charged election campaign was in full swing. Senator Dick Lugar of Indiana, a Republican who had been eager for a moderate alternative to Clintoncare, returned from a campaign swing through his state with discouraging news. "I'll tell you what my voters want. They don't want us to do anything on health care," Lugar reported. The same sentiment was heard in House races. A full-throttle advertising campaign by the insurance industry had paid off, building a sense among voters that health-care reform was not really necessary and could make matters worse. Some members of Congress doubted that voters would support any change at all.[5]

On September 19, Mitchell told Chafee he wanted to schedule four days of floor debate on the Mainstream proposal, followed by an up-or-down vote. But, he said, he needed more than four Republicans to vote to end a planned Republican filibuster because he couldn't count on all his Democrats. Chafee called us together—we were then eighteen members strong—but he could get only four Republicans, me among them, to support cloture. The next day, Gingrich told the president that if he continued with health reform, Gingrich would pull all the House Republican support Clinton needed to approve the General Agreement on Tariffs and Trade (GATT), a trade agreement that led to the creation of the World Trade Organization.

In the face of that sentiment, Senate Majority Leader George Mitchell decided not to bring any plan to the floor. The opportunity to "save" reform had slipped away. On September 26, Mitchell summoned reporters to declare health reform dead. The obstructionists had won. But they weren't gracious in victory. Bill Kristol declared his intention "to wrap health reform around the necks of every Democratic candidate in November's election," and Gingrich announced that regardless of the health reform result, Republicans would delay consideration of GATT until 1995.

In their 1996 book *The System: The American Way of Politics at the Breaking Point, Washington Post* journalists David Broder and Haynes Johnson did a postmortem on the health reform effort of 1993–94. I took some comfort from their assessment that I was seen as "the Senate's pre-eminent expert on the workings of America's medical marketplaces and on the complex set of questions that made reform so devilish a political issue." I think they agreed with what I told them: "It's a helluva problem when the parties have moved so far from the middle there's no room left for real leadership."[6]

Hillary Clinton's "Hillarycare" sales trip to Minnesota on September 17, 1993, is linked in my memory to the news I myself made on the Minnesota State Capitol steps the day before. I announced that I would not seek a fourth term in 1994.[7]

News stories announcing my decision made much of the ethics charges against me that were still churning through the federal judicial process. But as I told reporters that day, the political challenge those charges presented were not what dissuaded me from running. "This [decision] has to do with the future; it doesn't have to do with the past," I said.

I loved serving in the Senate when I could be a deal maker, the progressive thinker in the middle who could bring together people in both parties who sincerely wanted to enact sound policy. I grew frustrated when that role was not valued or was faulted by my fellow Republicans as partisan disloyalty. I took great pride in my Minnesota progressive Republican heritage, but sensed that the ideas that sprang from those roots were less and less appreciated in Washington. I also detected little interest in Republican input on the part of the Democratic president and many of his partisan allies. And I sensed that the prevailing trends in Washington would persist, further eroding my effectiveness.

A scorecard on the accomplishments of the 1993–94 Congress published by the *New York Times* a month before the 1994 election helps explain my dilemma. It mentions several dozen pieces of legislation either enacted or considered and then dropped. I was involved in at least half of the items listed, both matters done and left undone. Among the accomplishments are a number of instances in which I worked with Democrats to make their bills reflect progressive Minnesota values. That list includes a guarantee for American workers of up to twelve weeks of unpaid leave for medical emergencies and births; a directive that states provide voter registration forms in motor vehicle offices; a five-day waiting period for the purchase of handguns; making the forcible obstruction of access to an abortion clinic a federal crime, which I coauthored with Ted Kennedy; and a new higher education student loan program conceptualized by Boston University president John Silber, which I coauthored with Illinois Democrat Paul Simon. It's back today with the name "income sharing," and its opponents are the same private student loan industry that beat us then.[8]

I was also a player in the reauthorization of ISTEA, the Intermodal Surface Transportation Efficiency Act, which authorized needed expenditures in every state. Eighth District US representative Jim Oberstar, Minnesota's longest-serving Democratic congressman, and I teamed up to secure for our constituents a generous return on their federal gas tax dollars and to fund innovations such as my Intelligent

Vehicle Access to Interstates proposal—responsible for the "red-green" rush hour signal system—and Oberstar's expansion of bicycle and walking trails.

In each of those cases except ISTEA, I faced criticism from my own party—and on the matter of easier voter registration, an in-my-face scolding on the Senate floor from future Senate Republican leader Mitch McConnell. Minnesota's progressive Republicans were big believers in inclusive democracy. The party McConnell and Gingrich were building cared more about winning elections than assuring that all eligible Americans could vote.

Health reform tops the *Times*'s list of 1993–94 failures, as it does my own. The list includes other points of contention still familiar twenty-four years later: campaign finance reform, lobbying limits, the use of federal spending to stimulate the economy. I was heavily involved in efforts to pass a raft of environmental protection measures, particularly focusing on clean water. Powerful special interests got in the way then; they still do.

I was not alone in experiencing deep frustration. By my count, seventeen Republican senators who might fairly be labeled progressive had greeted President Reagan at his 1981 inauguration. By 1996, all but four of us had either departed or were retiring that year—and of those four, two, Jim Jeffords of Vermont and Arlen Specter of Pennsylvania, would eventually switch parties and a third, Indiana's Richard Lugar, would lose to a Republican primary challenger. By 1993, my progressive Republican colleagues and I were often comparing notes about the political heat we were feeling, not only from more conservative Republicans in Congress but also from our state Republican parties and Democratic operatives who eyed us as "targets of opportunity." To win reelection we likely would need to overcome serious challenges in both the primary and the general elections. We could expect to run defensive campaigns as we faced a barrage of attack ads that distorted our records. We would need to raise a prodigious sum of money and deal with the claims so much fundraising makes on our time and loyalties. We could do all that and win one more election, we told each other. But the prize would be continued service in a body in which our effectiveness was compromised. Over time, we knew, our diminished effectiveness would disappoint enough constituents to cost us an election.

Some of the same calculus was being worked by moderate Democrats who had been champions of bipartisan lawmaking. It was a sad day for me and for the Senate when Democratic leader George Mitchell announced that he would step down in 1994 after fourteen years. He was offered a nomination to the US Supreme Court that year by President Clinton. Selflessly, he declined in hopes of shepherding health-care reform through the Senate. I have no doubt that his disappointment over the fate of that work matched mine.[9]

My decision not to run was neither quick nor automatic. In fact, I had two versions of my speech prepared and ready to deliver as I drove to the state capitol on September 16—one announcing that I would not run again, the other that I would. The latter was the "cold feet" version. Fortunately, I was not bothered with such qualms that morning. The speech I chose to give was all about the joy of service. My aide Steve Moore and I sang the hymn "The Joy of the Lord Is My Strength" in the car as we neared the capitol. Steve says I had a huge smile on my face and a voice full of joy as I thanked my constituents for the gift of Minnesota values and ideas, and for the privilege of being allowed to take those ideas and values to Washington, DC.

I conveyed a similar message at the Independent-Republican state convention the following June—or at least I tried to. But as I presented the first-night keynote address, the delegates were distracted by a sideshow in the rear of the St. Paul Civic Center auditorium. Gubernatorial candidate Allen Quist had arrived for an on-air interview with Twin Cities talk-radio personality Barbara Carlson—the ex-wife of Minnesota's sitting Independent-Republican governor and Quist's IR primary rival, Arne Carlson. Barbara Carlson had arranged for the emblem of her program—a hot tub—to be installed on the convention floor and had invited Quist to join her in the tub for their conversation. As he obligingly waded into the warm water, a few hundred of his supporters gathered around and chanted "Allen! Allen! Allen!"[10]

It's hard to deliver a heartfelt valedictory when a circus act like that is splashing about in the same hall. I had been moved to see tears in the eyes of a few delegates who had been at the 1978 convention when Rudy Boschwitz and I and our similar families (four sons each) started our Senate journeys. But I was under no illusion that others in the room much cared about what I had to say. It was not my convention. I questioned whether it was still my party.

Quist, a forty-nine-year-old farmer and former political science professor and legislator from St. Peter, Minnesota, was this convention's darling. Though out of office for six years, Quist had nevertheless remained the outspoken hero of the evangelical Christians who flooded into the Independent-Republican Party in the 1980s. He had known some of them since his seventeen-year teaching career at Bethany Lutheran College in Mankato, a junior college affiliated with the very small and very conservative Evangelical Lutheran Synod, also based in Mankato. A father of ten, Quist lost his first wife in an auto accident, then married a leader in Minnesota's burgeoning Christian conservative political movement, Julie Morse. Her ambition fused with his to convince them and, apparently, plenty of others that it was possible for Quist to unseat an incumbent governor of their own party.[11]

That view involved a leap of faith. No opinion poll that spring made the case for the political plausibility of the Quist campaign. A Star Tribune Minnesota Poll in mid-May had found that Governor Carlson was viewed favorably by 56 percent of respondents—an approval rating that suggested he was in reasonably good standing with the voters. By contrast, Quist was still unknown to about half of those polled. Those who knew him didn't much like him. He scored 16 percent favorable and 23 percent unfavorable among all respondents.[12]

Those numbers should have told even political novices that Quist was unlikely to win a primary fight with Carlson. But that evidently didn't matter to the people who now had their hands on the levers of power in the Independent-Republican Party. Four years in office had not made Carlson a more sympathetic figure in the eyes of Christian conservatives. If anything, their antipathy for him had grown. Carlson had defended abortion rights and, in 1993, had signed into law a bill extending the existing ban on discrimination in state statutes to include bias based on sexual orientation. He had coped with a recession and a state budget deficit in 1991 by allowing counties to raise the sales tax. He was fiscally conservative enough to irritate many DFLers, who said his tightfistedness was too hard on the state's schools and infrastructure. But he had endorsed a major expansion of the state's role in providing health insurance and had ignored those in his party who demanded a rollback in state functions. On his watch, the state had recovered nicely from recession and was scoring high on a variety of measures of well-being. I was glad to endorse him for a second term.[13]

Quist, by comparison, promised that if elected, he would deliver a $1 billion state tax cut in 1995. If his bond with the convention delegates needed sealing, that likely did the trick. He waltzed to an easy first-ballot endorsement, winning 69 percent of delegate votes to Carlson's paltry 29 percent. The same delegates picked Rod Grams for the Senate seat I had held for sixteen years. Grams was a one-term congressman who had been a TV news anchor at KMSP-TV, a Twin Cities station affiliated with the conservative Fox network. His politics better matched Quist's than mine. Arne's lieutenant governor Joanell Dyrstad opted to challenge him in the September 13 primary. Also on the US Senate primary ballot, evidently because he simply could not stop running, was Harold Stassen himself, at age eighty-seven. (He would get more than 22,000 votes.)[14]

National political reporters buzzed in and out of Minnesota all summer, drawn by the spectacle of a state political party turning against a popular governor who, at least according to his party label, was one of their own. The *New York Times* was calling it a "Republican civil war," one reportedly being waged, albeit in less spectacular fashion, in at least ten other states. Carlson told the *Times*'s Richard Berke in June that his party had experienced a "complete religious takeover." The governor set out to prove that it was his party, not him, that was out of step with Minnesotans.[15]

Primaries in Minnesota may be intraparty elections, but they are not exclusive affairs. In a state that has opted not to require party registration, any voter can participate in either major party's primary. That meant that Carlson was well served by campaigning against Quist as if they were competing in a general election contest, addressing himself to all voters, not just party loyalists. He did just that in a barnstorming late-summer campaign, crisscrossing the state on a bus and touting a broad record of accomplishment.

Quist, by comparison, doubled down on attacks on Carlson's support for legal abortion in the campaign's final weeks, hoping that position would lure pro-life DFLers into the IR primary to vote for him. It was a less-than-plausible strategy, given that DFLers had a three-way gubernatorial primary of their own to settle and that staunchly pro-life DFLers had moved into the IR fold years earlier. Still, Quist had this much right: voters who typically favored the DFL were tempted to mark the IR side of the primary ballot that year—but not to support Quist. Carlson won the primary with nearly two-thirds of the vote. Tellingly, 150,000 more people cast votes in the IR primary in 1994 than had done so in 1990, a year that had also featured lively gubernatorial primaries in both parties. DFL turnout is typically larger than the Republicans' in Minnesota primaries, but that was not the case in 1994. More than 100,000 more ballots were cast to settle the Carlson-Quist contest than to decide whether John Marty, Mike Hatch, or Tony Bouza would be the DFL gubernatorial nominee. Marty, a state senator from Roseville who ranked among the legislature's most liberal members and who ran with DFL Party endorsement, narrowly won that race.[16]

Those results put Carlson in an enviable position. Marty, a champion of ethics in government and an early advocate for legalizing same-sex marriage and a single-payer health-care system, was arguably as far to the ideological left as Quist had been to the right. Quist may have thought he was insulting Carlson by calling him one of the most moderate Republican governors in the country. Instead, that charge bolstered Carlson's standing among centrist voters in both parties who were alarmed by the choices the two major-party conventions had made. Carlson embraced the "Independent" half of his party label as he cruised to an easy victory in November. He won a second term with 61 percent of the vote.

But the Carlson juggernaut did not extend to Joanell Dyrstad's contest with Rod Grams for the IR nomination to succeed me. Grams traded on his broadcasting celebrity status to win the primary with 59 percent of the vote and the general election against former DFL legislator Ann Wynia by some 88,000 votes. I liked Grams and endorsed him in the general election, though my mentor Elmer Andersen judged him too conservative for Minnesota and endorsed Wynia. Elmer turned out to be right.

An election defeat usually inspires soul-searching and some ideological adjustment on the part of the losing party. But Minnesota's Independent-Republican insiders did not feel like losers after the 1994 election, despite the drubbing experienced by the party's endorsed candidate for governor. Carlson was an anomaly, they assured themselves. His election was a last hurrah. The more important winner in 1994 was Grams, they said. The relative ease with which Grams convinced voters to allow a conservative Republican to succeed a progressive one in the US Senate was consistent with conservative gains all over the country.

Those gains were impressive indeed. Even though it occurred in the middle of President Bill Clinton's first term, the 1994 election deserves to rank among the decisive junctures in American governance. It brought Republicans into the majority in the US House for the first time since 1952 and elevated Newt Gingrich to Speaker of the House. Fifty-four House seats changed hands. Gingrich had promulgated a conservative policy manifesto called the Contract with America in the final weeks of the campaign, and claimed after the election that the voters had given Republicans a mandate to do what it said: cut taxes, shrink welfare, beef up spending on the military and law enforcement, and impose both term limits and a constitutional requirement of a balanced budget on Congress. Other analysts read the voters' message not as endorsement of the contract's agenda but as a housecleaning. Years of "ethical practices politics" had created the impression that congressional Democrats had become complacent and corrupt. Among those defeated were House Speaker Tom Foley of Washington and Illinois political titan Dan Rostenkowski, the "in-a-class-by-himself" income tax reformer who had been indicted earlier in 1994 on corruption charges.[17]

The geographical and philosophical heart of the national Republican Party shifted in that election as well. For the first time since Reconstruction, Republicans would outnumber Democrats in the sixteen southern states that had been deemed the "Solid South"—solidly Democratic, that is—through much of the twentieth century. With it came the long, racially charged southern history of cheap labor and acceptance of extreme income inequality as human society's natural order.

The 1994 national results left Minnesota's Independent-Republican activists convinced that despite Quist's fate, their thinking about what was best for the state and nation was spot-on. They were in the ascendency. All they needed, they told each other, was a clearer link to the national conservative movement. They needed to cease being the only state Republican party in the nation that used a distinctive name. They should again be the Republican Party of Minnesota.

That case had been made without success at the 1991 and 1993 state IR conventions. In 1995, its time had come. Party chair Chris Georgacas led the push to drop "Independent." Recent election results had "vindicated our Republican name," he said. Like-minded delegates wore buttons that said, "Simply Proud to Be a Republican." The most persuasive voice may have belonged to Allen Quist, whose popularity among the delegates who had endorsed him for governor the year before had apparently not been dented by defeat. He drew cheers when he proclaimed that Minnesota Republicans should make clear that "we are unabashedly and unambiguously part of the Republican revolution in the United States of America."[18]

Truth in advertising more than justified the name change, I suppose. But I regretted it nonetheless. By the party's own admission, there was no longer much that was distinctive about Republicans in Minnesota. Minnesota Republicans no longer saw an advantage in standing apart from the national party. They no longer sought to appeal to independents with a label that implied a philosophy only slightly right of the nation's ideological center and signaled a willingness to be creative in solving problems. They no longer cared to be cast as something other than—or something better than—committed partisans.

Arne Carlson would be in office through 1998. A few progressive Republican legislators would outlast him; two leaders among them, Dean Johnson of Willmar and Ron Erhardt of Edina, eventually would switch parties. But the progressive, problem-solving philosophy about the rightful role of government that had dominated the state Republican Party for a half century and made a difference for the nation during many of those years had nearly vanished from Minnesota ballots. It was the end of the Stassen line.

11 REVIVING THE MIDDLE

IT'S BEEN NEARLY A QUARTER CENTURY since Minnesotans could count on finding a progressive Republican option on their ballots. The Republican candidates on offer since the mid-1990s and the platforms they've embraced have increasingly rejected government at any level as a tool for solving society's shared problems—even as they have also, perversely, sought to use government to impose faith-based notions about social behavior on the whole society.

Instead of seeking to improve government's performance, latter-day Republicans have argued that government should retreat from fields such as environmental protection, education, energy, labor standards, and health care. Instead of encouraging state and local government innovation, they've sought to compel Minnesota to follow the libertarian dictates of large corporate special interests and the think tanks they fund—pressing for "no new taxes" pledges from candidates and pushing proposals such as anti-union "right-to-work" laws, an ID requirement for voting, restrictions on the growth of government spending, tax cuts for so-called job creators, and denial of government services to immigrants. Instead of embracing civil rights and equal opportunity for all races, they've put into office a president whose words and policies smack of racism. Instead of acting on the fiscal responsibility they've preached, the all-Republican federal government of 2017 has passed a tax bill that's forecast to produce record deficits.[1]

To be sure, another strain of progressive politics—the Democratic Party's version—has been available to voters on American ballots in the last twenty-five years. But many of the Democrats who embrace the progressive label espouse ideas that differ in significant ways from the thinking about government that characterized the Stassen line. For example, many of them are keen to see government as the monopoly provider of services, rather than using the government to set the framework within which private providers and informed citizens can act in the public interest. The drumbeat for government to become the sole provider of health insurance—the "single payer"—is a case in point. Many Democratic progressives call for federal action to address a wide range of problems—environmental protection and labor standards come to mind—rather than seeking ways to empower state and local governments to craft their own solutions. Seldom do Democrats talk about forging alliances with voluntary organizations or building more individual capacity for civic service. The Democratic Party's political alliance with public employees' unions has made it seem unresponsive to calls for more efficiency in the delivery of services. Progressive Republicans came to power in Minnesota in 1938 as enemies of government bloat and corruption; progressive Democrats today in many eyes have the opposite reputation.

In the absence of a progressive wing of the Republican Party, the philosophical gap between Democrats and Republicans has widened to such an extreme that it alone might suffice to explain the gridlock that has become frustratingly common when the two parties share control in Washington and statehouses. We now have what the founders feared: Two national parties to which practically every state conforms. But there's more to that story.

Newt Gingrich started something bigger than he and his allies likely knew when they demonstrated in 1993–94 the political potency of obstructionism. I'm told by some of them that they expected the norm of bipartisan lawmaking to rebound after Republicans gained control of the US House in 1994. But that norm had been demolished. In its place arose a fiercely rigid and disciplined partisanship that did not just discourage bipartisan cooperation but punished it. Those who strayed were threatened with primary challenges and the denial of campaign funds and positions of influence.

A sorry result has been the inability of Congress to pass major reform legislation with bipartisan backing. For example, Republicans love to claim that President Barack Obama and the Democrats did not give them an opportunity to "improve" the 2010 Affordable Care Act, which they tagged Obamacare. But it was the well-advertised Republican goal of making Obama a one-term president, the GOP refusal to confirm Obama's highly qualified appointee Donald Berwick to head the Centers for Medicare and Medicaid Services, and their unwillingness to supply a single vote at any stage of the enactment process that made the ACA an all-Democratic product. That gave a shaky foundation and an uncertain future to what should have been a major step forward for the country. To make matters worse, the "states' rights" party in nearly every Republican state stopped a new infusion of federal money into state Medicaid programs. And today they excuse their own refusal to help the poor access health care by their national "no able-bodied may apply" campaign. That's a shabby way for Congress to conduct its stewardship of an enterprise that's vital to American lives and amounts to nearly a fifth of the nation's economy.[2]

A trend toward a more imperial presidency—something the nation's founders would have abhorred—is another unfortunate consequence of radical obstructionism. During Obama's presidency, Republicans in Congress complained about his excessive use of executive orders. President Trump has more than kept pace with Obama in this regard, often to reverse what Obama had done. But both presidents were responding to a Congress that has repeatedly failed to act when it should. Through a combination of political risk avoidance and unwillingness to compromise, Congress has become adept at dodging decisions. Its members exhibit more interest in faulting the executive branch for its actions than in acting in the nation's interest themselves.

Another consequence of bare-knuckles partisanship, the perpetual election campaign, has been particularly disruptive to the lives of the people whom Americans send to Congress. Newt Gingrich urged members of his caucus not to move their families to Washington after their elections. Instead, he wanted them in and around the District of Columbia as little as possible—often just three days a week, half of the weeks of the year—and in their districts the rest of the time. While at home, they had two marching orders—raise money and make campaign appearances. The in-person "town hall meetings" on which members of Congress thrived thirty years ago have been abandoned for selective-issue online Q-and-A exchanges. The grueling schedules that senators and House members used to associate with the weeks preceding an election became the every-week rule. Nonstop campaigning has done much to erode the character of the policy-making branch of government. It also has deprived members of Congress of opportunities for the bipartisan relationships that once formed naturally when they lived near their legislative colleagues and attended school and community events and neighborhood parties in places like Falls Church and McLean, Virginia, or Chevy Chase, Maryland.

One consequence of this change was evident in Minnesota in 2015 when Second District Republican US representative John Kline announced his retirement after fourteen years in office. A generation ago, such a vacancy would have almost immediately attracted a small horde of ambitious office seekers. Many of them would have been midcareer state legislators, well prepared for the congressional work. But this time, weeks passed without strong candidates appearing. Several legislators who had been mentioned as plausible candidates demurred, saying they did not want to subject themselves and their families to the lifestyle of a member of Congress.[3]

The Second District seat was eventually won by a bombastic conservative radio talk-show host with no previous government experience, Jason Lewis. That illustrates another change: when choosing candidates, parties increasingly prize traits such as celebrity status and an attention-getting personality over demonstrated lawmaking skill and community service. Popular appeal is what counts, not proven ability in government. Winning elections has come to matter more than governing well.

Other long-standing norms have crumbled in the last two decades as the two parties' rivalry escalated. Respectful campaign rhetoric gave way to mean-spirited, often highly personal attack ads, debasing the nation's political dialogue. Fundraising to pay for those ads has made an ever-increasing claim on elected officials' time and attention. Redistricting and gerrymandering became virtually synonymous as the two parties turned to sophisticated computer modeling in attempts to map their way to the majority. With gerrymandering assuring safe seats to a large share of US House members, candidates no longer had an incentive to compete for independent or swing voters. Rather, candidates in each district's dominant party have been advised to appeal as strongly as possible to their fellow partisans and to concentrate on getting those voters—and those voters only—to the polls. It's no coincidence that voter turnout has decreased during much of this period.

In Minnesota's legislative races, a particularly disturbing trend has appeared in this decade. In history, economy, and culture—and in the governance structures largely established by Republican-controlled state government—Minnesota has been one state. Rural and urban Minnesotans have agreed to use state government to aggregate their resources and distribute them via need-based formulas for mutual benefit.

But since the 1980s, the Democratic-Farmer-Labor Party has so thoroughly controlled Minneapolis and St. Paul that the Republican Party barely has a pulse in the central cities. More recently, Republicans have become the dominant party in Greater Minnesota, appealing to voters with campaigns that drive a wedge between their districts and the metro area. They've claimed that "metro-centric" values are contrary to the values held dear by rural residents. They've criticized rural DFL legislators for voting in concert with those from Minneapolis and St. Paul. They've claimed that the metro area receives a disproportionate share of state spending. In fact, the opposite is true.

But it's hard to say how long an imbalance that favors Greater Minnesota will last, particularly since nearly all of the state's population growth in the past decade has occurred in the metro area.

The politics of resentment that has been ginned up in Greater Minnesota has lately stood in the way of funding urban mass transit and the Twin Cities–based University of Minnesota. That has put Greater Minnesota at risk of an urban backlash in future years. By the same token, it won't serve the nation's metropolitan areas well to entrust their futures to a single party and lose the benefits that democratic competition delivers.

These trends have been a hazard to the American experiment since its earliest days. I've thought often about President George Washington's farewell address with its warning about excessive partisanship. A "spirit of revenge" accompanies the "alternate domination of one faction over another," our wise first president warned in 1796. "This leads at length to a more permanent despotism. The disorders and miseries" which extreme partisanship brings "gradually incline the minds of men to seek security and repose in the absolute power of an individual. Sooner or later, the chief of some prevailing faction . . . turns this disposition to the purposes of his own elevation, on the ruins of public liberty."[4]

That brings us to President Donald Trump.

For progressive Republican voters like me, every recent election has required a discomfiting calculation about the lesser of evils. I am still a Republican. I am loath to disavow a lifetime of affiliation. What's more, I believe I'm upholding conservative principles when I espouse market-based approaches for delivering needed public services. But I have increasingly opted to vote for Democrats, particularly at the federal level. A Hillary Clinton lawn sign was planted in my front yard in October 2016.

Since Trump took office in January 2017, I have been frequently outraged, embarrassed, and deeply worried by much of what the president has said and done. But I also see his presidency as a direct consequence of the trends this book describes. Trump may have taken those trends to a new extreme, but he did not originate them. His disrespectful, ad hominem attacks on his opponents and his critics may be unpresidential, but they are akin to the attack ads that have become commonplace in congressional races in the past quarter century. The tax changes Trump championed and signed into law in December 2017 are highly skewed to favor the wealthy, but so have been many Republican policies since progressives lost their places in the party.

Trump's abandonment of the 2016 Paris agreement on climate change is in keeping with the pandering to corporate interests, particularly those of the fossil fuel industry, that Republicans have done for years in exchange for campaign lucre. His "America First" emphasis comes at the expense of foreign alliances that have served this nation well for more than a half century. But those ties have been disparaged for years by an isolationist and xenophobic strain in the GOP that predates Harold Stassen. It was dormant for decades but never died, and has rebounded with frightening vigor.

Trump won a minority of the votes cast for president in 2016, and polls show that his appeal is confined to a minority of Americans. But Trump is not an aberration in that respect. The changes in the American political system in the past two decades have allowed the nation to be governed by de facto minority rule for some time. I'm not only referring to the Electoral College system, which allowed Trump to win the presidency while trailing Clinton by nearly 3 million votes—though that fact should alarm anyone who understands that majority rule is crucial to legitimacy in a democratic system.[5]

I'm also pointing to the outsized influence of the political donor class; to a revolving door that spins elected officials and their staff members into lucrative lobbying positions on behalf of special interests; to campaign tactics and election laws that suppress voter turnout, especially among the non-white poor; to candidate recruitment and selection processes that vest too much power in too few hands; to the tyranny of the two-party system; and to a nationalizing of political campaigns that homogenizes local, state, and regional political distinctions, sapping the inherent strength of our federal system. Those trends have worked together to keep progressive Republican ideas and voices out of today's political dialogue. The same trends contributed to Trump's victory. It's telling that among sixteen leading Republican presidential candidates in the 2016 primaries, Trump was the least associated with the Republican establishment. Evidently, the party's insiders had left a sizable share of Americans feeling ignored, angry, and willing to take a risk on an unconventional candidate who said he would "drain the swamp."

Trump's first year in office showed that he is unlikely to alter those trends. He's demonstrated little interest in or aptitude for political reform. But in a perverse way, his presidency could yet be a catalyst for change. It could produce a backlash so intense that Americans are newly motivated to work for "a more perfect union."

The good news is that promising ideas have been proposed for moving the nation's politics in a democratically desirable direction. The story of Minnesota's progressive Republicans shows that it was possible not long ago for a centrist political movement to seize new ideas, build a constituency for them, win elections, and govern well. I submit that it still is—and that the Trump presidency is making that work urgent.

The remedies I favor start with the fundamental building block of democracy: the vote. American government can thrive only if it is a full and true reflection of "We the People." Today's government lacks that legitimizing distinction. In 2016 and for the last several presidential elections, only about three out of five eligible Americans have cast ballots. Minnesota's turnout has led the nation in those years, thanks to voter-friendly election laws—Election Day registration, no party registration requirement, easy third-party and independent-candidate access to the ballot, ample opportunities for absentee and early voting. Yet even in Minnesota, turnout has fallen in each of the last several presidential cycles, to 74 percent in 2016.[6]

To their credit—and at the urging of former Republican governor Arne Carlson, who displayed commendable elder statesmanship—Minnesota voters in 2012 rejected a Republican-proposed constitutional amendment that would have required a state-issued photo ID to vote. That's a favorite strategy of those in my party who want to make voting difficult for the low-income people who lack such ID cards. Minnesotans were wise not to buy the bogus claim that election integrity is at risk in the absence of a photo ID requirement. The rest of the nation would do well to follow Minnesota's lead in election laws. But even Minnesota can do more to encourage voting. Election Day should be a work holiday and it should occur on the weekend, perhaps over two days, to make it easier for people to get to the polls. More venues for early voting should be offered; they should be especially convenient in low-income neighborhoods where car ownership is less prevalent.

Minneapolis, St. Paul, and St. Louis Park have taken the lead on what could be a major game changer: ranked-choice voting. Ranked-choice voting allows each voter to express more than a single preference in a multi-candidate election. Minneapolis elections allow voters to rank up to three choices; in St. Paul, up to six choices have been allowed. As a result, elections that might have been won by a candidate with a relatively small plurality of the vote under the traditional voting method now produce a winner with a true majority, or something close to it. If, for example, ranked-choice voting had been used in the early Republican presidential primaries in 2016, Donald Trump would not have been able to score a victory by garnering only a third of the vote, as he did in New Hampshire's primary in an eighteen-candidate contest. He would have needed enough second-place votes from voters whose favorite candidate finished at or near the bottom of the pack to amass a vote total exceeding 50 percent. I think it's doubtful that he would have been the nominee under those circumstances.

Ranked-choice voting would do much to reverse the erosion of majority rule in America. It has other salutary effects, too. It reduces the incentive to engage in harshly negative advertising. Insult one's opponents in a ranked-choice election, and one's chances to garner second-choice votes are diminished, lessening one's chance of winning. Ranked voting is also friendly to the rise of third parties and independent candidacies—even as it allows voters who favor such candidates a chance to express their preference without functioning as "spoilers," inadvertently electing the candidate they like least. In that respect, ranked voting protects the two major parties, so long as those parties continue to enjoy wide support. But it also amplifies the voices that the two major parties currently ignore.

I've witnessed up close how even in Minnesota—a state that elected a third-party governor, Jesse Ventura, as recently as 1998—the current plurality-wins voting system discourages third parties. In 2010, I backed the gubernatorial candidate of Ventura's Independence Party, my former chief of staff, Tom Horner. He stood squarely in the Stassen line of progressive Republicans, and thus found no opportunity to run in today's Minnesota GOP. But he had appeal strong enough to win the endorsement of the *Minneapolis Star Tribune* and support from a number of luminaries in both parties. He ran an old-fashioned, highly informative campaign, appearing alongside DFLer Mark Dayton and/or Republican Tom Emmer in more than two dozen debates. Still, many voters told me they feared that a vote for Horner would lead to the election of the DFL or Republican candidate they favored least. To prevent that outcome, they reluctantly voted for a major-party candidate instead of Horner.

Tom finished in third place with 11.8 percent of the vote. No one can say whether Horner would have won if voters could have ranked their choices. But I'm certain his showing would have been much better—and even had he lost, I'm sure his ideas would have mattered more in the legislative sessions that followed. That showing in turn might have inspired more willingness to run for office on the part of able people who now refuse to consider the possibility. And it might have altered the criteria and manner by which parties select candidates. That's another part of the political process that's ripe for reform.

During the progressive Republican heyday in Minnesota, candidates were less often recruited by professional political operatives or people who already hold elective office. Rather, recruitment often happened locally, among friends who knew each other through service clubs and fraternal organizations such as the Jaycees and the League of Women Voters. Those organizations were and still are nonpartisan, but they played an important political role. They were builders of civic leadership capacity, offering their members experiences that instilled in them a spirit of community service. More than that: those community organizations schooled their members in creating and maintaining the working relationships that participatory democracy requires. That ability is underrated in today's politics, to the nation's detriment.

Today, some of the organizations that were important to civic leadership development in the twentieth century have faded away. But I've been heartened to hear about new grassroots efforts springing up since the 2016 election devoted to candidate recruitment—particularly among women. I'm also pleased to know that Minnesota groups including the League of Women Voters and the American Association of University Women are seeing membership increases. As baby boomers move fully into retirement and have more time for civic affairs, an opportunity exists for both the revival of existing civic organizations and the creation of new ones. I'm rooting in particular for the venerable Minnesota Citizens League to find a new lease on life, one that embraces its traditional role of policy analysis and advice. It could use a push from the corporate, union, and foundation leaders who recall the valuable role citizens once played in recommending remedies for public problems and are willing to finance a revival of that effort. I'm encouraged to know that more than five thousand policy-minded Minnesotans still "caucus" online, sharing and commenting on conversations with policy makers each week via the Civic Caucus, founded by the late and legendary Citizens League executive director Verne Johnson and chaired today by former Minneapolis city council chair Paul Ostrow.[7]

As partisan rivalry has intensified, legislative and congressional caucus leaders have played an outsized role in candidate recruitment. They swoop into a district with preconceived notions about who should run for office, aiming to supplant the judgments of local people with their own. They would do better to focus on shoring up their institutions' norms of order and civility, so that people of genuine talent and patriotic spirit will be willing to serve.

If that were their aim, much would change. The three-day congressional workweek would expand to four or five days, and members would be encouraged to move their families to Washington. The procedural shortcuts that empower caucus leaders to the detriment of other members would end. The ill-conceived "Hastert Rule," named for former House Speaker Denny Hastert, would be buried. No more would majority leaders refuse to bring up bills that were not supported by a majority of the majority caucus, as Hastert required in the US House. Genuine hearings and bipartisan bill markups in open committees would be the rule. Massive omnibus bills packed with unrelated items would give way to the single-subject rule, as set out in the Minnesota Constitution. What Arizona Republican senator John McCain calls "regular order" would be upheld. Implied in what John bravely said in 2017—even as he battled deadly brain cancer—is that the Senate procedural norms developed over two centuries serve the national interest and must outweigh partisan interests if the Senate is to play its rightful role as the nation's premier policy-making body. I have no doubt that the Senate leaders I much admired—Howard Baker, Bob Dole, and George Mitchell—would agree.

At the Minnesota legislature, the tendency for regular sessions to spill into the "overtime" of a special session should be curbed. I consider the legislature's move to annual sessions a mistake. Perhaps more than any other modern-era change in Minnesota's lawmaking process, that 1973–74 shift altered the composition of the legislature, and not for the better. People with substantial private-sector careers no longer felt able to serve. Minnesota was a smaller state fifty years ago when biennial sessions were the norm, and the legislative process then was not as open to public participation. Nevertheless, I be-lieve a return to biennial sessions is not only possible but also key to putting a needed focus on the state's long-range needs. The long interim between biennial sessions could be used for policy develop-ment by joint legislative committees, affording the time for legislators to deepen their understanding of complex matters. It would allow state leaders to better focus on not the next election but the next generation.

These suggestions would help not only attract able candidates but also bring more transparency and trust to the lawmaking process. But re-energizing the progressive middle in American politics will also re-quire curbing the influence of big money. More than any other force in American politics, the demands of big donors have propelled my party to the right and, to a lesser degree, the Democratic Party to the left. Big money infuses not only campaigns but also the careers of the nation's political class, as politicians and their staffs move through hugely lucrative revolving doors to become lobbyists and advisers to special interests. Politicians claim they are serving the cause of ethi-cal government through such small-bore measures as limits on free lunches and honorariums, while ignoring—and hoping the public will ignore—the huge influence-purchasing flow of special-interest money into campaigns, often via independent expenditures.

Americans are on to this scheme. They see that wealthy donors rather than "We the People" are in charge. That awareness has fueled a cynicism about representative democracy that makes this nation vulnerable to authoritarianism as never before. It can be fairly ar-gued that Trump was popular among Republican voters in 2016 in part because his personal wealth made him seem less susceptible to being "bought" by the likes of the Koch brothers. Americans desper-ately need a better way to pay for politics.

The US Supreme Court has made campaign finance reform very difficult by defining political contributions as constitutionally protected speech under the First Amendment. That is what the high court has held since the *Buckley v. Valeo* decision in 1976. In 2010, the court went further. Its 5–4 *Citizens United* ruling said that state and federal bans or limits on campaign spending by associations, including for-profit corporations, nonprofit corporations, and unions, were unconstitutional. The effect has been to open a floodgate of corporate money in American politics.

Amending the US Constitution to, for example, restore the restrictions on corporate campaign spending that were in place before the *Citizens United* decision is a tall order indeed. It's not as difficult to invite the court to reverse itself. State attorneys general and other Americans with standing should be mounting lawsuits that point out that corporate domination of political speech is not in the national interest. It's good news that nearly two hundred former governors and members of Congress from both parties—myself among them—are involved in a national effort, the Issue One ReFormers Caucus, urging more integrity and transparency in campaign funding.[8]

The high court has allowed reformers access to one potentially potent tool—donor disclosure. Yet that tool is too often denied to them by lawmakers who are only too happy to let big donors keep their identities and the size of their gifts—many tax deductible—shrouded from the public. The tax loophole that allows for such secrecy ought to be closed. When a lawmaker opposes disclosure, the voters ought to hear about it—preferably from nonpartisan watchdog organizations such as Common Cause and Minnesotans for Clean Elections. Supporting such groups financially in the Trump era is a timely act of patriotism. So is reviving discussion of an idea that was a favorite of the late Minnesota Republican representative Bill Frenzel—public campaign financing.

But as Minnesotans have witnessed on several occasions—including my own campaign in 1982—victory does not always go to the bigger spender. The antidote to big money can be small donations and volunteer action. Campaigns still need willing workers to operate phone banks, drop literature at doors, and spread the word.

Neighbor-to-neighbor organizing was key to the progressive Republican success story of the 1960s. It's still a potent political tool today.

On January 20, 2018, the first anniversary of Trump's inauguration, the nation was witness to a new level of federal government dysfunction. Despite controlling the White House and both chambers of Congress, Republicans were unable to pass legislation to keep government funded. For three days, federal offices were shuttered and services ceased. Though it was short-lived, that episode raised anew questions that progressive Republicans in Minnesota have asked for decades: What is the rightful role of the federal government? Might states and local governments—and incentivized citizens themselves—do a better job of meeting shared needs and solving shared problems?

My friend and policy mentor Ted Kolderie answers the latter question with an emphatic "yes" in his 2018 book, *Thinking Out the How*. Kolderie was the executive director of the Minnesota Citizens League during the 1960s and 1970s, when it had considerable influence on state and Twin Cities governments. His work as a national consultant in the years since then, particularly in education policy, has him convinced that Americans are witnessing the end of a mostly unsuccessful century-long experiment in nationalized domestic governance. "The national government is overloaded, national politics overwhelmed by its responsibilities," he wrote, citing failures in national education, health care, and urban development policy. "It is all the Congress and the presidency can do to handle foreign affairs, defense, homeland security, the economy. It has proved not possible to run domestic systems from the center."[9]

A better role for the federal government is one to which Minnesota progressive Republicans gravitated a half century ago: Use the power of the federal purse to set policy goals, and leave to states and local governments the "how" of achieving them. My old boss Governor Harold LeVander embraced that idea when it was called revenue sharing. The right-leaning American Enterprise Institute champions "localism." Kolderie calls this idea the New Federalism.

That idea is needed today in American politics as well as governance. Campaigns down to the local level have been nationalized since Gingrich and Texas representative Dick Armey wrote their Contract with America and directed Republican House candidates to align their campaigns with its message. Today, special-interest groups use independent expenditures to send cookie-cutter attack ads into congressional and legislative districts throughout the country. Candidates increasingly have little control over the messages their voters receive, and often have trouble being heard over the special-interest din.

Kolderie argues that a policy devolution to the states will arrive "of necessity" as the federal government falters. I think a shift to the states could use a push—and that push might come, perversely, from Donald Trump. His presidency may be doing more than any other event in my lifetime to cause Americans to recoil from over-reliance on the federal government and to reassert the power of community and local "by the people" government. That power is an American birthright. It is protected by the US Constitution. It was at the heart of the progressive Republican movement in Minnesota in the twentieth century. It's the best remedy I see to what ails America today.

An assertion of the power of community starts with deepening Americans' sense of mutual responsibility. We are all in this together—and as my late US Senate colleague Paul Wellstone often said, "We all do better when we all do better." We do ourselves and our country a disservice when we limit our regard for each other for reasons of race, gender, class, or status. We need to remind each other frequently that prejudice on those bases is not only immoral but unpatriotic.

Strategies for community building and democratic capacity building should now come to the fore. They can be as simple as inviting people to get acquainted with their fellow citizens and, in particular, with the candidates who seek to represent them. Social media has its place, but there can be no substitute for face-to-face human contact among those who are engaged together in self-governance. Relation-ships formed that way build the lasting trust that is essential between citizens and their government. I hear to this day from my former con-stituents, "I didn't always agree with you, Senator, but I voted for you because I always trusted you to understand what was in our best in-terest." That trust is crucial to an effective representative democracy.

I've long advocated for more intense civics education from grade school through college. That would reclaim the original purpose of public education, which was preparation for the responsibilities of citizenship. A requirement of national volunteer service for late teens is a long-discussed idea whose time should now come. Beefing up AmeriCorps to engage larger numbers of retiring baby boomers would be timely and smart. Employers should do more of what El-mer Andersen did for me: encourage employees to participate in civic activities on company time. Twin Cities corporations showed in 2017 a willingness to pony up more than $50 million to host the 2018 NFL Super Bowl. Think of how much good they could accomplish with a similar commitment to community-building work by their employees.

I am heartened by signs in Minnesota that a sense of community is quickening. In St. Cloud, Mayor Dave Kleis—a former Republican legislator in the progressive tradition—is busy in ways big and small building interracial understanding in a city that has seen an immi-gration surge in the last two decades. His monthly "dinners with strangers"—he does the cooking himself—have become an emblem of the welcoming spirit he's trying to instill in his city of 67,000. Then there is my Minnesota friend Dan Buettner, an explorer, author, and advocate for pursuing happiness through healthful communities. His "Blue Zone" pilot project in Albert Lea, Minnesota, produced a community-wide commitment to healthier living and changed how people think about their communities in many other places. In St. Paul, a new watchdog organization called St. Paul STRONG—of which I am a member—is applying grassroots pressure on city offi-cials to keep their decision-making processes transparent and inclusive. Mayors like Jim Hovland of Edina and Ben Schierer of Fergus Falls are consciously reaching across the partisan aisle to build networks of support. In municipalities throughout the state, schools increasingly are doubling as community centers providing health care, recreation, and gathering places for all.[10]

Small local steps like these can revitalize a democratic nation. I'm convinced that when democracy flourishes at the local and state level—and "when every state is heard from" in the halls of Congress—a great America will be even greater. For more than a half century, we progressive Republicans proved the power of these ideas in Minnesota. I'm eager to join my fellow citizens to do so again.

NOTES

Note to Introduction

1. A compilation of national poll results asking Americans whether they consider the nation headed in the right direction or on the wrong track can be found at www.realclearpolitics.com.

Notes to Chapter 1

1. *Minnesota Legislative Manual, 1939,* 209.

2. *Immigration in Minnesota: Discovering Common Ground* (Minneapolis: Minneapolis Foundation, 2004).

3. Steve Werle, *Stassen Again* (St. Paul: Minnesota Historical Society Press, 2015), 32–44.

4. Alec Kirby, David G. Dalin, and John F. Rothman, *Harold E. Stassen: The Life and Perennial Candidacy of the Progressive Republican* (Jefferson, NC: McFarland & Co. Publishers, 2013), 7–13; Werle, *Stassen Again,* 54–56.

5. Theodore C. Blegen, *Minnesota, A History of the State* (Minneapolis: University of Minnesota Press, 1963), 287.

6. Lori Sturdevant with George S. Pillsbury, *The Pillsburys of Minnesota* (Minneapolis: Nodin Press, 2011), 58–69.

7. The platform is available at http://www.theodorerooseveltcenter .org/Research/Digital-Library/Record/ImageViewer?libID=0282587, accessed Sept. 17, 2016.

8. John Earl Haynes, *Dubious Alliance: The Making of Minnesota's DFL Party* (Minneapolis: University of Minnesota Press, 1984), Ch. 2.

9. Harold E. Stassen, *Where I Stand!* (Garden City, NY: Doubleday & Co., 1947), 1–5.

10. Olson is quoted in George H. Mayer, *The Political Career of Floyd B. Olson* (Minneapolis: University of Minnesota Press, 1950), 171.

11. [Republican State Central Committee], *The Keynote Speech of Harold E. Stassen, Candidate for Governor* ([St. Paul]: The Committee, 1938), copy at Minnesota Historical Society (hereafter, MNHS) Reference Library.

12. The Governor's Fishing Opener, a major annual event on today's state tourism calendar, began in 1948: http://www.mngovernoropener.com/faq.

13. Harold Stassen's inaugural message, Jan. 3, 1939, can be found at https://www.leg.state.mn.us/docs/2007/other/070500.pdf.

14. "Report on the Civil Service System for 1939–1940," Minnesota State Civil Service Department, Nov. 15, 1940, 3–6.

15. *The Statehouse Review: A Quick Summary of the 1939 Session of the Minnesota Legislature* (St. Paul: Minnesota Legislative Research Bureau, 1939), 185, https://www.leg.state.mn.us/docs/2018/other/180505.pdf.

16. Neal R. Peirce, *The Great Plains States of America: People, Politics, and Power in the Nine Great Plains States* (New York: W. W. Norton & Co., 1973), 116.

17. *Statehouse Review, 1939,* 174.

18. Jack Alexander, "Governor Stassen," *Life* magazine, Oct. 19, 1942, 126. On the names for the legislation, see Stassen, *Where I Stand,* 139, and Kirby, Dalin, and Rothman, *Harold E. Stassen,* 13.

19. Sturdevant with Pillsbury, *The Pillsburys of Minnesota,* 267.

20. Werle, *Stassen Again,* 94.

21. Kirby, Dalin, and Rothman, *Harold E. Stassen,* 17–19.

22. *Life* magazine, Oct. 19, 1942, 123–24.

23. Kirby, Dalin, and Rothman, *Harold E. Stassen,* 23, 31–32.

24. Elmer L. Andersen, *A Man's Reach,* ed. Lori Sturdevant (Minneapolis: University of Minnesota Press, 2000), 111–15.

25. Werle, *Stassen Again,* 206–7, 209. In his support for Jean LeVander King, Stassen was, as usual, ahead of his time. In 2018, Minnesota Republicans have endorsed a woman for the first time to run for the US Senate. State senator Karin Housley is the leading contender in a three-way primary for the GOP nomination to challenge Democratic US senator Tina Smith.

Notes to Chapter 2

1. Bernhard LeVander, *Call Me Pete: Memoir of a Minnesota Man* (Reno, NV: Dawson Creative Ltd., 2006).

2. On the vote, see David T. Beito, "Henrik Shipstead against the UN," History News Network, Aug. 1, 2005, http://historynewsnetwork.org/blog/13436.

3. Frank P. Leslie, *The Resurrection of the Republican Party of Minnesota, 1932–1950* (Wayzata, MN: Maplewoods, 1971). A brief history of Mount Olivet Lutheran Church history can be found at http://www.mtolivet.org/about-us/history.

4. Robert Esbjornson, *A Christian in Politics: Luther W. Youngdahl* (Minneapolis: T. S. Denison & Co., 1955), 131–38. 1952 Survey of Churches and Church Membership: Religious Bodies Data [States & Counties], Minnesota Population Center, National Historical Geographic Information System: Version 11.0 [database], Minneapolis: University of Minnesota, 2016.

5. Daniel Elazar, *American Federalism: A View from the States* (New York: Thomas Y. Crowell Company, 1966); Virginia Gray and Wyman Spano, "The Irresistible Force Meets the Immovable Object: Minnesota's Moralistic Political Culture Confronts Jesse Ventura," *Daedalus: The Journal of the American Academy of Arts and Sciences* 129 (Summer 2000): 221–30. This special issue of the journal, titled *Minnesota: A Different America?,* was published in book form as Stephen Graubard, ed., *Minnesota, Real and Imagined: Essays on the State and Its Culture* (St. Paul: MNHS Press, 2001).

6. Esbjornson, *A Christian in Politics,* 134.

7. Charles Adrian, "The Origin of Minnesota's Non-Partisan Legislature," *Minnesota History* 33 (Winter 1952): 155–63, http://collections.mnhs.org/MNHistoryMagazine/articles/33/v33i04p155-163.pdf.

8. Esbjornson, *A Christian in Politics,* 319–28.

9. Theodore C. Blegen, *Minnesota: A History of the State* (Minneapolis: University of Minnesota Press, 1963; 2nd ed., 1975), 552–55.

10. Tom Jardine, "All Bets Were Off when Luther Youngdahl Declared War on Minnesota Gamblers," *TC Magazine* (Apr. 1983): 65–69, 109–10.

11. An example of the national notice Youngdahl received: Rufus Jarman, "The Governor and the Gamblers," *Saturday Evening Post,* Dec. 13, 1947.

12. The quotation is in [Luther W. Youngdahl,] "Centennial Inaugural Address of Governor Luther Youngdahl to the Legislature of Minnesota, January 6, 1949," MNHS Reference Library.

13. [Luther W. Youngdahl,] "Budget message of Luther W. Youngdahl, delivered to a joint session of the 56th session of the Minnesota Legislature, Jan. 19, 1949," MNHS Reference Library.

14. Mayer, *Political Career of Floyd B. Olson,* 122, 139.

15. Andersen, *A Man's Reach,* 120–57.

16. Ben Cohen, "Legislator and Lawyer Arthur Gillen Dies at 86," *Minneapolis Star Tribune,* Aug. 2, 2005, 6B.

17. Stanley W. Holmquist with Fred Lee, *Memorable Reflections: Education Is the Life of Democracy* (N.p: n.d., 2001), available at Minnesota Legislative

Reference Library (hereafter, MLRL); "The Record of the 1947 Legislature," *State Governmental Research Bulletin* no. 21 (Dec. 1947), available at MLRL.

18. Wilfred Bockelman, *Culture of Corporate Citizenship: Minnesota's Business Legacy for the Global Future* (Lakeville, MN: Galde Press, 2000), 104; Phil Jenni, "A Short History of the Citizens League" ([N.p.]: Citizens League, 1993), from *Citizens League Matters*, copy in author's possession.

19. On labor conflict, see Lois Quam and Peter Rachleff, "Keeping Minneapolis an Open-Shop Town," *Minnesota History* 50 (Fall 1986): 105–17.

20. John E. Brandl, "Policy and Politics in Minnesota," *Daedalus* 129 (Summer 2000): 209.

Notes to Chapter 3

1. Andersen, *A Man's Reach.*

2. Tom H. Swain with Lori Sturdevant, *Citizen Swain: Tales of a Minnesota Life* (Minneapolis: University of Minnesota Press, 2015), 93–98.

3. Iric Nathanson, "The Grand Consensus, Part III: Minnesota's Progressive Legacy—Civil Rights," Think Again MN, http://www.thinkagainmn.org/the-mn-miracle/195-progress-on-civil-rights, accessed Jan. 14, 2017; inaugural message of Governor Elmer L. Andersen on Jan. 4, 1961, can be found at https://www.leg.state.mn.us/docs/pre2003/other/I600.pdf.

4. Iric Nathanson, *Don Fraser: Minnesota's Quiet Crusader* (Minneapolis: Nodin Press, 2018).

5. Steven Dornfeld, "Gordon Rosenmeier: The Little Giant from Little Falls," *Minnesota History* 64 (Winter 2014–15): 148–57.

6. Minnesota population trends can be found at www.mncompass.org.

7. Minnesota Legislature, Legislative Research Committee, Publication No. 100, Minnesota Reapportionment, Jan. 1965, 11, available at MNHS Reference Library.

8. Peirce, *Great Plains States*, 120–22.

9. Doug Head obituary, *St. Paul Pioneer Press*, Feb. 6, 2011.

10. Lyall Schwarzkopf, *Memories of My Life: Politics, Government Administration, and a Loving, Caring, Fun Family* ([Minnesota?]: n.p., 2009), and interview of Schwarzkopf by Lori Sturdevant, Feb. 20, 2017.

11. Schwarzkopf interview.

12. David Peterson, "Judge Robert Forsythe Once Led State GOP," *Minneapolis Star Tribune*, June 15, 2007.

13. "GOP Official Pays Tribute to Viehman," *St. Cloud Times*, Aug. 15, 1961,

10; John Gizzi, "Modern Conservatism Marks 50 Years since First Big Win," June 26, 2013, http://www.newsmax.com/John-Gizzi/Young-Republicans -Goldwater-Reagan/2013/06/26/id/512047.

14. Schwarzkopf interview.

15. Swain with Sturdevant, *Citizen Swain*, 125–28.

16. Iowa house election results from 1964, https://en.wikipedia.org/wiki /United_States_House_of_Representatives_elections,_1964#Iowa.

Notes to Chapter 4

1. Sturdevant with Pillsbury, *Pillsburys of Minnesota*, 316–27.

2. Dr. Theodor LeVander obituary, *Quad City Times*, Mar. 8, 1996. For biographical info on Harold LeVander, here and below, see the Minnesota Historical Society's biography, http://collections.mnhs.org/governors/index. php/10004227, and Robert Whereatt, "LeVander, Affable 1-Term Governor, Dies at 81," *Minneapolis Star Tribune*, Apr. 1, 1992, 1A.

3. "Pete LeVander Practiced Law with Respect, Dignity," *Minneapolis Star Tribune* obituary, Jan. 2, 2009.

4. Iantha Powrie LeVander obituary, *St. Paul Pioneer Press*, Nov. 30, 2009. Her papers are at MNHS.

5. The Kelly in the firm's name is Fallon Kelly. In 1958 President Eisenhower appointed him US district attorney for Minnesota; in 1970, LeVander appointed him to the Minnesota Supreme Court, where he served for ten years as an associate justice. Today the law firm they headed is known as LeVander, Gillen and Miller. The firm's history can be found at http://www .levander.com/Our-History.shtml.

6. Harold Levander, "What's Right with America," speech delivered Memorial Day, 1965, copy supplied to the authors by Jean LeVander King.

7. David Lededoff, *The Twenty-first Ballot: A Political Party Struggle in Minnesota* (Minneapolis: University of Minnesota Press, 1969).

8. Peirce, *Great Plains States*, 120. The archives of the party's auxiliaries are available at the MNHS Reference Library: see http://www2.mnhs.org /library/findaids/00751.xml.

9. Lebedoff, *The Twenty-first Ballot*, 180.

10. "A Comparison of Similarities in the 1966 Minnesota DFL and GOP Party Platforms," Newsletters and Publications, Publications and Reports, DFL Party State Central Committee Papers, MNHS Reference Library; Sturdevant interview with Wayne Popham, Apr. 14, 2017.

11. "Programs for People," Minnesota Republican Platform, adopted at the Minnesota Republican State Convention, June 23–25, 1966, 28; population statistics from Minnesota Compass, www.mncompass.org.

12. Chuck Slocum, "The Candidate for Governor Who Worked a Miracle," *Minneapolis Tribune,* June 20, 1986, 17A.

13. Speech transcript provided to the authors by Jean LeVander King.

14. Ted Kolderie, *Thinking Out the How* (Edina, MN: Beaver's Pond Press, 2017), 53, describes the willingness of state representative Bob Renner of Walker, Minnesota, to play that role. Similar comments were made to the author by state representative Alfred France of Duluth; Tom Berg, *Minnesota's Miracle: Learning from the Government that Worked* (Minneapolis: University of Minnesota Press, 2012), 15.

15. Jackie Germann, "Sales Tax Issue Must Be Studied, Holmquist Says," *St. Paul Pioneer Press,* Nov. 27, 1966; Robert J. O'Keefe, "Duxbury Ready for Sales Tax Proposal," *St. Paul Pioneer Press,* Jan. 5, 1967.

16. Paul Sevareid, "Sales Tax Inevitable? Minnesota Holds Out," *Suburban Life* magazine, Nov. 23, 1966.

17. Bob Weber, "Sales Tax Passage Predicted," *Minneapolis Star Tribune,* Mar. 9, 1967.

18. Frank Wright, "Sales Tax Bills Obscure LeVander Plan," *Minneapolis Tribune,* Mar. 13, 1967.

19. Bob Weber, "Sales Tax Passage Predicted," *Minneapolis Star,* Mar. 9, 1967, 1A.

20. Peter Vanderpoel, "LeVander Tax Stand Ires Wright," *St. Paul Pioneer Press,* Apr. 7, 1967.

21. Citizen's League, "Tax Relief and Reform Proposal," May 5, 1967, available at https://citizensleague.org/wp-content/uploads/2017/08/Policy ReportFiscalMay-67.pdf.

22. *Minneapolis Tribune,* Apr. 23, 1967; The Minnesota Poll, Apr. 23, 1967, and May 14, 1967.

23. Lori Sturdevant, "A Governor's Reticence Spoke Volumes," *Minneapolis Star Tribune,* May 6, 2007.

24. William C. Johnson and John J. Harrigan, *Governing the Twin Cities Region: The Metropolitan Council in Comparative Perspective* (Minneapolis: University of Minnesota Press, 1978), 30–31.

25. John Watson Milton, *For the Good of the Order: Nick Coleman and the High Tide of Liberal Politics in Minnesota, 1971–1981* (St. Paul, MN: Ramsey County Historical Society, 2012), 207.

26. Elizabeth H. Haskell, "Managing the Environment: Nine States Look

for Answers," report produced by Woodrow Wilson International Center for Scholars, Smithsonian Institute, Washington, DC, Apr. 1971, 123; Stephen J. Lee, "Operation Save a Duck and the Legacy of Minnesota's 1962–63 Oil Spills," *Minnesota History* 58 (Summer 2002): 105–23.

27. Roberta Walburn, *Miles Lord: The Maverick Judge Who Brought Corporate America to Justice* (Minneapolis: University of Minnesota Press, 2017), 233–37.

28. Briana Bierschbach, "Why Lawmakers Want to Fundamentally Change How the Minnesota Pollution Control Agency Does Business," *MinnPost*, Feb. 16, 2015; Matt McKinney, "Protestors Decry Death of Citizen Board at Minnesota Pollution Control Agency," *Minneapolis Star Tribune*, June 23, 2015.

Notes to Chapter 5

1. Milton, *For the Good of the Order*, Ch. 6.

2. Peirce, *Great Plains States*, 122–24.

3. Today, the successor to the Five Percent Club is called the Keystone Program. It honors the Minnesota-based companies that donate at least 2 percent of their pretax profits to charity, either through cash or in-kind contributions. Find more at http://www.minneapolischamber.org/pages/MinnesotaKeystone.

4. "A Citizens Guide to the 1969 Legislature," *Minneapolis Tribune*, June 1, 1969.

5. Mitau biography supplied by Macalester College, accessed June 18, 2017, https://www.macalester.edu/academics/politicalscience/mitaulecture.

6. A map of the eleven regions is available from the Minnesota Department of Employment and Economic Development: https://apps.deed.state.mn.us/assets/lmi/areamap/edr.shtml.

7. Gordon Slovut, "How Major Proposals Fared During Legislative Session," *Minneapolis Star Tribune*, May 29, 1969.

8. Milton, *For the Good of the Order*, 244–45.

9. Kolderie, *Thinking Out the How*, 83; William C. Miller and James L. Weatherby Jr., "Financial Aspects of the Tax Reform and Relief Act of 1967," Minnesota AFL-CIO Federation of Labor, 1968; "Citizens Guide," *Minneapolis Tribune*.

10. "Citizens Guide," *Minneapolis Tribune*; "Minnesota School Finance History," Minnesota Department of Education, Apr. 2016, 4.

11. "LeVander Visits State Deserter," *Minneapolis Star*, July 18, 1968.

12. "A Message to the People of Minnesota from Their Governor," transcript of LeVander's remarks, Jan. 26, 1970, courtesy of Jean LeVander King.

13. In the governor's office, we had been aware of Eugene McCarthy's eagerness to leave the Senate since shortly after the 1968 election, when LeVander was visited by Warren Burger. A St. Paul native who affiliated early with Harold Stassen, Burger by 1968 was on the District of Columbia Court of Appeals, the nation's busiest appellate court. It wasn't a social call. Burger had been sent by President-elect Nixon to ask LeVander if he would agree to appoint a Democrat to McCarthy's US Senate seat, if Nixon would appoint McCarthy as US ambassador to the United Nations. McCarthy would accept the appointment only if LeVander would appoint a Democrat to succeed him, Burger said. LeVander refused to make that promise. Eighteen months later, Nixon appointed Burger chief justice of the US Supreme Court. On Head's entry into the race, see "Now Who? Goetz? Head?" *St. Cloud Daily Times*, Jan. 27, 1970; William Fox, "Head Says Aims to Be Same in New Race," *Minneapolis Star*, Feb. 11, 1970 (United Press International story).

14. Jim Klobuchar, "Like Mac, He Shall Return," *Minneapolis Star*, June 20, 1970.

15. Milton, *For the Good of the Order*, 274–349.

16. A concise summary of the modern-era revenue sharing program is offered by James Cannon, a former aide to Republican New York governor Nelson Rockefeller, in "Federal Revenue Sharing: Born 1972, Died 1986. R.I.P." *New York Times*, Oct. 10, 1986.

17. Elmer L. Andersen, *I Trust to Be Believed,* ed. Lori Sturdevant (Minneapolis: Nodin Press, 2004), 29; Kolderie, *Thinking Out the How*, 59–69, describes the league at the time he took the reins as executive director.

18. Kolderie, *Thinking Out the How*, 32–34, 91–93.

19. "Head, Anderson View 3 Major State Issues," *Minneapolis Sunday Tribune*, Oct. 4, 1970, 10B.

20. Gerald W. Christenson, *A Minnesota Citizen: Stories from the Life and Times of Jerry Christenson* (Arden Hills, MN: G. Christenson, 2005), 118–23. Future State Planning Agency director Gerald Christenson's 1969–70 PhD thesis at the University of Minnesota documented differences in per-pupil spending among six sample districts in the metro area. The gap between the wealthiest district, Hopkins, and the poorest, Anoka, in per-pupil spending at the elementary level was nearly 50 percent. The endorsement is at "Douglas Head for Governor," *Minneapolis Tribune*, Oct. 27, 1970, 12.

21. Kolderie, *Thinking Out the How*, 92–93.

22. "Kidnap-Hijack Plot Foiled," *Minneapolis Star*, Nov. 13, 1970, 1A.

23. Andersen, *A Man's Reach*, 270–71.

24. The term "Minnesota Miracle" is believed to have first been used by the US Advisory Commission on Intergovernmental Relations in its February 1972 report, "Federalism in 1971: The Crisis Continues." It called the actions of the 1971 Minnesota legislature "the outstanding fiscal case study of the year." The term is often attributed to a *Time* magazine cover story on Minnesota, headlined "The Good Life in Minnesota," Aug. 13, 1973.

25. Milton, *For the Good of the Order,* 357; Lori Sturdevant, "An Architect of 'Minnesota Miracle' Is Rooting for Another One," *Minneapolis Star Tribune*, Dec. 28, 2000, A23.

26. Berg, *Minnesota's Miracle*, 39.

27. Berg, *Minnesota's Miracle*, 37; "1970s Politics in Minnesota," a memorandum to the author by Ernest A. Lindstrom, Nov. 2, 2016.

28. "Breaking the Tyranny of the Local Property Tax," approved by the Citizens League board of directors, Mar. 20, 1969; Kolderie, *Thinking Out the How*, 87–89.

29. Journal of the Minnesota House, Extra Session 1971, Tuesday, Oct. 12, 1971, MLRL.

30. Division of School Finance, Minnesota Department of Education, "Minnesota School Finance History, 1849–2015," Apr. 2016, available at MLRL website, https://www.leg.state.mn.us/docs/2016/other/160495.pdf; Kolderie, *Thinking Out the How*, 93–94.

Notes to Chapter 6

1. Authors' interviews with Robert Brown, 1973–75 Minnesota Republican Party chairman, Aug. 15, 2017; Sturdevant interview with Chuck Slocum, 1975–77 Independent-Republican Party chairman, Aug. 8, 2017.

2. Dornfeld, "Gordon Rosenmeier," 148–57.

3. Slocum interview.

4. "Behind the Proposed Republican Party Name Change," *Minneapolis Star*, Nov. 15, 1975, 6A.

5. Durenberger interview with Minnesota Supreme Court retired associate justice Paul Anderson, Aug. 2017; "Blackmun's Bust: A Show of Servility to MCCL," *Minneapolis Star Tribune*, Mar. 24, 2000, A22.

6. Sturdevant with Pillsbury, *The Pillsburys of Minnesota*, 299–300, 347–48; Sturdevant interview with Lois West Duffy, Aug. 27, 2017.

7. *Minneapolis Star,* June 22, 1974, 1A.

8. Lori Sturdevant, *Her Honor: Rosalie Wahl and the Minnesota Women's Movement* (St. Paul: MNHS Press, 2014), 88.

9. *St. Cloud Daily Times*, June 17, 1974, 4A. Conventions in those years gave fractional votes to members of affiliated or auxiliary groups.

10. National Academy of Sciences, http://www.nasonline.org/member -directory/deceased-members/54296.html?referrer=https://en.wikipedia .org/. On the walking subcaucus, see https://www.dfl.org/sd46/wp-content /uploads/sites/126/2016/02/Walking-Subcaucus-Procedure-FINAL.pdf.

11. Margaret Morris column, "Nuptial Notes," *Minneapolis Sunday Tribune*, Aug. 22, 1971, 6E; *Minneapolis Star Tribune*, June 14, 1990, 15.

12. "Minnesota: State of the Arts" is available at the MLRL.

13. The report is available at https://citizensleague.org/wp-content /uploads/2017/08/PolicyReportGovernmentSept-72.pdf.

14. *Minneapolis Sunday Tribune*, Dec. 19, 1976, 1A.

15. *Minneapolis Tribune*, June 19, 1977, 4A.

16. "Durenberger Confirms He'll Run for Senate," *Minneapolis Tribune*, Apr. 23, 1978, 1A.

17. "Durenberger to Run for Senate Opening," *St. Paul Pioneer Press*, Apr. 23, 1978, 1A.

18. Betty Wilson, "Short Rallies, Takes 3,747 Lead," *Minneapolis Star*, Sept. 13, 1978, 1A.

19. Tony Sutton, "The Reluctant Senator," unpublished book manuscript in Durenberger's possession, 2017; "Minnesota Election Results: 1978," Office of Minnesota Secretary of State Joan Anderson Growe, 1979, https://www.leg .state.mn.us/archive/sessions/electionresults/1978–11–07-g-sec.pdf.

Notes to Chapter 7

1. Eric Pianin, "Durenberger Humble in Office of HHH," *Minneapolis Tribune*, Nov. 10, 1978, 1A.2.

2. An enlightening description of the variations in culture and political philosophy in the various American regions can be found in Colin Woodard, *American Nations: A History of the Eleven Rival Regional Cultures of North America* (New York: Penguin Books, 2012).

3. Drew DeSilver, "The Polarized Congress of Today Has Its Roots in the 1970s," FactTank: News in the Numbers, Pew Research Center, June 12, 2014, http://www.pewresearch.org/fact-tank/2014/06/12/polarized-politics-in -congress-began-in-the-1970s-and-has-been-getting-worse-ever-since/.

4. Jim Dawson and Steve Berg, "Heart Attack Kills George Thiss, 55, Durenberger Aide," *Minneapolis Star Tribune*, Dec. 3, 1983, 1B.

5. "The Neas Years," 141 Cong. Rec. S6028 (May 3, 1995), entered into the record by Senator Carol Moseley Braun of Illinois.

6. Neas told his Guillain-Barré story in the *Washington Post:* "I could move my fingers but within days, I'd probably be totally paralyzed," Jan. 11, 2016.

7. See analysis by Steven J. Allen, head of the Capitol Research Center's Investigative Unit, Oct. 7, 2014, at https://capitalresearch.org/article/we-have -lost-the-south-for-a-generation-what-lyndon-johnson-said-or-would-have -said-if-only-he-had-said-it/, accessed Oct. 21, 2017.

8. "Survey Tells Why Bush, Reagan Tie," *Minneapolis Star*, Feb. 27, 1980, 1A.

9. "The Mood of the Voter," *Time* magazine, Sept. 15, 1980.

10. "The Recession of 1981–82," Federal Reserve History, https://www .federalreservehistory.org/essays/recession_of_1981_82, accessed Oct. 28, 2017; "Presidential Job Approval," The American Presidency Project, http:// www.presidency.ucsb.edu/data/popularity.php?pres=40&sort=pop&direct =DESC&Submit=DISPLAY, accessed Oct. 28, 2017.

11. Steve Brandt, "Quie Sets 8.3 Percent Budget Cut," and Lori Sturdevant, "Property Tax May Rise with New Budget," *Minneapolis Tribune*, Aug. 20, 1980, 1A.

12. "Spannaus, Perpich Lead Quie 2–1," *Minneapolis Tribune*, Oct. 25, 1981, 1A.

13. Lori Sturdevant, "Gov. Quie Showed a Lame Duck's Advantages," *Minneapolis Star Tribune*, Sept. 20, 2008.

14. Lori Sturdevant, "Quie Says He Will Not Run Again," *Minneapolis Tribune*, Jan. 26, 1982, 1A.

15. Whitney's progressive positions on abortion and same-sex marriage were described in Amanda Terkel, "Wheelock Whitney, GOP Businessman, Fights Ban on Marriage Equality in Minnesota," *Huffington Post*, Oct. 10, 2011, https://www.huffingtonpost.com/2011/10/10/wheelock-whitney-minnesota -gay-marriage-ban_n_1003533.html.

16. Betty Wilson, "Dayton, Durenberger Trade Charges of Distortion," *Minneapolis Star Tribune*, Oct. 26, 1982, 1A.

17. "Durenberger Criticizes Energy Plans of Reagan," *Minneapolis Star Tribune*, Oct. 7, 1982, 3B (Associated Press story).

18. "Dave Durenberger for Senator," *Minneapolis Tribune*, Oct. 24, 1982, 12A.

Notes to Chapter 8

1. W. Scott Lamb, "35th Anniversary of Reagan's 'I know you can't endorse me. But I endorse you' to Evangelicals," *Washington Times*, Aug. 21, 2015.

2. Authors' interview with Glen Taylor, Apr. 11, 2017.

3. Joe Kimball, "Conscience Won't Let Him Follow Party Line," *Minneapolis Star Tribune*, Feb. 21, 1986, 1B.

4. Lori Sturdevant, "IR Legislators Determined to Bring Minnesota into a Self-Reliant State," *Minneapolis Star Tribune*, Feb. 21, 1986, 1B.

5. A transcript of Reagan's address can be found at https://reaganlibrary .archives.gov/archives/speeches/1986/111386c.htm.

6. Andrew Chamberlain, "Twenty Years Later: The Tax Reform Act of 1986," The Tax Foundation, Oct. 23, 2006, https://taxfoundation.org/twenty -years-later-tax-reform-act-1986/.

7. "In Poignant Public Letter, Reagan Reveals That He Has Alzheimer's," *New York Times*, Nov. 6, 1994, 1A.

8. Jason Manning, "The Bork Nomination," The Eighties Club: The Politics and Pop Culture of the 1980s, http://eightiesclub.tripod.com/id320.htm.

9. The use of "borked" as a verb may have originated with William Safire of the *New York Times*: http://www.nytimes.com/2001/05/27/magazine/the -way-we-live-now-5–27–01-on-language-judge-fights.html.

10. Reagan is said to have first invoked this rule during his 1966 campaign for governor of California. David C. Wilcox, "The 'Eleventh Commandment,'" Enter Stage Right, Apr. 8, 2002, http://www.enterstageright.com/archive /articles/0402/0402eleventhcommandment.htm.

11. Sturdevant interview with Jimmie Powell, former Durenberger aide and Republican staffer on the Senate Environment and Public Works Committee during the 1980s, on Nov. 22, 2017.

12. Steve Berg, "Acid Rain Plan Called Waste of Time, Money," *Minneapolis Star Tribune*, Jan. 9, 1986, 3A; "Setting the Stage for an Acid-Rain Compromise," editorial, *Minneapolis Star Tribune*, Apr. 24, 1986, 18A; Berg, "Durenberger Again Targets Electric Utility Companies in Effort to Curb Acid Rain," *Minneapolis Star Tribune*, May 1, 1987, 7A; "Finally, a Clear-Air Coup," editorial, *Minneapolis Star Tribune*, Nov. 3, 1990, 14A.

13. "Poisons in the Water Glass," editorial, *Minneapolis Star Tribune*, May 19, 1986, 10A.

14. Kenneth F. Gray, "The Safe Drinking Water Act Amendments of 1986: Now a Tougher Act to Follow," *Environmental Law Reporter*, 16 ELR 10338 (1986), https://elr.info/sites/default/files/articles/16.10338.htm.

15. "Congress Overrides Clean-Water Bill Veto," *CQ Almanac* (1987), https://library.cqpress.com/cqalmanac/document.php?id=cqa187–1144980.

16. The act is available at https://www.congress.gov/bill/100th-congress /house-bill/791.

17. Betty Wilson, "Minnesotans in Poll Favor Dukakis over Bush 2-to-1," *Minneapolis Star Tribune*, Apr. 22, 1988, 6B; "Sierra Club Gives Endorsement to Durenberger," *Minneapolis Star Tribune*, June 8, 1988, 8B.

18. Paul Klauda and Dennis J. McGrath, "Dukakis, Dole Strengths Analyzed," *Minneapolis Star Tribune*, Feb. 25, 1988, 6B; Betty Wilson, "After Caucuses, Real Battle Begins," *Minneapolis Star Tribune*, Feb. 25, 1988, 1B.

Notes to Chapter 9

1. "Party Control of the House of Representatives, 1951–present," MLRL, https://www.leg.state.mn.us/lrl/history/caucus?body=h.

2. Neil MacNeil and Richard A. Baker, *The American Senate: An Insider's History* (New York: Oxford University Press, 2013), 221.

3. Bill Frenzel, "Wellstone Plans Spell Disaster," *Minneapolis Star Tribune*, Nov. 2, 1990, 19A.

4. Binyamin Appelbaum, "How Party of Restraint Shifted to 'No New Taxes,' Ever," *New York Times*, Dec. 22, 2012; "Bill Frenzel, Minnesota Republican and Fiscal Authority in the US House, Dies at 86," *Washington Post*, Nov. 10, 2014.

5. Don Phillips, "The GOP Whip's Alter-Ego," *Washington Post*, July 17, 1989.

6. Robert L. Jackson, "The Resignation of Jim Wright: Speaker's Downfall," *Los Angeles Times*, June 1, 1989; Sam Howe Verhovek, "To Jim Wright, What Goes Around . . . ," *New York Times*, Jan. 5, 1997.

7. Helen Dewar, "Counsel Urges Senate Denunciation of Durenberger," *Washington Post*, June 13, 1990.

8. Cliff Haas, "Senate Formally Denounces Durenberger for Misconduct," *Minneapolis Star Tribune*, July 26, 1990, 1A.

9. Greg Gordon, "Durenberger Gets Probation, Fine," *Minneapolis Star Tribune*, Nov. 30, 1995, 1A; Greg Gordon, "Durenberger Accepts Plea Bargain," *Minneapolis Star Tribune*, Aug. 22, 1995, 1A.

10. Gallup historical trends, "Congress and the Public: Congressional Job Approval," Jan. 10, 2018, http://news.gallup.com/poll/1600/congress-public .aspx.

11. "Durenberger, Perpich Low in Job Approval, Poll Shows," *Minneapolis Star Tribune,* July 29, 1990, 4B (Associated Press story).

12. Andersen, *A Man's Reach,* 379.

13. Betty Wilson, "Two IR Gubernatorial Hopefuls Fight for Crown of 'Purest' Abortion Foe," *Minneapolis Star Tribune,* Apr. 18, 1990, 1B.

14. Allen Short, "Allegations Rock Governor's Race," *Minneapolis Star Tribune,* Oct. 15, 1990, 1A; Allen Short and Paul McEnroe, "When Did Grunseth 'Wild Years' End?" *Minneapolis Star Tribune,* Oct. 18, 1990, 1A. See also David Hoium and Leon Oistad, *There is No November: The Rise and Fall of the Jon Grunseth for Governor Campaign* (Inver Grove Heights, MN: Jeric Publications, 1991).

15. Robert Whereatt, "IR Team is Carlson-Dyrstad," *Minneapolis Star Tribune,* Nov. 2, 1990, 1A.

16. Jon Jeter, "Boschwitz Campaign Letter Angers Some Jews," *Minneapolis Star Tribune,* Nov. 4, 1990, 1B.

17. The story of the charter school bill's enactment is told in Ember Reichgott Junge's *Zero Chance of Passage: The Pioneering Charter School Story* (Edina, MN: Beaver's Pond Press, 2012). Ted Kolderie's role is related in his *Thinking Out the How.*

18. National Commission on Excellence in Education, "A Nation at Risk: The Imperative for Educational Reform," Apr. 1983, https://www2.ed.gov /pubs/NatAtRisk/index.html.

19. David E. Sanger and David Johnston, "With One Filing, Prosecutor Puts Bush in the Spotlight," *New York Times,* Apr. 11, 2006.

20. Kimberly Amadeo, "The Rising Cost of Health Care by Year and Its Causes," updated Oct. 26, 2017, https://www.thebalance.com/causes-of -rising-healthcare-costs-4064878.

21. For Rockefeller's own take on the commission's work and failure, see Senator John D. Rockefeller IV, "The Pepper Commission Report on Comprehensive Health Care," *New England Journal of Medicine* 323 (Oct. 4, 1990): 1005–7.

22. Lori Sturdevant, "Consider Carlson's Example on Health Care for Poor," *Minneapolis Star Tribune,* Mar. 27, 2011, 10P; Lori Sturdevant, "As Always, Arne Carlson Speaks His Mind," *Minneapolis Star Tribune,* Sept. 27, 2009, 10P.

Notes to Chapter 10

1. Gwen Ifill, "Clinton Proposes Making Employers Cover Health Care," *New York Times*, Sept. 25, 1992.

2. Robert Pear, "How Bush and Clinton Differ," *New York Times*, Aug. 12, 1992.

3. Glenn F. Bunting, "Gingrich's Politics Got Boost from Nonprofits," *Los Angeles Times*, June 25, 1996.

4. Paul Starr, "What Happened to Health Care Reform?" *The American Prospect* (Winter 1995), http://prospect.org/article/what-happened-health -care-reform.

5. Adam Clymer, "Bipartisan Group Nearly Ready to Give Up on Health Care Bill," *New York Times*, Sept. 22, 1994; David W. Brady and Daniel P. Kessler, "Why Is Health Reform So Difficult?" *Journal of Health Politics, Policy and Law* 35 (2010): 161–75.

6. Haynes Johnson and David S. Broder, *The System: The American Way of Politics at the Breaking Point* (New York: Little, Brown and Co., 1996), 444–45.

7. Dennis J. McGrath, "He'll Leave the Senate Behind; Durenberger Decides Not to Run Next Year," *Minneapolis Star Tribune*, Sept. 17, 1993, 1A.

8. "The 103rd Congress: What Was Accomplished and What Wasn't," *New York Times*, Oct. 9, 1994, 16.

9. Alex Altman, "Middle East Envoy George Mitchell," *Time* magazine, Jan. 22, 2009.

10. Sharon Schmickle, "Durenberger Gets his Last IR Hurrahs at Convention," *Minneapolis Star Tribune*, June 18, 1994, 1A.

11. Dane Smith, "Quist: Call Him Humble or Call Him Weird, He's Giving Carlson a Run for Governor," *Minneapolis Star Tribune*, Apr. 10, 1994, 1A.

12. Dane Smith, "Carlson to Make Case to Hostile Audience // Statewide numbers not kind to Quist," *Minneapolis Star Tribune*, June 12, 1994, 1B.

13. "Talking Taxes," *Minneapolis Star Tribune*, Aug. 21, 1994, 24A.

14. Dane Smith, "It's No Palace Coup: IR Schism Has Deep Roots," *Minneapolis Star Tribune*, June 17, 1994, 1B; Robert Whereatt, "IR Delegates Give Quist a Historic Win," *Minneapolis Star Tribune*, June 18, 1994, 1A.

15. Richard Berke, "Religious Right Gains Influence and Spreads Discord in the GOP," *New York Times*, June 3, 1994. The states Berke cited as witnessing Christian conservative surges within the Republican Party were Texas, Virginia, Oregon, Iowa, Washington, South Carolina, Florida, New York, California, and Louisiana, as well as Minnesota.

16. Sharon Schmickle and Allen Short, "Quist Scrambling to Close Gap Between Himself and Carlson," *Minneapolis Star Tribune*, Sept. 10, 1994, 1B.

17. Jeffrey Gaynor, "The Contract with America: Implementing New Ideas in the US," a report by the Heritage Foundation, Oct. 12, 1995, https://www.heritage.org/political-process/report/the-contract-america-implementing-new-ideas-the-us. The Heritage Foundation is credited by some sources for the content of the 1994 Contract with America.

18. Dane Smith, "IR Party: We're Simply Republican," *Minneapolis Star Tribune*, Sept. 24, 1995, 1A.

Notes to Chapter 11

1. David Leonhardt, "Just Say It: Trump Is a Racist," *New York Times*, Jan. 12, 2018; "Tax Bill Is a Missed Opportunity That Makes Fixing Our Fiscal Challenges Much More Difficult," Committee for a Responsible Federal Budget, press release, Dec. 20, 2017, http://www.crfb.org/press-releases/tax-bill-missed-opportunity-makes-fixing-our-fiscal-challenges-much-more-difficult.

2. Berwick was finally appointed to the CMS position as a recess appointment—that is, when Congress was not in session—after the ACA was signed into law. David Ignatius, "With Donald Berwick's Appointment, the Doctor Is (Finally) In," *Washington Post*, July 9, 2010.

3. Lori Sturdevant, "An Open Seat in Congress? Tough Sell," *Minneapolis Star Tribune*, Sept. 18, 2015.

4. The text of Washington's farewell address is available at http://avalon.law.yale.edu/18th_century/washing.asp.

5. For a discussion of the nation's drift toward minority rule, see E. J. Dionne, Norman J. Ornstein, and Thomas E. Mann, *One Nation After Trump* (New York: St. Martin's Press, 2017), 27–32.

6. Jennifer Bjorhus and Mary Jo Webster, "Minnesota Likely No. 1 Again in Voter Turnout," *Minneapolis Star Tribune*, Nov. 11, 2016.

7. One of the grassroots efforts is More Women on the Move in Rochester, Minnesota. Heather Carlson, "Run, Jane, Run: Revived Group Encourages Tomorrow's Female Political Leaders," *Rochester Post Bulletin*, Oct. 26, 2017. On the Civic Caucus: www.civiccaucus.org.

8. Information about the caucus is available at www.issueone.org.

9. See Kolderie, *Thinking Out the How*, especially section seven, for his case for a renewed federalism (quotations 213–14).

10. Jay Walljasper, "Blue Zones Project Helped Albert Lea, Minn., Find the Benefits of Walking," *Minneapolis Star Tribune*, May 23, 2015.

INDEX

ABOUT THE AUTHORS

★

DAVE DURENBERGER was a Republican US senator from Minnesota from 1978 through 1994. A native of Collegeville, Minnesota, and an attorney, Durenberger was chief of staff for Minnesota governor Harold LeVander. He was the founding chair of the National Institute of Health Policy at the University of St. Thomas and has written books on health policy and national security policy and a biweekly newsletter on health policy and politics. He and his wife, Susan Bartlett Foote, live in St. Paul.

LORI STURDEVANT is an editorial writer and columnist covering state politics and government for the *Minneapolis Star Tribune*. A native of Dell Rapids, South Dakota, Sturdevant is the author, coauthor, or editor of eleven books and a three-time winner of the Minnesota Book Award. She and her husband, Martin Vos, live in St. Paul.

When Republicans Were Progressive was designed and set in type by Judy Gilats in Saint Paul, Minnesota. The text typeface is Poppl Pontifex. The display face is Franklin Gothic Condensed. The book was printed at Versa Press in Peoria, Illinois.

CPSIA information can be obtained
at www.ICGtesting.com
Printed in the USA
BVHW071924281118
534235BV00001B/3/P